A LIFE IN PIECES

*Reflections on
Alexander Trocchi*

A LIFE IN PIECES

*Reflections on
Alexander Trocchi*

edited by
Allan Campbell and Tim Niel

First published in Great Britain in 1997
by Rebel Inc., an imprint of Canongate Books Ltd,
14 High Street, Edinburgh EH1 1TE

Copyright editorial arrangement and forewords
© Tim Niel and Allan Campbell 1997.
For all other copyright acknowledgements, see page 304.

ISBN 0 86241 680 9

British Library Cataloguing-in-Publication Data
A catalogue record for this book is available on
request from the British Library

Typeset by Sarah Merrill Mowat
Printed in Finland by WSOY

FOREWORDS

When I first came across Alexander Trocchi, about four years ago, he was subterranean; long-dead and largely forgotten, existing only as a tiny footnote in the careers of William Burroughs and Allen Ginsberg. What vague awareness there was of him took the form of 'Wagnerian' fable (to borrow Terry Southern's term), built on heroin, pimping and an eye-popping list of famous friends. Part of this had been fuelled by an enthusiastic, but at times, wildly inaccurate, biography on Trocchi, entitled *The Making of the Monster*, by journalist Andrew Murray Scott. Intrigued, I wanted to know more.

Others were already on the trail of 'the Troc'. Irvine Welsh and Kevin Williamson – surprised and pleased to discover an international Scot who was as disparaging about his native country's parochialism as they were – talked him up a storm in the pages of *Rebel Inc.* magazine. Trocchi seemed to have a currency for a certain clandestine group of young Scots writers. I phoned up Alan Warner, who had just published *Morvern Callar*. Like Trocchi's *Helen and Desire*, it too featured a feisty female protagonist. Warner denied any connection, but admitted that he admired the subversive qualities of Trocchi's pornography. In another conversation, novelist Barry Graham confessed, rather alarmingly, that he cried when reading certain passages of *Cain's Book*.

Clearly, Trocchi was beginning to resurface. A more detailed picture of the Scot-on-the-make appeared in 1994 in James Campbell's *Paris Interzone*. 'He possessed an Olympian regard, which, tempered with a generous manner and a way with people of every class and type, made him a natural leader in the literary coteries of the Left Bank,' noted Campbell, before adding the kicker: 'Or, if you chose to see it from a different point of view, as some people did, a born manipulator.'

Yes, contradictions and ambiguities abound in Trocchi's story, which is why, along with his writing, it is so compelling. 'Be careful you don't become notorious instead of famous,' someone once warned him. 'It was a remark which disconcerted the outwardly imperturbable Scot,' continued Campbell, 'for it exposed an aspect of his nature he was not happy with, an emotional loose wire, a likelihood of spiritual damage.'

I suspect that one of the principal reasons, over and above our regard for his writing, that Tim and I gave up the best part of two years producing a television documentary and editing a book on Trocchi was to get closer to understanding that spiritual damage. Most obviously, this manifested itself in the transformation of his cherished literary debut into a pornographic quickie and devoting much of his life to heroin. This is not to suggest moral judgement on our parts, just that we too had, in our more timid way, 'wondered how far out a man could go without being obliterated'.

Allan Campbell, April 1997

I had been familiar with the basics as far as Alex Trocchi was concerned for a number of years (about six or seven) when I was approached to direct a half-hour documentary about him. Allan Campbell, whose idea it was, was to produce. In the end we shared the jobs. I felt fairly sanguine about it all, at least at first, but as time went on I felt less so. For a start I read the books, which I'd avoided up till then. *Young Adam* didn't seem so unfamiliar – it was essentially a normal novel; but *Cain's Book*, it rapidly became clear, was a more difficult thing altogether, much less inclined to stick to the rules. It was obviously autobiographical – about Trocchi's own experiences as a junkie in New York, and his childhood in Glasgow. It was also obviously a philosophical tract, and moment by moment it was a novel as well. There were characters in it. There was surprising, blistering, beaten prose. It was very good indeed, and it was also, clearly, going to be difficult to deal with in a half-hour film.

After that I reread the excellent essays collected in the *Edinburgh Review*, and realised that exactly the same problem was going to apply to Trocchi's life. Depending on your standards for success, a graph of his life booms first in the early Fifties, then busts for the next thirty years. Or it booms until the early Sixties, and busts for twenty-five; or it booms until the early Seventies, and busts for ten. Probably until 1975 or thereabouts, Trocchi had something to warm him up in the mornings, something he could say to himself that made getting out of bed seem not just worthwhile but actually a contribution, almost an altruistic act.

Trocchi and his money were soon parted. The money was rarely his in the first place. His career is spotted with anecdotal evidence of small cons, wiped clean (or cleaner) with his generosities. There are begging letters to publishers who pirated his work, and an orderly queue of less canny bookmen still waiting for books, advances duly paid, that Trocchi either would not or could not ever have written. Wherever the money came from it was never in his pocket long. There are stories of atrocities, or what would be atrocities by any other person's standards – wife pimped, drugs pushed to the underaged. But all this is oddly balanced by the fact that many of the people to whom he did the wrongs in question were willing, even happy, to give interviews twelve years after his death to the effect that his life had not been worthless, that the person they remembered was valuable. At which point you begin to suspect that a fragmented moral impulse was at work, at least sporadically, that Trocchi's life was lived with a whole heart to which others had only incomplete access.

Editing the film was a nightmare. We decided to call it *A Life in Pieces*. That was the easy bit – choosing the title. Dustjackets frequently claim that the author of the book contained within has been everywhere, done everything, and that's fine, because it's always either untrue or anything but obvious from the book itself. But Trocchi *was* a pig farmer, a straight-a university student, a family man, a pimp, a heroin addict, a bargee, a translator, a pornographer, a dealer in books and stamps, a forger, a success, a failure, beautiful, ugly, a hit with the girls, a dirty old man, friend of the famous, fuckwit next door, a pundit, a revolutionary, an alcoholic, an editor, deserted, partnered, bereaved, and last but not least, a novelist; at least seven of his books of fiction were printed during his lifetime. He should have been famous, rich, but he was robbed. He made least of all, relative to his expectations, from the two bestsellers, *Cain's Book* and *Helen and Desire*. He spent thirty years, give or take, in the public eye, but behind him at the end there was nothing to see: no money, not enough 'proper' books, and, in the words of one interviewee, not enough *professionalism*.

All this in thirty minutes. At one point Allan and I made vague appeals for a fifty minute slot, but fortunately for us no one was listening. An extra twenty minutes would have been no help at all.

Our first tack was to try editing the film as a series of fragments. It seemed to make sense, at first, given the extraordinary extent to which his life refused to hang together, but in fact what happened instead was that within the first fifteen minutes we had exploded the film completely. There was nothing to carry from one film to the next, apart from his face, which photographs at any end of his life serve remarkably well. But then there's a problem there too; one moment, the snappy young editor plots the wider distribution of his leading-edge literary magazine, the next your embarrassing old uncle grins madly – possibly toothlessly – from under a fez and inside a tatty kaftan patchworked out of pyjamas and curtain braid. In the end there's only so much experimentation allowed in a BBC1 slot, and the film shrank back together. While we were watching the finished product with a mixture of relief and disappointment, Allan reminded me that he had approached Rebel Inc. at Canongate with the reams of additional research and interviews that we had always known would prove too difficult for inclusion, and been rewarded with interest in a possible book.

This *A Life in Pieces*, we hope, is considerably better. It's full of gaps, and in several places there probably ought to be explanations that aren't there, but Trocchi was more comfortable than most with the fact that his life – like everyone else's – was not a whole, that it was made up of things that don't fit together. Any ordinary biography tries to have its cake and eat it by excluding every paradox but one from the plot of what is actually a novel. These are the facts, from as many perspectives as possible.

Tim Niel, April 1997

CONTENTS

AFTERWORDS

INTRODUCTIONS

MY FATHER HAD FALSE TEETH:

from *Cain's Book*

Alex Trocchi

We sat there after we had fixed and watched wood burn. The white box-wood burned quickly. Tom Tear leaned forward and added a few sticks to the blaze. He is a tall man in his late twenties, lean, with a beautiful, pale, lean face expressionless often as porcelain, the nose long, the eyes half-closed and heavily lidded under the drug.

I also am tall. I was wearing my heavy white seaman's jersey with a high polo neck, and I sensed that the angularity of my face – big nose, high cheekbones, sunken eyes – was softened by the shadows and smoothed – the effect of the drug – out of its habitual nervousness. My eyes were closed. My elbows rested on my thighs and my hands were clasped in front of me. Tom Tear is a negro who sometimes speaks dreamily of the West Indies.

At that moment I felt impelled to speak and I said: 'My father had false teeth.'

I was aware that I flashed a quick intimate glance first at Tom, across Fay's line of vision, and then, turning my head slightly, I caught the glint of appraisal in her pale protruding eyes.

'Yes,' I said, and my face grew radiant, encouraging them to listen, 'he had yellow dentures.'

Tom's teeth – they are long and yellowish and give his mouth a look of bone – were clenched in a tight smile, the pale lips falling away, exposing them. It was almost a mask of ecstasy, *part of the game*, I might have said in some contexts, in some rooms.

Fay's face was more reserved. Swinish? More like a pug than a pig. Her untidy dark hair tumbled into her big fur collar. A yellow female pigdog, her face in its warm nest beginning to stir with knowing.

'He was outside in the hall, spying on the lodgers,' I said. 'My father was a born quisling, and he had false teeth.'

Tom Tear's face was patient and serene. The flicker of the fire stirred in the sparse black stubble on his lower face, making the hairs glint.

I went on for the friendly silence: 'While he was in the hall his false teeth were squatting like an octopus in a glass of water on the kitchen dresser. The plates were a dark orange brick colour and the teeth were like discoloured piano keys. They seemed to breathe at the bottom of the glass. The water was cloudy and tiny bubbles clung to the teeth. That was the kitchen where we lived, and they sat there like a breathing eye, watching us.'

Fay's bluish lips had fallen apart in a smile. She made a grunt of understanding through her decayed teeth. Fay is forty-two. She has lived all her life in this city.

Tom Tear leaned forward and threw more wood on the fire. Wood is plentiful. We gather it, when we can be bothered, on the streets.

'He went on tiptoe about the hall for nine years,' I said, 'in tennis shoes and without his teeth. The hall was No-man's Land.'

Tom Tear nodded as he leaned back again away from the fire. His right cheek, which was all I saw from where I sat, was impassive, long and smooth.

'If someone came to the front door he came flying back into the kitchen for his teeth. He came in puffing and blowing with his hand on his paunch. He wore a colourless shirt with a stud in it and he went round in his shirtsleeves and this old grey, sleeveless pullover.' I paused. A white stick darkened and burst into flame. 'When he grew older he became less frantic about the teeth,' I said, smiling. 'He slipped them into his mouth furtively in front of the visitor as though he suddenly remembered and didn't want to give offence. Perhaps he no longer need defences.'

'He had given up by that time,' Fay said. She looked straight into the fire.

We were all silent for a moment. I felt I had to go on. I said: 'I'll tell you a story . . .'

SORT OF A BLESSED CURSE

Patti Smith

In 1972 I was working in the basement of a bookstore called The Strand on Broadway and 12th Street. A lot of people worked in that basement, it seems that half the New York underground worked in that store. I used to pick up some interesting used books there, really cheap. One day I came upon *Cain's Book*. I have always been interested in Cain as a symbolic, biblical character. I didn't know anything about Trocchi but I liked it so much, the whole rhythm of the writing. Even with all of its complex subject matter, the thing I found most profound about it was that it seemed such a great, generous example of the act of writing, of the writer commenting on the act of writing. Genet does quite a bit of that. So you're not only invited to enter their world but you're also watching some of the writer's process. I was very taken with that and it became my bible for a while. Some people took it as the drug user's bible but for me it was the writer's bible.

To me, his descriptions were like seeing Newark, the Hudson River and the whole barge scene for the first time. Often someone besides a fellow countryman, maybe a stranger, reveals the best part of your own homeland to you. I thought it was great. I mean, I loved that book. I still have it – I just bought another copy! I didn't like the new cover, so I tore it off. I have several falling-apart copies around.

I thought *Cain's Book* seemed very natural, sort of like jazz. That's one thing I liked about him. He was able to move in and out of time frames, just like a film maker. I think he had a lot of the film maker in him. If he had been born in France he would have worked with Jacques Rivette or Godard because he could move time frames, I thought, very gracefully. It worked for me. *Cain's Book* is in the Top 20. You know, it's not *the* book, but it was really important to help me develop the nomadic writer's process. Hell, he had his typewriter on the barge. When I find I'm having trouble writing I just go back and read some of it and I always have to put it down because it always makes me want to write. That's a really beautiful thing.

Tom Verlaine gave me a 1974 copy of *Poems of a Millionaire*.[1] Then I read his Helen Seferis books and *Thongs*. I loved *Helen and Desire*, it was a very big influence on me in the late Seventies when I wrote *Babble*. You know, the study of pornography as an art is very interesting. You have certain aspects of Genet or Burroughs or Cocteau, various people who explored that, and Robert Mapplethorpe in his photography. I thought Trocchi's writing was so good, it was pornography presented as such a dream-like, almost visionary experience. I was quite taken with those books and they did influence a lot of my own attempts at merging art and pornography. I was directly influenced by him.

I looked at it as very high pornography. I can't get into a political argument about those kind of things, it's not my fight. It was just so well written and transporting, very much in the rhythm of my thinking and my energy in the Seventies. I'm not in that same place now but it very much coincided with my writing pursuits and my thoughts about literature then. I tried in my own way to go beyond it. But still, in all, *Cain's Book* is the one I cherish the most. All artists [like Trocchi] gravitate towards outsiderdom, not even in a conscious way, it's part of the process, it's in the veins or in the lifeblood of every artist because you're set apart because you have certain gifts that other people don't have or certain perceptions that other people don't have. You're immediately set apart by the nature of your gift. It's not society's fault, it's sort of a blessed curse.

Trocchi is an artist, like Brion Gysin. His work isn't for everybody, doesn't have to be for everybody. In that way, William Burroughs' writing is a lot more universal. I don't think Trocchi cared about being a universal writer. The universal nature in his work is between artists or certain heightened individuals. He won't be forgotten. He might have a certain place, but his place is unique and will be revered.

A SCOTTISH GEORGE BEST OF LITERATURE

Irvine Welsh

When did you become aware of Trocchi?
I read and enjoyed *Young Adam*. There was a real cynicism in the outsiderness of his voice, which was attractive. It was a breath of fresh air after all those horrible, sickly celebrations of Scottishness which some Scottish writers feel obliged to do. They feel that because of Scotland's relationship with England they've always got to be nice and watch what the neighbours might say; but the neighbours don't care. He seemed to have a vision which wasn't constrained by other people's narrow definitions of Scottishness. He was off in his own world.
Did his work help you in any way to find your own voice or subject matter?
No, not really, because I was quite disappointed in *Cain's Book,* which is regarded as his classic. I thought it was just a sub-Burroughs junkie type thing; it didn't appeal much. It was just an existential, middle class figure mythologising drugs and the junkie experience. *Trainspotting* was a reaction against that, against the Burroughs-Trocchi dark, Bohemian figure

who was a big drug-taker. What I was saying is that it's now, it's different; it's a chemical society, it's a mass experience. It's as likely to be a working class person in a network of friends – a community – that's involved in any drugs scene, rather than this existential rebel.

His intellectualising of drugs didn't correspond with your feelings?

I don't think so. His intellectualising of drugs and his rationale of the lawless outsider was dated by history. Britain – the West – has obviously always been a drug culture. But in the Eighties, first with the heroin scene taking off then, more importantly with the whole ecstasy and acid house culture, what happened was that drugs became a mass experience. As Matthew Collin said, it became an unremarkable part of everyday life, rather than something seen as the badge of the outlaw.[1]

Can you explain, though, why there has been an increasing interest in Trocchi again?

There has been tremendous interest from people like Kevin Williamson, Barry Graham, and newer Scots writers.[2] That's a reaction against the old Scottishness. Trocchi was from the opposite camp, the antithesis of Hugh MacDiarmid. There's a new generation of writers now . . . I remember reading the introduction to *Dream State* and to me it was a load of nonsense.[3] It was not new poetry, it was just the same old, tedious, tired debate about Scotland's role and Scottish self-determination. What I see as the newer thinkers in Scottish writing are looking way beyond this. Trocchi is a much more appropriate role model because of his internationalist lifestyle and his attack on Scottish parochialism and the tedious nationalistic issues which every Scots writer is supposed to engage in. Writers in Ireland are traditionally supposed to write about 'the Troubles' while writers in Scotland are supposed to write about the role of Scotland in the Union. It's so limiting, and the reaction against that was; we can't be bothered with all this stuff. So Trocchi was an appropriate role model; an internationalist and an empowering figure for a lot of writers trying to escape the shackles of Scottishness.

For some, Hugh MacDiarmid remains a symbol . . .

For me, he's a symbol of all that's horrific and hideous about Scotland and Scottish culture. When you look at Trocchi's life, l don't think it adds up to a great deal of substance, it's more what he's perceived to symbolise. His life doesn't really impress me; it showed a lot of self-indulgence, petulance and misogyny. He was a Scottish George Best of literature. He wasted a lot of his talent through that self-indulgence, through not being able to discipline himself and control his darker side. *It comes as a surprise to some younger Scots writers to find that someone like Trocchi was even connected to their home country. Do you go along with that?* Yes, he's very un-Scottish. I think he was quite embarrassed about it. People say he was a quintessential Scot in so many different ways, but it's a lot of nonsense. He was always an internationalist, a traveller; he could have been any nationality. I think he was embarrassed by the parochialism, in the same way that Beckett grew to be embarrassed about being Irish and hated going back to Dublin. At least he got dragged back there occasionally, kicking and screaming. I don't think you could have dragged Trocchi back to Glasgow once he'd left. What you're fighting against isn't being perceived as being Scottish – which would be pretty ludicrous with the stuff that I write – but against somebody else's perception of Scottishness, somebody who is putting a straightjacket on you. The idea of disowning somebody like Trocchi is quite sinister because it's proscribing; it's cultural Nazism.

FROM THE *EDINBURGH REVIEW ENCYCLOPAEDIA*

Howard Slater

ALEXANDER TROCCHI

Born 1925, he attended Glasgow University and was awarded a scholarship, subsequently leaving Britain to travel and write. He lived in Paris, putting in a brief attendance at the Sorbonne in 1951 and between the years 1952–55 edited the magazine *Merlin* with poet Christopher Logue.[1] This was a journal largely ignored in its day but now renowned for publishing work by Robert Creeley, Italo Svevo, Pablo Neruda, Eugene Ionesco and Samuel Beckett. As editor, Trocchi wrote several incisive editorials calling upon his contemporaries to be 'alive to the snares of language'. He saw the magazine as a means of combating the rigidity of opinion, hoping that the writing published would influence others to analyse their own attitudes and become more critical. These editorials culminate in the lengthy essay, *Words and War*. Associated with the magazine, a small publishing group produced several volumes under the name *Collection Merlin*, issuing the first English language editions of

Beckett's *Molloy* and *Watt* as well as Genet's *A Thief's Journal*. Whilst in Paris Trocchi attempted to have published in Britain his first novel, *Young Adam*, which had already been published in France under the pseudonym Frances Lengel. He was also working on *Cain's Book*, the novel that brought him notoriety through the legal action that was taken against it. A little known side of Trocchi is his involvement with the French avant-garde of the Fifties, namely the Lettrist International, a group of dissident surrealists, and later the Situationist International, an amalgamation of experimental artists and revolutionary theorists that included Asger Jorn and Guy Debord.

On leaving France in 1957 Trocchi journeyed to New York, the setting for *Cain's Book*, and at one time was present in Venice, California. His stay in the U.S.A. saw him associating with the 'Beat' writers, forging a friendship with William Burroughs through mutual use of heroin.[2] Trocchi had to leave the U.S.A. as his involvement in the New York drug scene made him a target for the authorities. It was Norman Mailer who gave him some money and false papers, enabling Trocchi to return to Britain via Montreal.

Cain's Book was first published in Britain in 1963 and is the work by which Trocchi is most widely known; the novel uses memory as its main guideline, merging sections of journal with reminiscences and a keen sense of Self. Despite its categorisation as a 'junk-scene' novel, Trocchi develops the theme of the 'outsider' in a disquieting and immediate manner. Throughout it, Trocchi's acute self-consciousness develops a criticism of writing itself, questioning the role of the novel as opposed to more practical and concrete attitudes, those that suggest that imagination can be inscribed onto the environment without the aid of a specific medium. What makes *Cain* successful is its author's internationalism, his awareness of a variety of viewpoints.

Young Adam, written and published before *Cain* in 1961, is a precursor of the *nouveau roman* and deals primarily with capital punishment and the workings of judicial proceedings whilst embryonically tracing an 'existential' strain in its principal character. In the course of his life, Trocchi's other literary pursuits included work as a translator; *I, Jan Cremer, Girl on a Motorcycle* by Andre Pieyre de Mandiargues, *The Centenarian* by René de Obaldia, Valentine Penrose's *The Bloody Countess* and Jean Douassot's *La Gana*. He also penned several 'pornographic' novels under the name of Frances Lengel; these being *Thongs*, *Helen and Desire*, *School for Sin*, *White Thighs* and *Sappho* for Girodias' Olympia Press.[3] Within this work there is a marked erotic interest and in places the anti-authoritarianism and hedonism that characterise Trocchi is prevalent. In 1971 a collection of a 'life's poetry' was published under the title *Man at Leisure*. These poems led Burroughs to describe Trocchi as a 'modern metaphysical poet'. Four stories dealing with loneliness and alienation were issued in Calder's *New Writers 3*.

An area of Trocchi's life that has been neglected is his position within the British underground scene where his energy, enthusiasm and unselfish attitude did much to disseminate the uncompromising ideas he had developed throughout his life.

The focal point of his activity in the early Sixties was project sigma, an organisation of a worldwide linking up of intellectuals, poets and writers to effect a revolutionary transformation of Western Society. The methods deployed by sigma are eclectic, ranging from the setting up of sigma centres (free universities) to participation in global chain-letters (Potlach), from architectural projects (shadow cities) to developing new forms of publishing (cards / billboards).[4] Trocchi was careful to stress that such activity had already begun, independent of any individuals, that it had always aimed 'to bring all informations out into the open, to attack stock responses that paralyse social intercourse'. These activities were expected to 'snowball' and effect a change within individuals that would undermine prevailing institutions. Trocchi instigated this project with his essay 'The Invisible Insurrection', warning that as soon as a revolt is defined it 'provokes the measures of its confinement'. This led Trocchi to develop the idea that a sigmatic revolt would be an 'outflanking'; subversive methods would be employed in order to avoid recuperation. A key tactic was the opposition of play to work, 'Homo Ludens' being a theme throughout his novels and underground pamphleteering, and sigma was to be a promoter of play, urging others to apply themselves to a greater creativity that would aid self-discovery. Central to the role of play was the notion that with increasing automation looming, people must be prepared to deal with the accompanying 'leisure'.

A *Sigma Portfolio* was created gradually and distributed, containing essays by Michael McClure, Robert Creeley, R. D. Laing, Stan Brakhage, Colin Wilson and others. Trocchi himself wrote further essays: 'Tactical

Blueprint', 'Potlatch', 'Sigma General Informations' and 'Projects (Beyond the Portfolio)'. After a year of great activity in 1964 project sigma 'disbanded'. In an archive note Trocchi suggests that a lack of courage and overt competitiveness were mainly responsible for this. During the Sixties, Trocchi participated in other underground events; at the Edinburgh Writers' Festival of 1962 his arguments with Hugh MacDiarmid gained attention, and the 1965 Poetry Festival at the Albert Hall saw him acting as compere. In the early Seventies Trocchi was active in the thwarted campaign to commute Michael X's sentence to life imprisonment.

Alexander Trocchi died in 1984 leaving a body of work that remains to be collected and republished.

Further reading:
Edinburgh Review 70: Trocchi issue
Ken Knabb (ed.): *Situationist International Anthology* (Bureau of Public Secrets)
Jeff Nuttall: *Bomb Culture* (Paladin)

GLASGOW

1925 30TH JULY. Alexander Whitelaw Robertson Trocchi born in Glasgow to Alfredo Luigi and Annie Trocchi.

1942 4TH JANUARY. Annie Trocchi dies of acute bacillary dysentery.

1942. Trocchi begins a degree in English, Political Economy and Logic at Glasgow University.

1943 5TH FEBRUARY. Trocchi is called up. He begins training as a pilot in the Fleet Air Arm, transfers to the Royal Navy and completes basic training in 1944.

1946 16TH NOVEMBER. Trocchi is demobbed and returns to Glasgow University as a student of English and Philosophy.

1947 15TH JANUARY. Trocchi marries veterinary student, Betty Whyte.

1948 15TH JANUARY. Jacqueline Anne Trocchi born.

1950. Trocchi completes degree at Glasgow University. Despite the high expectations of his tutors, Trocchi receives only a second class degree.

1950 MAY. Trocchi is awarded the Kemsley Travelling Scholarship. Trocchi, Betty and their daughter, Jacqueline, tour Europe.

1951 30TH MAY. Margot Francoise Trocchi born.

FREE TO CHOOSE FROM THE BEGINNING:

from *Cain's Book*

Alex Trocchi

When I was four I fell from a swing and broke my arm. When it was set in plaster I asked for a big box with a lid on it, like the one the cat slept in. I put it in a corner near the fire in the kitchen and climbed into it and closed the lid. I lay for hours in the dark, hearing sounds, of my mother's moving about, of others coming and going from the kitchen, and inside sensing the heat of my own presence. I was not driven from my box until after my arm was healed, and then at my father's insistence. It was a stupid game, he said, and the box was in the way. A boy needed fresh air.

My mother was proud and my father was an unemployed musician with the name of an Italian.

The blue-black hairs on my father's legs gave to his flesh the whiteness of beeswax. I associated him with the odours of pomade and Sloan's liniment. The bathroom was his lair and his unguents were contained in a white cabinet affixed by four screws to a green wall. The pomade came in a squat jar with a red cap, the liniment in a flat bottle on whose label was an engraved likeness of Joseph V. Stalin. Because of his strange moustache I always thought of Mr Sloan as an Italian. It was not until today that it occurred to me to suspect that he wasn't. The name of the maker of the pomade was Gilchrist, and yet it too was oily and glistened in my father's scalp.

In my father's obsequiousness there was an assurance, but as he grew older he became reflective during the winter months. His step quickened, his distances were less ambitious. He spent more time in smokerooms over coffee and didn't move out again into the street until the waitresses had begun to sweep away the fag-ends which had been trodden into the carpet and to polish the glass tops on the tables. At that point he glanced at the clock he had been aware of since he came in, pretended to have found himself once again in time confronted by an overlooked appointment, and walked purposively to the swing doors. In one of his ungloved hands he carried a small leather briefcase which contained the morning paper, the evening paper, and a pale blue box of deckled notepaper with envelopes to match. Sometimes he stopped abruptly on the pavement and fingered the lapel of his heavy coat. He'd looked guiltily at the feet of the people who passed him on either side. And then he walked more slowly. Every so often, just in that way, he remembered his angina. The word stuck in his throat. He was afraid to die on the public thoroughfare.

Sunday. My father would be awake before the milk and the morning papers were delivered. He slept four or five hours at most. After the death of my mother he lived alone. At nine he shaved. Not before. The number of such necessary enterprises was very meagre. He had to spread them thinly over the day, as he spread the margarine thinly over his bread, to prevent the collapse of his world. The fort wall was a frail one between my father and his freedom. He shored it up daily by complex ordnance. He was chosen for by an old selector system of tested rites. He gargled, watching his eyes in the mirror. He polished his shoes. He prepared his breakfast. He shaved. After that he staved off chaos until he had purchased the morning paper. Births, marriages, and deaths. He moved up and down the columns at the edge of himself. But with the years he achieved skill. Either way he was safe. If none of the names meant anything to him he could enjoy relief; if a friend had died he could after that first flicker of triumph be involved in solemnity. His hours were lived in that way, against what was gratuitous, and he was all the time envious . . . at the brink. There is no suspicion so terrible as the vague and damning awareness that one was free to choose from the beginning.

EDWIN MORGAN

What were your impressions of the youthful Trocchi?
When I met him first of all, he was already a student at Glasgow University and I had just started lecturing in the English department there. He didn't talk very much about his family or his background. He was regarded generally as a man of tremendous potential. He was a really brilliant student in many ways, he was capable of doing extremely good work, not just in English (that was my department) but also in philosophy as his degree course. And they felt the same on the philosophy side – he was capable of absolutely first class work. It was generally thought that he probably would get a first honours degree.

On the other hand, it was also quite clear, that he was in some ways erratic . . . He would suddenly take some idea in his head which was not related to the course he was taking up, or the work he was doing, it was something totally different, perhaps regret it and very often, his life would fly off at a tangent. Like the time he started the pig farm at the very time he should have been doing serious work for his final examinations. So, although we were disappointed he didn't get the best kind of degree that he should have got, we weren't perhaps totally surprised. But this made it all the more interesting. He was a very interesting character. I think we all felt – I certainly felt – that he would be remarkable for something. We weren't very sure whether it was for good or for evil, I think! But we felt he was a very remarkable character, with a very keen brain. But, at the same time, a man who would behave perhaps in psychologically very sudden, strange aberrational ways . . . which couldn't be related very readily to the intellectual side of him.

Did he still have a certain charm?

He had charm, yes, he had charm. I think everyone felt that. He had a kind of magnetic quality. But at the same time, again, there was a curious double-take about all these things. The charm was there and it was generally thought and felt by his contemporaries, by students and also by the staff, I suppose. But there was always something slightly . . . dangerous or sinister or untrustworthy about the man too. You would never be quite sure whether you should put your life in his hands – and the charm in that sense was always slightly double-edged. But, I mean, it was there, no doubt about it. He had a great ability to get speaking to people, get talking to them, get interested in what they were doing, very quickly, get them drawn into his orbit as it were. He was a great manipulator of people. Even as a student this was true, I think.

What was expected of him academically?

When he got his degree in the end, it was disappointing from our point of view as those who would lecture to him. We felt he could have done better, but at the same time, he got a scholarship. He was clearly regarded as being worth more than the degree he got. He got a scholarship and went to France. It was just underlining the fact that he had this great potential for interesting people in what he was thinking and doing, which made him move very quickly into intellectual and cultural circles in Paris . . . Almost in an uncanny way, getting to know some of the famous writers of the time, like Genet, Sartre and Beckett.

TAPEWORM
Alex Trocchi

Desire for opium, alcohol – any narcotic or woman or power or the cigarette you finished two hours ago and the empty packet in front of you.
The past is dead and useless. There is a tapeworm in your bloodstream.
The crocus has faded. Doesn't matter what anyone else says. And this
coldblooded bastard inside saying write write write, all over and over
again when you'd much rather get hold of the bottle and sink into the
state when all you want is some shapey piece of the other sex to play the
flute with. But then you haven't got the money for that all the time. In
fact you've got about two quid and then you're flat and all the while this
lump of psychological cancer, this impersonal hook of worm has got
you dangling like a piece of dead beef at the end of a butcher's chain.
And it is not going to let off the pressure – not a dog's chance – until you
sit down and write two thousand words that you can read over again
without belching. So you don't write? All right. You go to the pictures. It
is a picture for adult audiences or at least that is what the censor calls
them and you see some bugger who doesn't get seen getting into bed
with some other bugger's wife but who is found out afterwards by cir-
cumstantial evidence and then the fireworks begin and the drama leaks
oozily on via two violent deaths (crime does not pay) to a final stasis
where the wronged bugger gets himself tied up again to another piece of
skirt whom we are led to believe is some sort of suburban Desdemona
who has no interest in these things and whose papa is going to get the
wronged bugger a job in a bank where he can earn enough money to
support his wife and breed children. She is the type of bitch who is going
to keep one large burst eyeball on him and who is going to ditch him for
some good clean bloke if he gets his shirt dirty. But of course that doesn't
happen in the picture and the lights go on and you are left sitting in the
one and ninepennies with nowhere to go and a sick feeling in the pit of
your stomach.

And now you go outside and the night is cold and the rain is coming
down like a box of blue rivets. You think of Bach and the second movement of the concerto for two violins and how many children he had and
you wonder how that guy ever did it. You move into a doorway for shel-
ter and you find that it sells fish and chips. You go to the counter and you

are served by one of the sweetest little curls you have ever seen. Oliveskinned from Napoli. She is about seventeen and she has dark crinkly hair like most Italian girls. Her eyes are black diamonds with a touch of the snake about them and she has lips like those things you see advertising various beauty products. Only hers are real. They move softly like a slow-bleeding wound. But you don't get any ideas because her old man is standing there at the chiprange and he has a neck like a gnarled oak and a forearm like a ten pound cod. And anyway you have only two quid in the whole world and your tapeworm has got St Vitus dance. You go out and your feet are walking to wherever you left your typewriter. You are crucified and you have got to make the best of it. You know that what you write is going to be no good and that if it is good it won't be published because it is immoral. And you begin to wish you'd bought that bottle after all. And then you get to thinking you've had a bum deal and this merely puts you more clearly on the romantic side of the fence – you've got to believe a helluva lot to be a classicist, that is to say if there are such people. Which is hard to believe. And you begin to think that Rimbaud was dead right when he migrated. That man was dead right in a lot of things. But then you've got no guns – you swapped the Luger you brought back for Mario Praz's *Romantic Agony* so now you can't even blow your brains out – and you wouldn't know where to get any. And anyway the niggers are a lot smarter now and can probably get guns easily enough without making you rich by playing the intermediary. So it seems this tapeworm's got you nailed alright. It seems you've just got to fiddle away and snatch something to drink, eat or sleep with between meals – the tapeworm's meals, I mean, the hungry bastard!

You are walking slowly because you are a man as well as a bloody poet. You get to thinking that this whole set-up does not delight your nostrils. At the same time you do not want to change anything except perhaps the colour of your shoes. You walk too much. Your shoes get dusty and you could do with another half-inch of sole on them. But you do not want to build ridges or societies for the pacification of the nations. Let them bleed themselves white. The process of disintegration will at least provide some punk of a historian with a job and furnish at least four philosophers with a brand new philosophy of history. Incidentally it will provide men like yourself with some very interesting and variegated pigments for a mural or something. Viz. Guernica. Very interesting. It is very interesting indeed how superbly coloured are some of the most hideous diseases under a microscope. The orchid is fatal. You think to yourself that there is positively no use being indignant about it. You decided long ago to accept everything. Even the tapeworm. To do him justice – though God knows if a tapeworm deserves justice – he is very good when he is satisfied with his fodder. He sleeps then. And you are compensated by a sharp tingle of pleasure somewhere between your navel and your throat and by a supercharged desire for Betty your wife. It is then that you derive an intensified electric pleasure from her moist body. She is magnificent. You accept then. Past, present and future. They are all part of the present after all – what you wrote yesterday is as good as it is today – and the present is you. The future is as much part of you as your own daughter. You are the future. All of it that concerns you anyway. It does not appear suddenly in company like an unpleasant diarrhoea. It is here, now, at this instant. It exists in embryo as the product of your own perverted copulation, and if it turns out to be a bastard, well, you know who to blame! You should look after your wife better.

You get to thinking a lot when you are being probed on the backside by the tapeworm. Perhaps it's a sort of defence mechanism. Something glandular. You begin to think in circles. You think for example that the whole set-up stinks of stale meringue, musty taffeta and faded rosewater. A distinct odour of decay. The aforesaid items having originally been introduced to tone down the smell. You needn't have worried! The original stink disappeared long ago when its source solidified, that is to say when the apple disappeared down old Adam's gullet. By the time that pimp had reached the stage where he swallowed more than an apple, well, that was that as some folks say who want to be conclusive. By that time he was as dead as the bird who fell on his head on a concrete surface. After that he was worrying only about the next world and the price of a ticket on the bus. And incidentally he was the first silly bugger to clamour for the right to hard labour. Dead from the brainpan downwards. No. You needn't have worried about the smell. The hard, the dead, the negative exhales no odour. But then you get to thinking that perhaps this cadaverous hulk is made more interesting by the sham scent treatment. And this is the way you've got to argue if you're going to accept. You can have no truck with those coons who talk big about accepting one minute and produce a fistful of blueprints the next. And you have a sly thought to yourself that there are a lot of these bastards. So long as you're not a member of the official school of British Watercolourists you can accept the hypocrisy of a cheap blonde's mascara, and what's more, love it! You remember reading somewhere about the scarlet women of Ancient Egypt and what these janes didn't know about magnetising the female torso you could put in your tooth. After touching it up with gold, green, grey and blue paints and draping a smoky-coloured something about as dense as a spider's web from hiplevel the guaranteed magnetic locus was upwards of four hundred yards. And if some modern skirts object in principle to these artifices, then it probably wouldn't be very practical for them anyway.

You are now reaching the hovel where you have temporarily installed your typewriter and your wife. You hesitate darkly at the bottom of the gaslit stair waiting for the woman whom Eliot said was also hesitating somewhere about the streetlamp. But of course she doesn't show up. And she is probably very mercenary anyway. So you light a cigarette and give the rudder to the tapeworm who is by this time about as sleepless as a lion rampant. You enter and Betty greets you with a big smile and a cup of coffee, and looking at her standing there like one of those enchantresses out of a fairy book you decide that if Caesar Borgia had wanted that little Italian curl at the chip shop then he would have been welcome to her as far as you are concerned. You decide that your wife has got all that it takes. After a while when she has shown a bit of leg and generally indicated that she desires your conjunction in the dance of the seven veils she begins to realise that this is one of those nights when the tapeworm has got you nailed. She is a good kid. Quietly she goes off to bed by herself and leaves you about as happy as a gooroo on a desert island.

You are sitting there in front of the typewriter. Like all other machines this wonderful invention needs an operator. You stare at the keyboard and it stares back at you as though it was disgusted. You big helpless bastard, it says, why don't you die? Sometimes you are sorry you have not pawned this contraption. It is one of those eternal manifestations of the cosmic pressure. But somehow it was always the last thing you had to pawn and you never needed to pawn it. At last you have a brainwave. You will play a game of solo. The more you think about it the more you like the idea. You have been alone a long time. Always as far as you can remember. Except perhaps sometimes when you are making love to Betty. You are alone now. And you begin to think that that is okay by you – at least you should know how to play solo . . .

My deal. Up through the hollow shadow-ribbed vault as far as the darkness. The bent ones. The feared ones. The edge of the rain metallic, final, a drawn dagger. And cold wet bodies under sodden smelling undergarments sticking to the expectant skin of soft-bellied harlots. I make a cut. I win. The cataracts are loosened as far as the flesh of my brain. I listen blackly to the drip drip drip of oil of cloves in the cavity of an old tooth. The pain sinks. I swell into being. I am the chancre of the cosmos. They hate me. But I have all the aces. l am an old hand at this game. With my terrible lever I shall prise their balance into Limbo. Not that I give a sweet damn really. Just that they get in the way – these moral philosophers, university professors and youth leaders, all the carbolic-soaped legion.

Men call me mad. It is true that I love bad smells and all sinful unclean things generally. I love bandits and poets and raped women, chinks and lascars and diseased negresses. Everything in fact from the navel downwards. Above the navel I am not such an expert. But then who really wants to be except moral philosophers, university professors and youth leaders? And you know what you can do with them. I can argue on their ground too – these buggers who worship the big brain and hide their penis in the urinal at the end – but who wants to argue with them anyway? Not me, by the good St Michael, not me! But perhaps I am mad too. If upside down means mad. I hang by my tail from the high wire. I put five fingers to my nose. Don't worry. I won't fall. You see, I've got the aces. I like a full fleshy thigh better than algebra. Laugh that one off you knackerless punks! I like sexy jube-jubey women better than pencils or metaphysics and what's more, I think deontology stinks! Put that in your pipes you noumenal jackanapes! Further, as logicians say, I like to trace with my tongue the soft line of down hair faintly over flesh from navel to cunt – I like to do that better than all your psychological bellyache with space-time and ultimate essences. I prick a balloon. I turn over my wilkies. I buy myself a packet of fags and a good stiff drink and I say to hell with thinlip, scragneck, knock-kneed virgins of thirty-five and their masculine paraphernalia. Agreed. May they inherit big brains and walk on tubular crutches till the cows come home. Then Charon ad holocaust. Pull the plug on them. They HAD their chance. Let them wallow in their own spume. Me? Give me a bed and a woman who knows when to take her scanties off – I'll be alright! My trick, gentlemen, I t'ink!

The man with the blue chin leads his queen. He is very, very efficient. He has studied economics at one of our liberal universities. They say he has fixed an automatic tabulator inside the lobe of his left ear. I hear it ticking now. He calculates he can trip me. The poor misguided bastard hasn't seen my fist! But this much I give him. He's thorough. He plays according to the rules. If I'm long-suited in Clubs he's caught me with my pants down. But as it happens I've got four aces and a string of trumps as long as a chorus-girl's leg. I grin. I take the first space-ship as far as Jupiter and I talk Rimbaud to the Caliph's daughter whose hips look like something out of Matisse. She is a very interesting conversationalist. But she is more interested in the practical than the theoretical. Which is as it should be. I don't disappoint her.

As I have remarked before I am not interested in the pure in mind, flesh or spirit. May they inherit nothing. I am not interested in the white radiance of eternity. Later I decide it's about time to take a sock at this blue-chin with the university education. I flick an ace. I bend down and grab hold of his right shoe and twist it upwards towards the roof. He is hanging like a stuck pig from the chandelier reciting Karl Marx and Harold Laski. I tell him what he can do with these birds below plain level. I tell him what he can do with the London School of Economics and with this slow fungus he calls the proletariat. I draw my tomahawk and I remove his scalp. It is a very bloody business. Somehow the operation is not a surgical success. The top of his skull is hanging open like the lid of a box and I am surprised to see what this lug uses for a brain. It consists of two rotating wheels not unlike typewriter spools and a ribbon perforated like one of those pianola things winds from one to the other. By the length of it I guess this bastard must have taken an honours degree. I close the lid and stick a label on it – returned empty.

A smiling fat priest with face-flaps like a bulldog has just revoked. I can see that by the glassiness of his cheap-bead eyes. I decide to watch this bird very carefully. I consider him a lot more dangerous than the blue-chin I have just scalped. He is one of those chameleons who changes the colour of his coat to suit the company. He has read St Paul and likes being a Roman very well. But if this cheapskate thinks I am not going to notice he has revoked then he had better offer me a percentage. Otherwise I'm going to blow him. And on due consideration I decide I'm going to blow him anyway. I don't like his crap line about the negative value of this world. I think this world is a very nice place indeed. I have no desire to change it. I leave that to the moral philosophers, the university professors and the youth leaders and I hope that the imposition breaks their bloody backs or something equally unpleasant. A Christian is a bastard who refuses to accept the present in and for itself, that is to say, to accept life in all its aspects. In the conflict between sex and death he swings a club on the side of the latter – as if the said latter needed any boob to swing a club for it! This sack-faced bird in the white collar is extremely eloquent in his demands for (a) mutilation – a detruncated man, and (b) a general diminution of intensity in living, catabasis; life minus its mysterious pointed flame. And I have no use for this philosophy which is anti-orgasm. The orgasm is the fire in the black vault, it is the dark deed in the hotel bedroom. I look up a dictionary. Orgasm: n. immoderate excitement or action (Gr. orgasmos, orgao: I swell). And now we know. Orgasm defines the vibrant, the vivid, the volcanic, the living, the Antichrist. Dilation, expansion, pregnancy, brutalisation, nakedisation – Orgasmos the Galegod! I look this guy right in the eye and I say to him that he is all washed up. I tell him I am going to blow him which I proceed to do in the name of the good god Orgasmos with a stick of dynamite which I always carry round for that purpose. When the air clears I think to myself that some day I shall write a history of religion. But then I got to thinking that I could do that in three or four lines and I decide to do it pronto. So here goes. Some bastards begin to find life tough. The cosmic pressure is too tough for them and as they are weak-livered skunks they don't see that they can do very much about it. So they begin to deny that it is one hundred per cent authentic. It is to be considered as a sort of insurance premium, something for your own good like a bad bottle of tonic. You can cash in on it later. There is no more efficacious method of getting rid of a bastard than by denying his reality. But it is difficult to see what you can do with an impersonal bugger like death. So a good God is invented and He will see you alright. Then these guys got to thinking that there are some bright moments too in this world, e.g. sex. But as they had already written off this world lock, stock, and barrel as a 'mere transient thing' they had to levy a tax on this world's pleasures. And that is where the sin of the flesh comes in. But as these birds have only had experience of transient pleasure and as that is all bound up with sex they find it very difficult indeed to say just what this supersubstantial pleasure in the next world will be like. And so they say it is playing harps. And they call that symbolic. A history of heresy is far more interesting. It is the long struggle of sex and life against the death-instinct implicit in Christianity. I dedicate this history of religion to the schools and the colleges and suggest that they remove all the rest from their libraries. Don't those buggers know there is a paper shortage?

I am now leading out my string of trumps. I am pulling teeth like a dentist with thirty years' experience. This young man with the thick-lensed spectacles is looking decidedly uncomfortable. He is a poet and for this reason I spare him. But at the same time he is one of those coons who accept one minute and who talk of the utter dearth of all moral values in the modern world just a moment later. So he has got it coming to him. I can't allow him to pervert the minds of the young. So I compromise. Without saying anything I prod him a quick left to the solar plexus and send him home to his mama. I have now thirteen tricks in front of me and I decide that solo is a very interesting game!

You sit back and you are very happy to realise that the tapeworm is having a drop of shuteye. You smoke a cigarette. You go to the bedroom and you find that Betty is still awake. She gives you a long look and in a few moments you decide that the world is a very rosy place indeed.

PARIS

1952 JANUARY. Trocchi settles in Paris. He meets Jane Lougee and forces Betty to accept a separation. Betty and the children settle in Mallorca.

1952 15TH MAY. First edition of *Merlin* magazine published. One thousand copies are printed.

1953. *Collection Merlin* publishes *Watt*, by Samuel Beckett — Beckett's first English-language publication. Later titles will include Jean Genet's *Thief's Journal* and Beckett's *Molloy*.

1953 JULY. Olympia Press publish Trocchi's translation of Guillaume Apollinaire's *Les Onze Mille Vierges*. Trocchi uses the pseudonym of Oscar Mole.

1954. Olympia Press publish the dirty version of *Young Adam*. Trocchi uses the pseudonym Frances Lengel for this and all his other dirty books for Olympia.

1954 3RD JUNE. Trocchi divorces Betty Whyte.

1954 10TH AUGUST. Jane Lougee returns to America.

1955. *Merlin* ceases publication.

DEAR JACK AND MARJORIE

Alex Trocchi

Dear Jack and Marjorie,

We travelled Newhaven-Dieppe because it was cheaper. The sea was calm, the sun shining and the deck was crowded with a merry band of pilgrims to Rome for the Holy Year – some Celtic society or other, each member with an immense buttonhole of green and yellow ribbon. They sang in Gaelic.

On the steamer we tasted French bread for the first time – like our Vienna loaves only longer, tastier, with a thicker crust. The meal consisted mainly of bread and various highly seasoned cooked meats.

Dieppe still shows its scars. Rubble, gutted buildings, fallen masonry. The railway line is unfenced. The train runs out of Dieppe at the level of the street beside vans, loaded bicycles and costermongers' carts.

By the time I'd got the registered luggage through the customs at the Gare St Lazare it was after 8 p.m., nearly twelve hours since we left London. Betty and little Jacqueline were naturally very tired. We ate a ham sandwich and drank Cinzano. Then Jacqueline disappeared. We found her a few minutes afterwards playing with a beautiful white cat which was attached to a disapproving lady by a lead of red patent leather! Apologies in our hesitant French, bows, and we retreated to our own table. In search of a hotel . . .

We had very little ready money and were reluctant to deliver ourselves into the hands of a French taxi driver. I left Betty and J. in the station cafe and went down the steps into the street. The night air was aglow with multi-coloured neon. There was a cafe, with tables on the pavement, at every corner. Vendors of roasted chestnuts, peanuts, shrimps, crabs, mussels, oysters. A conscious surrealism in all the posters. The traffic frantic, uncontrolled. In Paris one doesn't halt at crossroads. One slips subtly forward driving on the brake and on the horn.

It was ten o'clock when I returned to St Lazare. I had found a small hotel in the 10th arrondissement, near the Place de la Republique. A week later, in the same district, we got a furnished room where we could cook, a small room on the fourth floor of a dilapidated hotel. For this room – its condition is appalling – we pay more than ten pounds a month. This is one of the anomalies of present-day Paris. The Parisian, as a rule, pays a ridiculously low rent. The foreigner pays about ten times as much. Restaurant meals for all are very expensive. It is much cheaper 'doing for oneself'. The shops are stacked with exciting kinds of food but prices are far higher than at home.

A violinist lives in the next room. I began to despair of my French because I couldn't understand a word he said. Laboriously I tried to follow him. Politely, he spoke more slowly, stressing the infinitive of the verb and waving his hands about in the air. It was only after a week that I found out he was a Brazilian and couldn't speak French. He knew about ten words of the language and flung them about with a vicious Latin-American fluency that seemed to proclaim him a master of the tongue.

The 'intellectual elite' – if one is to believe the management of the cafe 'Deux Magots' – is at St Germain des Près. It is here that the night-clubs offer one 'Les soirées existentialistes'. It is all this long hair, the talk, the obvious tourist traps, that lead me to think (I may change my mind) that the creative centre is in the process of moving on. For the time being, I prefer Montmartre. If it is one big tourist trap at least it is a professional one, whereas the set-up in the Boulevard St Michel and St Germain strikes one as amateurish, a superstudents' union where the students are not necessarily superior. They make a lot of money, anyway, in Montmartre. I'm sure there must be some virtue in making money. I never seem to make any myself. We had been in the furnished room for less than a week when we became aware that we were not alone. We were infested with 'peen 'eads', a breed of bug that grows red on bloodfeasts. I had read about them – in Miller, in Celine, in Elliot Paul. But although I granted their existence, I had previously looked upon them (*qua dramatis personae* in autobiographies) as a sort of poetic licence, an appendix of the garret dweller in post-Dostoyevskian fiction. I had been wandering about Montmartre one night and returned to the room rather late. I fell asleep quickly. Then I was aware that the light was on and Betty, clutching her nightclothes about her, was telling me to waken up – bedbugs! Gorgeous fat creatures glutted with our blood, minute ones spumed hungry from the walls. We spent an hour searching every crevice in the sheets, blankets, mattress. We found a spent match beneath the mattress. Doubtless a bugtrap of a previous tenant. The Brazilian next door tells me he has fought the advance of 'la peste' for three months. An extremely dapper little man, he is frantic but helpless. And for the moment we are helpless too. But we will move as soon as possible.

Yours always,
Alex

JANE LOUGEE

When did you first meet Trocchi and how was Merlin *founded?*

I met Alex in the fall of '51, I believe, and we were immediately attracted to each other. I had become involved with a literary magazine that was going to be established.[1] We met Alex and he really was going to be a very fine editor but the magazine fell through and Alex and I went on and did the first issue of *Merlin*.

What was it about Trocchi? People seem to react very strongly to him.

He was very secure in his being. He appeared to be very secure about his talent and you knew that this was somebody who really could write. He was very self-assured.

What was the idea behind Merlin? *What were your intentions?*

It was a very exciting time in Paris because a lot of students were coming from the States on the GI Bill. There were writers who really had no place to have their writings published and we felt this was a wonderful opportunity. The name was suggested by Christopher Logue. He had been very interested in falconry; a merlin is a lady's falcon. It's very keen and sharp-eyed and goes for its prey. We were interested in writing that expressed some degree of change in life, the changes that were happening in the world, having just gone through a World War. We were interested in creative writing that showed some degree of experimentation, if you will. It was exciting because we got many manuscripts that expressed just those things. None of the other magazines seemed to be handling it. We did.

Can you explain what your role was and how you worked with Trocchi?

I was involved in making the mock-up of the magazine and choosing the print and how it looked. And also I read. I wasn't a writer but I had studied with Auden and with Roethke and had an ear and an eye for what I considered good writing. With Dick [Seaver] coming on as Alex's assistant, that was just fine because they worked wonderfully well together and were in agreement.

What was life in Paris like with Trocchi?

It was a very exciting time to be with Alex. To the other writers, he was obviously someone to be with and a delight to be with. He was funny and amusing and light-hearted and gay and posturing, which one recognises throughout his later work. *Young Adam* was his key first novel and he was in the process of working on it. It was extremely exciting to be with him as he wrote the chapters for it, to watch him sit down at the type-writer (which was my typewriter, incidentally) to type this thing out chapter by chapter. It was all in his head without really having to do any re-vising, it was very exciting. Now, having it published was a problem, I think, because already first chapters had been turned down in England, so he was concerned. This was a problem, what to do. I think he felt that the magazine would somehow enhance his chances of having *Young Adam* published.

MERLIN

Autumn 1952: volume 1, number 2

EDITORIAL

It is not sufficient to deplore the state of modern writing in general. Who is bad, and why? Generalised obloquy is not enough.

MERLIN would not exist if its publisher and its editor did not believe that good writing was being written. It is the editor's object to find that good writing, some of which he believes was printed in *MERLIN* number One, and to publish it.

Some ways of talking about literature are more useful than other ways of talking about literature. All ways of talking involve the use of distinc-tions. That is all right so long as those distinctions are not allowed to *harden*, that is to say, if we abandon them as soon as they cease to be useful. Most of the traditional categories are merely distinctions, hal-lowed by antiquity, which have been allowed to harden, and which, in the hands of unscience, have become an inquisitorial rack to which the flesh of contemporary writing is to be twisted. James Joyce's *Ulysses* broke one rack for the intelligent; they saw that it did not amount to much to say that it was not a novel, the significant point being that it was obviously a great work of genius. That was more than could be said for the productions of most of his contemporaries. Since then there have been other instances of rack-breaking; instances, but the principle does not appear to have been grasped, even by the intelligent reading public. That principle may be stated simply: *all categories are utilitarian; when they cease to be recognised as such, they become obnoxious.*

The categories die hard. Their utilitarian nature has been obscured by the poet's mistrust of, and his ignorance of the methods of, science. The floundering octopus of metaphysics has, quite naturally, made things worse. The poet was a useful ally against an intelligent approach to the universe. But now, in 1952, it is high time the poet let 'big brother' sink. *The experience of the poet and the experience of the scientist are not mutually contradictory.*

It is by a suspension of (or a failure to achieve) the scientific habit of mind that the poet attains that immediacy of experience which was natural to the primitive who experienced time, for example, concretely and promiscuously, as periodicity and rhythm. For the poet, *qua* poet, time is not a concept; it is something in which he is emotionally involved. The poetic habit of mind is an archaic one. The poet is situated beyond the problematical in a personal cosmos whose vital centre he is and which grows away from him on all sides into the warm flanks of *mystery*.

This mystery is inexpugnable.

But it is so simply because it is not a problem. Mystery cannot legitimately be said to be either *known* or *not known*. There is nothing suprarational about it. It is merely non-rational, logically neutral. The cosmos which contains it is, figuratively, the shadow of the poet himself; it is the colour, the complex vibration of his own emotions. It is a private *expressional* cosmos.

That cosmos has no relation whatsoever to, nor does it invalidate nor make nonsense of, the cosmos of exact science. The cosmos of exact science, in so far as it is valid (i.e. in so far as it can claim to be true or false) is purely *descriptive*. It is vital at the beginning to understand that the poetic experience is not valid in this sense, that being an expressive reaction towards something it simply *is* and is neither true nor false.

The poetic experience *is*. But it is also more or less formalised, and thus it has a technical aspect and thus there are problems of poetry. Scientific criticism must restrict itself to those problems and to the description of how they have or have not been solved by this or that poet. As soon as it encroaches on the personal cosmos of the poet, evaluating this or that content *out of relation to the work itself*, it ceases to be descriptive and becomes expression of the second order. Most so-called scientific criticism is second-order expression. The critical utterances of Henry Miller, which make no pretence of being scientific, differ only in degree from those of his detractors. At the same time, his are more engaging because, unlike them, he makes no solemn or pedantic allusion to the critical machinery of Aristotle. His 'information' comes directly from the Holy Ghost. We can accept it for what it is.

Poetry may well be *in its expressive content* 'a criticism of life': a science dare not have such a content.

The expressive element clings to most literary categories with the pertinacity of an old wart, is so embedded in some instances that category and fungus are indistinguishable. Certain words – the scientist has discarded many of them – handed down to us from primitive times (and still current in the press, the schools, the law courts) have pernicious structural implications. They reflect the assumptions of unscience in past epochs, strangle thought, and give structure to human institutions (honoured, God help us! for their antiquity) which, likewise false to facts, are the more pernicious because of the authority vested in them. To think we must use language. Language is, from the point of view of meaning, a system of implicatory relations, an apparatus for thinking with. If the apparatus is faulty, if certain implications are stultifying – and twentieth-century science has proven them to be so – then language itself can be the greatest obstruction to clear thinking. It is not only literature which suffers when the poet allies himself with the metaphysician against science.

No one asks the poet to give up writing poetry; what is demanded is that he should recognise for once and for all that it is poetry that he is writing, that he is dealing with what is emotionally significant and not necessarily with propositions which are true or false. As for the critic let him distinguish second-order expression from science; when he has done this there is no danger in either.

MERLIN will hit at all clots of rigid categories in criticism and life and at all that is unintelligently partisan.

To say that *MERLIN* is against obscurantism in criticism is not to say that it is against obscurity in poetry.

MERLIN is for any innovation in creative writing which renders creative writing more expressive.

Paris, 15 September 1952

ALEXANDER TROCCHI AND THE BEGINNING OF *MERLIN*

Christopher Logue

Between 1952 and 1955 I saw Alex, as he was to me, several times each week; but in the twenty-eight years following his departure from Paris until his death in 1984 we met no more than fifteen times, seldom alone, and twice in police courts. This, then, is only a personal recollection describing his effect on myself; an impression of his nature as it was when we were close.

He was a handsome man. Broad, easy on his feet, with a gliding walk, body tipped forward from the waist, and usually talking in a confidential way to whoever was with him, when he drew himself up to look before entering the traffic his six-foot two surprised. Taken in Mallorca by I am not sure who, my photograph of him seated at a cafe table proofreading the extract from Beckett's *Molloy* that appeared in *Merlin*, issue five, shows a face comparable to Burt Lancaster's, a man full of worldly confidence, charming enough to assure those left behind, 'Spanish printing costs half that of French' – when we knew it cost a quarter – without causing resentment, and thereafter to spend the balance on an excellent time in the sun.

As well as his liking, it seems to me now that such times were his due. Then, though, I was apt to look down my nose at sensual pleasure, but not in his presence. Encouraged by his good will, I feared his comradely sensuousness except when in trouble and kept our talk from intimate things. In those days I would let myself fall in what I mistook for love two or three times a year. When things went wrong, as they often did, I asked for his help. 'Believe me, old man,' he would say, 'she is keen on you. Cut your hair, persuade her to sell her father's car, and go to the south. But with you it's always the same – either All Off, or, Give Me The Gun.'

Once, in the second of these moods, I decided to go to the sea, hire a dinghy, pass out of sight of land, consume my bag of sleeping pills, and die. Perhaps I meant it. Losing my glasses, I did not replace them; returning to Paris from London, I avoided Alex and went by train to Perpignan. Next day I walked as far as Canet Plage, looked for, failed to find my dinghy, and then sat, trying to think of nothing until Alex, having heard of my flight and taken the following train, found me in tears. And of course he had jokes, good words, and two couchettes booked that evening for Paris, plus money enough for an expensive supper in the dining car. What is more, he had persuaded our wealthy acquaintances, Clement and Matilda Heller, to keep me in their apartment until I was myself again.

Six months earlier Alex and Alice Jane Lougee – whose will and whose money supported *Merlin* throughout – had moved themselves and the magazine's office out of the Hotel Verneuil into the store-room of a shop that sold African curiosities – tom-toms, canoe-paddles, shark's tooth necklaces, and so forth. Its proprietor had gone mad; and his girl, who was left in charge, never opened its shutters. The storeroom measured ten metres by five and, apart from a huge cupboard with curtains instead of doors, was unfurnished. Money was short. The storeroom was rent free. Alice Jane's father, a local banker from Limerick, Maine, sent her food parcels.

At the time of their move I was again confused by love and demanding Alex's advice on an almost hourly basis. I would ban all save Alice Jane from our conferences. When matters had taken yet another turn for the worse, she, who kept her council, would go to the cupboard, remove the latest food parcel, then cut us slices from the rich fruit cake that they always contained. My ban was a nuisance to others of the *Merlin* lot. They too needed advice, literary chat, and cake.

Prominent among them was Henry Charles Hatcher. While most of us wore what we had – in Alex's case sandals, check socks, green or gray cords, a windcheater – Charlie dressed well. Suit, shirt, links, tie, carrying a leather briefcase, he was an exceptionally polite and courteous man whom Alex would introduce as, 'a poet – but designing jewellery for cash'. At first, this made me discount Charlie; you hustled in order to read, write, or load; otherwise something was wrong. But my mind changed when I saw his fine drawings of bracelets and collars to be, watched him make a guitar in his hotel room, ate the suppers he bought me by playing it to the patrons of a club called Les Amis du Guitar – who knew about such things – and thereafter draw, paint, varnish, back, gild, box in a box that sucked, then give to the girl he was later to marry, a set of Tarot cards that shuffled like oil.

Alex and I made a plan. He would invite my present love to the storeroom for a talk about 'your and Christopher's case'; I would hide in the cupboard in order to learn what my chances were. 'It is a bad thing,' Alex said. 'Give me your word never to mention it. And regardless of what you overhear, you must not emerge until she and I have gone for a drink.' It worked: I promised and hid, she came, they talked, Alex drew nothing from her, and then they left, leaving me, with the bunch of flowers I had concealed, bursting to be out and after them, after her, when a hand holding a knife came through the bottom of the curtains, dipped into the parcel and began to cut a large slice of cake. I drew the curtain and looked into Charlie's shock-popped eyes. Then I ran off with my flowers.

Six years ago Austryn Wainhouse, whose translation of de Sade's *Philosophie Dans Le Boudoir* helped to finance an issue of *Merlin*, invited Alex and me to supper in a London restaurant. The food was bad; but the sight of Alex enjoying it was worse. He had liked well cooked food and had known where to find it. It was I who had needed instruction. During the meal we talked about the past. I asked Alex to remind me how he came to be in Paris and how *Merlin* started. He had been awarded a travelling scholarship by Glasgow University and set out for Spain, intending to finish his first novel, *Young Adam*, while there. Circumstances marred this plan. He and Betty, his first wife, left their two children in the care of a French couple who lived just outside Paris. Alex went to the Isle of Man to visit, perhaps to borrow money from, his brother, returned to France to collect the children and during this trip met Alice Jane. In Paris since the summer of 1951, she had been introduced to Alan Riddell, an Australian poet who wanted to start a literary magazine called *Lines*, and a fellow American, Victor Miller, who said he would finance it. Alice Jane was to be the assistant editor, and the magazine was to be based in her studio apartment at Auteil. Then Miller vanished. So Riddell introduced Alice Jane to Alex, who became coeditor of the nonexistent *Lines*.

I knew very little of this. Alex and I remembered our first meeting differently. He said, and now I think he was right, we met on the staircase of a wretched hotel in the rue de la Huchette, just north of Ile de la Cité. Being almost without money, he had taken a room among its permanent guests, the Algerian street pedlars who sold nick-nacks and carpets to tourists. *Le Canard Enchaine* published a cartoon of one such salesman saying to his prospective customer: 'Madam, it is me, not the carpet that smells.' Soon afterwards Betty and the children went to live in Spain; Alex sending them money each month. Then he moved into Alice Jane's studio and *Merlin* was planned, him to edit, and Alice Jane to finance it with the allowance she got from her father. Alan Riddell left Paris for London and started to publish *Lines*.

It was not easy to get Alex's goat. Now and again I could half manage to do so by traducing his favourite philosophers, A. J. Ayer and A. Korzibski – '. . . the obvious Alfreds, schmuckdoodles thick enough to think logic more than a game invented by cantankerous schoolmasters in order to fox the children of Greek slaveowners . . . ' then his first sharp words would turn to '. . . very well. Logue has said it. You believe it. And that settles it . . .' or: 'Very well, old man. I would not want it said I invited a friend to lift his head onto the block; but nor is it wise to keep so fine a communications centre in the sand. True, the chief use of logical discourse is highlighting fallacy. But to spot the dotty upshot in fair, or maybe wicked, words, is just as useful as to invent King Kong. And what's more – evil men fear it. They do not fear poetry. They quote it.'

'I want to do it like Keats,' I said, anxious to change ground. 'He did not bother with argument.'

'The only evidence for that is his failure to talk Fanny Brawne into bed. With respect, old man – and speaking as your first editor – if you can do it like Keats, so much the better for us both. But can you? Is this,' putting his finger on my manuscript, 'as good as

> O latest born and loveliest vision far
> Of all Olympus faded hierarchy!
> Fairer than Phoebe's sapphire-regioned star,
> Or Vesper, amorous glow-worm of the sky

because if you think it is, let us say no more – except that I might be wrong – and as you are not in love at the moment, see if we can get to know that young lady over there.'

I angered him twice. The second time coincided with the end of our friendship; the first resulted in an exchange of letters. Prior to my leaving on a visit to Italy, Alex, Charlie, Alice Jane and I had a meeting during which I slighted Charlie's poems. Alex's first letter reached me in Rome. He answered my answer, thus:

> *Chez Meyer*
> *8 rue du Sabot*
> *Paris*
> *October 1952*

Dear Chris,

By this time you will have received the little bomb of yesterday. I hope that it got you bloody angry and then that on thinking it over you realised that I wouldn't have written like that unless my esteem and liking for you were what they are, very high indeed. Of course, I exaggerated; but then you do and you have. I wish you would write to Charlie, politely, with no grain of irony, in good faith, asking him not the meanings of words which can be found in any dictionary but for the associative transitions, which means in the case of Q.M.S. and in the case of T.G.F., the basic reference. Remember, Chris, that Charlie is much older than we are, rather petty in some ways, and, unaccepted by those older than him he is bloodily sensitive to hostile criticism from the young. I don't know how you two fell originally into your respective shooting attitudes; I suspect because you (or because Charlie thought you) crowded him; it must have been something like that, because of all the poets he had ever met Charlie had more respect for you than any other. As a matter of fact he still has, but defensively and because he's not always objective he admits to this respect only to me and when we're alone. Again, you have a tendency to interpret silence or tonguetiedness as admission or capitulation. It's not always so. Another point I don't think you have given enough weight to. I think in an extra-literary way it can be accepted as evidence of Charlie's good faith: his qualifications are such that he was offered (subject to his being able to speak fluent French – the ass admitted he couldn't) 250,000 francs a month to be the head of the Graphics Department of E.C.A.! This only a couple of weeks ago, from qualifications tendered in writing two years ago! Charlie has literally given away every comfort to write poetry. To know that alone of a man without reference to his writing is enough to convince one of the seriousness of his intentions.

I don't consider it fair of you to hold a pistol at my head, and that, and that alone, was what prompted me to write a letter which must have hurt you. God knows, with Betty and the children crying out for money in Spain, and with the finances of the magazine in a poor state, with so many letters to be written to agents and subagents who can't be bothered replying, a threat like that from you who are closer than any of them was a body blow. Do you, Chris, respect my judgement or don't you? I don't claim to be almighty God; but where I know myself to be ignorant I think I am a good listener, and shrewd enough in deciding between advices. If you do trust me as a friend and as a fellow-writer and your being in Rome is going to lead and relead to 'incidents' like this, then for God's sake get back to Paris where your friends are, and where in spite of our own poverty we can give you some help.

Young Adam is finished and sent off to London. I am looking around for a cheap typist to have a good copy for America. The money when and if it comes will, needless to say, go to *Merlin* and its dependents.

Write soon, I'll ignore any letter occasioned by the bomb, and sent before you receive this.

Yours always,
Alec

Philip Oxman, the American scholar-poet who lived in Paris at the same time as ourselves, said this of Alex: 'He was strong. Well able to survive shocks that would have been the end of many. He had a sharp, intuitive, understanding of others; relating easily and sincerely to them. Of course you avoided him having decided to commit suicide. Whatever theory he held – and I heard him through several – he was firmly on the side of life, even in his self-destructiveness. He would have laughed and charmed you out of it. The trouble was, he never kept still. He was not a vessel in which intuitions can age. True, he was often unscrupulous; borrowing money without knowing or caring how it could be repaid. But he lent it just as easily; carrying whatever he had, his pocket his bank, hardly expecting its return.'

Each issue of *Merlin* cost, roughly, £430. As comparisons: the train fare to Paris from London was £12; my hotel room (clean but small, 'guests and cooking forbidden') £6 a month. Most of what Alice Jane did not supply, Alex supplied. Contributors were seldom paid, or paid in kind: they included Ayer, Beckett, Creeley, Genet, Ionesco, Neruda, Sartre, as well as the debutants. Writing this piece soon after the publicity surrounding the death of the mass murderer, Joseph Mengele, I notice that issue three of *Merlin* included what must be one of the first accounts in English of his atrocities – as well as the first publications of part of Beckett's *Watt*.

In January 1952 my lower teeth began to ache. Twice a day I opened a capsule of Tuinal, mixed the powder with oil of cloves, and rubbed the paste along my gum. After a week of this I accepted Philip's offer to take me to his dentist.

Philip lived at 31 rue de Seine, an *hotel particulier* owned by Ronald Duncan, Isadora's elder brother, a lively, Druidic figure of seventy-six, who wove his own soutanes, baked his own bread, wrote and published his own books, and had divided his vast house into a large number of very small apartments each of which he rented for over two hundred dollars per month, collected his rents at 6.00 a.m. on the first day of the month, cut off the lights, the heating, and the minuterie between 9.30 p.m. and 7.30 a.m., and was, as Philip said: 'An active miser of the most exceptional stamp'.

Philip opened his door, looked at my swollen face, and began to dress. Knowing my fear of dentists, he had laid his plans. On the bus, he said: 'Beit Kiewicz is a no-nonsense Pole. He will want to get on with it. During the war he fixed the teeth of Allied spies.'

'Voila, Anglais. Au chaise,' Dr Kiewicz said. I opened up and began to recite to myself. Then, my repertoire consisted of some fifty items. If I could get as far as 'Easter 1916', and as far into that as *Hearts with one purpose alone*, I told myself I could face the terrible cross-nosed pincers, and the soft wrench as the root left its socket.

'Bon,' he said, after twenty seconds. 'On va.' And led the way to his Renault.

'We are going to his hospital. He has to extract three of them. Big ones. He says you stink of pus,' Philip said as we drove.

It was a state hospital. Dr Kiewicz left us in a wide, ground floor passage with stools along one of its walls. Three of them were occupied by men wearing pyjamas made of blue canvas. After a few minutes one of the men began to piss. Philip and I watched his urine trickling across the floor. Nobody spoke or moved.

'This is a lunatic asylum, isn't it?' I said.

'Yes,' Philip said. 'St Anne's. One of the biggest.'

As I was getting to my feet two orderlies in bloodstained whites came down the passage, took my elbows, lifted me to, then through, a pair of yellow rubber doors that were hinged at the top, on, through another such pair, into an operating theatre, onto its table, and by the time Dr Kiewicz appeared, saying: 'Lumiere et gaz,' had stripped me to the waist, laid me flat, strapped my wrists and ankles to the table's top, and fitted the hissing mask across my face.

'Au revoir, Anglais,' said the bearded one.

'Holy shit!' said Philip, when, on our way to Auteil, I mentioned the strapping down.

Alice Jane still had her studio in Auteil at that time. Philip had asked her if she would let me stay the night.

And what a lovely room it was, and sight they were, both in the one large bed, as yellow as the hospital's rubber doors, recovering from jaundice.

'You look pale,' said Alice Jane.

'Better get into bed, old man,' said Alex, and moved over.

I stayed a while. Either we played canasta or talked philosophy and books. Our tastes were not dissimilar. The usual moderns: Eliot, Pound, Yeats, Joyce, Faulkner; the usual ancients. He had landed up in Paris by accident; I was there because I could not find my way in London. I had some verse written; he had nearly finished *Young Adam*. Perhaps I persuaded Alice Jane to call the magazine *Merlin*. I was very keen on Pound's versions of Troubador poetry at the time, and had read a number of books on falconry; it was the bird, not the wizard, that counted: particularly the one that sits on the wrist of the wimpled girl in a tapestry belonging to Musee de Cluny.

Alex would have liked the magazine to represent a coherent philosophy. We all knew that it did no such thing. Rather, we got ourselves into print, published some of the established writers we admired alongside, helped to make Beckett's reputation among those who cannot read French, and included political and philosophical comment as well as fiction and verse. I say 'we did'; I mean, Alex did. For without him the magazine would not have existed.

Its first issue appeared on the 15th of May, 1952. One thousand copies. Aside from those sent on a sale-or-return basis to Amsterdam, London and New York, the magazine had two outlets. George Whitman's Librarie Mistral 'Dans le vieux quartier de Saint-Julien-le-Pauvre la poesie vivante vous donne rendezvous. 37 rue de la Bucherie – at the end of Quai Saint-Michel opposite Notre Dame – Noon to Midnight – open house every Sunday afternoon – you are invited for tea', and Gaït Frogé's English Bookshop at 42 rue de Seine. I doubt if more than three hundred copies of each issue were sold.

Alex and I quarrelled for the second and last time while at a party in Notting Hill Gate. Because I was in the middle of leaving Paris and he had been travelling, we had lost close contact. When we had recounted our doings, Alex told me that he was going to live in New York and had decided to take heroin on a regular basis. I forget my reply; but I know that my words, unlike his had our positions been reversed, were hasty, self-righteous, dismissive, heedless that he was confiding a dangerous proposal concerning himself to one from whom he had a right to expect something better than anger. After all, he had befriended me, published me, persuaded others to publish me, had helped to curtail my suicidal urge, overseen the publication of my first book, and borne with my so-called love affairs.

Alex was obstinate, headstrong, clever. *Cain's Book* is far and away the best of its kind. I do not think I could have altered his course. But I could have tried. And failing that, have kept contact. Like many of us, he cherished his errors and was proud of his defects. I know that later he brought confusion on himself and disaster to others. It was not his way when I knew him.

LETTER FROM PARIS

Alex Trocchi

NIMBUS: volume 2, number 1 (June – August 1953)

During the summer, while we were away on vacation, Sartre attacked Camus in *Les Temps Modernes*. The attack was sudden and uncompromising. There has been no subsequent reconciliation and there is no reason to suppose that there will be. Sartre remains adamant in his judgment, his position being the logical development of that expressed in his *Situations*. Camus has withdrawn into a largely emotional isolation, into the position of non-participation outlined in his *L'homme revolté* and since Sartre and Jeanson combined to attack him, his public utterances have been few. Sartre, the pamphleteer, the man of action, flies to Vienna with a new, as yet incomplete manuscript on his lap: for him Camus is a thing of the past: 'If you want to write again, the magazine is at your disposal. But next time, I shall not answer' – he is sharpening his scalpel to cut out a more recent cancer.

To understand the present literary situation in France it is necessary to go back to the defeat of Nazism. At that time the *N.R.F.*, which had remained in existence throughout the German occupation and which was, to say the least, suspect, ceased to appear, and at that time it must have appeared to the resistance heroes that there was no question of its renaissance. Celine, Montherlant, Giono, Cendrars, Chardonne, Drieu, to name only a few who were denounced as collaborators at the time of the liberation, were all in varying degrees discredited; Sartre and Existentialism replaced Breton and Surrealism as the most powerful single force in French letters; Malraux, Camus, Aragon, and Eluard emerged unscathed; Gide continued to be the grand old man and Claudel and Mauriac went ambiguously on. The displacement, indeed dethronement, of Surrealism by Existentialism was inevitable in the new historical context, the former being a largely negative attitude, the latter, although pessimistic, being vibrant and a philosophy of action. To paraphrase M. Julien Gracq, Sartre emerged with both a position *and* an audience, and won on both the swings and the roundabouts.

Between the wars it was still just possible for the French writer to retain his position as an individualist, to show his sympathy for the mass without actually communicating with it, by satirising the class who manifested their liberality by providing his bread, the clothes of his mistress, or his Delage, depending on the voltage of his titivations. Such a writer, according to Sartre, was a parasite on a parasitical class. His work, critical of, but specifically directed to, the bourgeois, was clever, amusing, but from the point of view of social change, utterly ineffectual. It made no impact whatsoever on the proletariat. Such a writer was in a very real sense 'out of key with his time'.

After the Nazi occupation, as gradually before the Allied advance the hellish interior of Germany was revealed, many writers began to feel that the 'gentleman of letters' was perhaps an anachronism. The 'creative' writer had a position rather than an audience, and, as that position was conferred upon him by a politically inconsequential section of the bourgeoisie, his work had no significance outside the sphere of *superior amusement;* however profitable, it amounted to little more than intellectual masturbation. In short, 'creative' writing was no longer a force that counted; it was ignored by both Stalin and MacArthur. It was such considerations as these which led Sartre, with a ruthlessness which is characteristic of him, to condemn all writing which was not *engagé.*

Existentialism in all its ramifications, epistemological, psychological, and political, is a philosophy of crisis with an essentially practical impact; for this reason, with a man of Sartre's energies at the helm, it had not even to contend, after Europe had been razed for a second time, with the perennially vague doctrines of the Surrealists. Existentialism was in and Surrealism out, and Sartre sat in the throne vacated by Breton.

Almost from the beginning the utterances of the French existentialists were political and, from a certain point of view, naive. "Those who take upon themselves the governing of others,' wrote Merleau-Ponty, 'can no longer be judged by intentions but by results.' Statements like 'a man is what he does' or 'a man defines himself through his acts', while for the philosophical analyst they are merely definitions and for the cynic platitudes, do nevertheless have a vital significance at a time when the ancient certitudes, authorities and functions have reached an extreme depth of decay; when, in brief, there is not only a 'power vacuum' but a crisis in language, that is, in the tools of thought. They imply that in the present historical context with the atomic threat to civilisation, and when there is lacking the margin of comfort and abundance that allows for fatuousness, it is no longer enough to profess liberal opinions; they include the urgent question: what are you *doing?* The point is that if you pretend to be 'above' politics, i.e. the contemporary situation, then however amusing your professions and ingenious your pleadings, you are *in effect* contributing to the maintenance of the present repressive *status quo*; you are, moreover, still demanding your share of diminishing supplies. What, should I starve? Have I not the right to eat? That right, goes the reply, is strictly commensurate with your right to vote. That, as we shall see, was the basis of Sartre's condemnation of Camus. It is the footrule by which Sartre measures all things human, literary expression included: *what is the practical result?* For the fact is that Sartre considers the self-appropriated pedestal of the writer ludicrous and unrealistic. After having massively extinguished others, we are confronted by the growing possibility of our own mass extinction. Is the writer who will fiddle while Rome burns worthy of any consideration? What kind of consideration can he expect from the Romans? Because of his intelligence and powers of expression he may be viewed either as a criminal or a lunatic. Anyway, the pyromaniac can claim very little attention: he who persists in regarding humanity as divisible into master and slave classes must have a strong back as well as a vigorous hand.

Members of the reigning literary oligarchy in the United States are clambering over one another to avoid responsibility. Alan Tate, who come what may is going to be an optimist – has he not God and Mr Taft on his side? – sees Existentialism as a 'paranoid philosophy of despair'. One of the *Partisan Review* editors, Mr William Barrett, criticising Sartre for 'meddling' in politics, protests his own unworthiness:

> It is time we recognised that there is such a thing as 'literary' politics, to be taken no more seriously than 'literary' philosophising, 'literary' psychology, and the rest of these adulterated products. During the thirties, of course, 'literary' politics was the universal pastime; the mood of the period was some excuse, but that period has now passed, and literary men and fellow travellers (?) ought to be told that politics is a special discipline, with its own data and rules, concerning which one ought occasionally to think before one talks. [*Partisan Review*, September 1949]

Barrett has sold his birthright as a social critic for a stale meringue and a Cadillac convertible; he can expect nothing but contempt. One would formerly have thought him (and his coeditors) to have a more intelligent approach to politics than Senator McCarthy.

Neither Diderot, D'Alembert, Voltaire, nor Rousseau was content to be a political eunuch. Sartre is in good company. The fact is that politics pervades the existence of every man, circumscribing action, defining and limiting personal possibilities, and to say that one is not interested in politics is tantamount to saying one is not interested in life.

In 1945 the time had arrived for the writer to take stock of himself. The war was over, but the world was dividing into two camps, East and West. New and unimaginable destructive weapons were being forged to 'make the world safe for democracy'. Sartre and his associates, facing up to the crisis, asked themselves the following questions:

What is writing?
Why write?
For whom does one write?

The answers to these questions were given in 1947, in that important if ambiguous series of essays entitled *Situations*. However much one might disagree with his individual judgments about this writer and that, the main impact of the book is clear and decisive: no writer who is worth his salt will be content to poeticise and reap his reward in being invited to address ladies' clubs. What about Belsen? What about Auschwitz? What about the Korean war? Is it to stretch the limits of our imagination to assert that in the history of our civilisation the development of atomic physics is more significant than the appearance of *Finnegan's Wake?*

Historical parallels are unrealistic. It may or may not be true that this or that particular writer in the past was not intimately concerned with politics. Attitudes as well as language are in constant need of modification. The twentieth century implies atomic physics, mass psychology, symbolic logic, mass production, mass movements and mass slaughter. The danger is NOW. The fault lies not with science but with politicians. The writer is not 'above' politics; he is not even 'out' of them. Barrett in his ingratiating way has merely promised his employer he will behave with docility and cause no trouble; he is, if we are to believe him, 'below' politics, and will be content to leave political questions in the hands of those who have undergone a 'special discipline', that is to say, to the mercy of the rogue's gallery of the China Lobby and the financiers who back them.

Thus, in France after the war, the *engagé* writer came into fashion and has more or less remained there ever since. But that is not the end of the story.

Gradually, in spite of the international situation, or perhaps because of it, the forces of reaction have begun to play an increasingly prominent part in French politics. Such is the fear of Russia that it has become almost a crime to have been an active member of the Resistance Movement, and today laws exist that discourage the application of the epithet 'collaborator'. Nevertheless, things have not and probably will not, come to such a pass as they have in the United States where a liberal in a prominent position or a dissident Bourbon is almost certain to be called before a loyalty board.

I have heard it said recently that Existentialism is dead; the only meaning that can be given to such a statement is that tourists are no longer amused by the moth-eaten but wistful big-busted small girls in tight black trousers who conglomerate in the Mabillon on the Boulevard St Germain. Sartre is more active than ever – he *has* to be – and both Camus and Sartre will tell you that Camus was never an existentialist.

Apart from an unsatisfactory account of the polemic in the *Partisan Review*, the quarrel between Sartre and Camus has received little attention outside France. The most comprehensive English-language treatment of the episode appeared in the Paris-American quarterly, *Merlin*, early this year. Richard Seaver, who wrote the article, ends on the following note: 'Practically all of the contemporary truth makes its appearance in one form or another in their bitter contest; that, in a word, is its significance.' With *L'homme revolté*, fatigued but acclaimed, his reputation secure and his bank account adequate to his needs, Camus returns from the contemporary situation in intellectual disgust: all revolutions repudiate their own first principles, therefore I shall take no part in a revolution and cannot approve of those who do. The substance of the attack on him in *Les Temps Modernes* can be summed up in two sentences of Jeanson:

> It is especially when a person is not at grips with any great injustice himself that he can be wary of combating it for fear of provoking an even graver injustice.

And,

> ... you were in history precisely when you undertook to disengage
> yourself from it ... your protest against history was in reality
> directed against *its practical urgencies* ... the attitude you sanctioned
> consists in *maintaining* history, that is, maintaining one's position
> *before* it, but forbearing to undertake anything *in* it.

The virulence of Sartre's attack on his former friend can perhaps be explained only in reference to events in the literary world since the Liberation. In 1945 Sartre's position was unassailable. It remained so until approximately 1948. By that time, a non-'committed' literature (Aymé,
Anouilh, Peyrefitte, old Mauriac again, etc.) existed side by side with
what was 'committed', the surrealists were and still are making convul-
sive attempts at a come-back, the old brigade, Cocteau, Prévert, Giono,
Mauriac, those whose wartime activities were suspect or contemptible,
were again publishing, and the politico-economic schism between East
and West was already clearly defined, with the result that the two Communist giants, Aragon and Eluard, were already to some extent suspect.
Sartre made no effort to conceal his attitude towards those writers who
ignored contemporary events. From the beginning *Les Temps Modernes*
had a political aspect. Thus, in spite of his furious attacks on the Communists in the late Forties, he was in one sense closer to Aragon and Eluard
than to most of his contemporaries. Within the Communist fold, Aragon
had already become such another pamphleteer. By the time *L'homme
revolté* appeared, anti-Soviet feeling in the West and the West's readiness
to founder, flop, and snigger away its responsibilities, to bury them beneath style and soft complaints, had already prepared the way for the
reappearance of the *N.R.F.*; it is small wonder that when Camus retreated
from politics, in effect turning a blind blue eye to the resurgence of reaction in France, Sartre turned to attack him. Since *La Nausés* Sartre has, it
would seem, almost deliberately written second-rate novels because he
wanted to say something to a wide audience. Even his plays, first class
theatre as they are, are sometimes overloaded with message.

This brings us to the present time. It is by no means the whole story.
Many writers, including Samuel Beckett and Jean Genet, have not even
been mentioned. Both writers have appeared in *Les Temps Modernes*, the
latter, 'Saint' Genet, has been eulogised by Sartre in a series of articles

which have now been collected and published by *Gallimard*. Genet, a professional burglar, seems to Sartre to be the epitome of 'man in revolt', a man who does rather than a man who deliberates. Beckett's characters (Molloy, Malone, Watt) are so inactive, so vegetable, that they are also in a queer and disquieting way in revolt, and the impact of the man-vegetable is perhaps even more powerful than that of the burglar-saint.

And now the wheel has come full cycle with the appearance in January of this year of the new (old) *N.R.F.* This event is practically coeval with the amnesty for collaborators. Paulhan, its editor, has stated that if the collaborators were traitors during the German occupation then the French Communists are traitors now. Whether or not he really believes this is uncertain. His argument, like all political argument, is not one that can convince on a purely logical plane; the dialectic is psychological; he will convince those who are ready to be convinced – too many; we are at liberty to oppose his attitude.

The *N.R.F.* is not a bad magazine. It is a very rich one. It assembles together under one cover a glittering array of talent, even if that talent is for the most part over sixty, by now short in the wind, and thoughtful chiefly of the pleasures of comfortable retirement. Without doubt it will continue to print much work that is well-written. With the *Gallimard* machinery and discipline behind it, it can summon all but the most scrupulous. It is, however, essentially an old man's work, conspicuously elegiac, a miscellany of well-written prose, scraps and scrapings, reminiscences, fragments.

The difference between the literary situation in Paris and that in London is an age-old one. It is parallel to the difference between London of the age of Dr Johnson and London of today. In the former, the writer was an important figure who brushed shoulders and crossed swords and invective with statesmen. In London of today he is a frail exile in his own city, and if he has become 'famous' he is either not living in London at all, but in the country or abroad, or else he is on the editorial board of some publishing house or other from whose august windows he blinks sadly down at streets which are all but unconscious of his existence. London is too big. But Paris today is in some respects similar to the London of Dr Johnson, and his counterpart, more deadly serious, but a man with an audience and a man with a reputation, is the dynamic M. Sartre.

(Editors' Note: Mr Trocchi is the editor of the Paris Quarterly, *Merlin*.)

Describe the position that Trocchi occupied amongst the Merlin *coterie. How was he viewed?*

Alex was the clear leader of the *Merlin* writers. I met him in 1952, through the auspices of a man named Patrick Bowles, an aspiring South African writer, who was living in Paris. We happened to meet one day at the Deux Magots, as I recall, at St-Germain-des-Prés. I had just written a piece for a magazine called *Points*, which Patrick had read, and he said, you ought to meet this guy named Alex Trocchi, he's just started a magazine called *Merlin*.[1] So we went around the same day to Alex's hotel, which wasn't far away, I can't remember what street it was on. The room was three-quarters taken up with a bed, there was a table and he and Jane Lougee were living there. He said, well why don't you write something for us? in his inimitable Scottish accent. Who's the most notable writer who you know who might be unknown and who you think is worthy of our attention? And I said, I have just been reading a man who I think is most extraordinary. He was James Joyce's secretary, a man named Samuel Beckett. And Alex said, Beckett . . . Beckett? I think I've heard of him. I said, he is published, he's now writing in French and I have read three or four of his books. He has just written a play which I believe is going to be produced. He said, well, why don't you write a piece on him? Alex was tall, very prepossessing, very impressive, with a wonderful twinkle in his eye. Obviously bright as hell and I thought, okay, a piece on Beckett, that might make sense. I did write it and it appeared in *Merlin*, number two, Autumn 1952. I was all of twenty-two. I would suspect that Alex was twenty-four or five at the time. He seemed much more mature than most of us. Alex had already been married, had two children and had left his wife. That seemed to us a whole life at the age of twenty-five. But very much in charge. Everything he did he felt was part of his destiny and I think his destiny included being a major writer or a major force in European literature.

Merlin was founded on the premise that there was no serious literary magazine after World War II the way there had been after World War I. Although there were two or three such as *Points*, he did not feel that these magazines were 'serious' and if you read the editorials in issues number one and two you can see that *Merlin* was dead serious. It was political, it was an avant-garde approach, it was the thought that for good writing to exist, it has to move forward the way Joyce moved literature forward with *Ulysses* and later with *Finnegan's Wake*. Beckett, it turned out, was the worthy successor of Joyce, although we did not know it at the time, but in that piece I made a prediction that Beckett would turn out to be one of the major writers of the twentieth century. I doubt that any of the fifteen hundred readers (fifteen hundred is about the number we printed of the magazine) shared that view, but we sent a copy of *Merlin* number two to Beckett. Meanwhile, the other members of *Merlin* who could read French were beginning to read Beckett as well. Alex could not, but people like Austryn Wainhouse read him and recognised that he was a major writer. Alex was the towering figure of that *Merlin* group. I would say not only in that *Merlin* group but among the English language writers, critics, whatever we were, in Paris. He was the clear leader.

He also was a wonderful conman, which we didn't know at the time but we began to perceive as time went on. Jane Lougee, I believe, who was madly in love with him, was also being conned by him. She was a relatively wealthy, young, very attractive American from Bangor, Maine, whose father owned a bank in a little town called Limerick and how she and Alex met is a whole other story. She was mesmerised by him and was financing the magazine, with pretty limited funds. I think she had enough money to finance the first three or four issues after which it became a question of finding funds elsewhere and also of trying to move from printer to printer, since credit grew short for non-payment from the previous issue, you had to find another printer. But Alex had very clear ideas of what literature should be, of its relationship to science, of its relationship to politics and I would say *Merlin*, among the literary magazines of the post-war era, was the most politically motivated and politically sensitive magazine.

It also aspired to be very high quality. It also should be said, it was a voice for Alex Trocchi. It was a voice he could use as a springboard for other ambitions and I think he used that to the fullest.

What was Collection Merlin?[2]

Collection Merlin grew out out of the magazine *Merlin*, obviously. A year or two after we published the magazine for which we were having great problems making payment, we decided in for a penny, in for a pound. Why not do some books? We had one ready which was *Watt*, Samuel

Beckett's last book written in English, which he had given us to excerpt for the magazine and which we had read and decided we should really publish. We also had Jean Genet's *Our Lady of the Flowers*, whose translator Bernard Frechtman worked with us on the magazine; he contributed some translation to the magazine itself. With those two major works we decided to go ahead and publish books. We ultimately published eight or ten books, of which those are certainly the two best, most famous and the two most enduring.

Was Trocchi a radical?

Alex was a radical. He was a born radical. He was certainly in rebellion against parochial Scotland and probably parochial England. And Paris was the place to exercise that kind of rebellion. There was a great ferment after World War II. You had Sartre and Camus who were in rebellion against the French establishment, both politically different but trying to forge something new, both in literature and in politics, and I think Alex saw himself as the equivalent in the English language. When I first met him there were no drugs involved in his life. His radical stands were concentrated on literature. When literature began to pale as rebellion, or was not paying off in the way that he had hoped, the sexual experimentation took its place, and I think drugs followed thereafter. He was a true rebel in the sense that the establishment was abhorrent to him and he would do whatever he could to fly in the face of it and to outrage it, *épater les bourgeoises*, as the French would say, and Alex spent a great deal of his life trying to *épater les bourgeoises*.

When Trocchi turned up in Paris, he was already married to Betty and had two children, yet he was gadding about, doing as he wished . . .

I really didn't know much about that. That was already his past. I think I saw the children once, two absolutely charming little girls, and Betty who seemed like a lovely lady. She came through Paris at one point and we met, but . . . Alex turned his back entirely on them, both financially and as a parent to his children.[3] I don't know what's become of them but . . . in those days he was so charismatic, so handsome, so . . . prepossessing that one forgot that he already had a past, even when he was that young. It was a past that indicated, certainly a carelessness or an uncaring about others around him for whom he should have had some responsibility, in the basic sense of the term, and the later pattern certainly seems a continuation of that.

You said that Trocchi was the man most likely to amongst the Merlin *coterie . . .*
Alex was enormously articulate, both verbally and in writing and he was able to write with a facility and an intelligence that I had rarely seen. I think I was the first to read *Young Adam*, and I acted, as it were, as a first editor on that and actually re-typed the manuscript for him incorporating changes, etc. Although it was very much influenced by Camus, by *L'Étranger*, it was nonetheless a very developed, mature piece of work for a twenty-four or -five year old and on the basis of that and on the basis of his non-fiction writing, his editorials, there was no question, I think, in any of our minds, that among the group in Paris, Alex was the person who could become the major writer of our generation, or certainly one of the top two or three, and I think that would be shared by Austryn Wainhouse, Patrick Bowles, Christopher Logue and those who were close to *Merlin* as well as probably George Plimpton.

When *Young Adam* was typed and ready to be sent out we had had, via *Merlin*, two or three queries from American publishers, including a man named Mark Jaffe, who was a very highly esteemed editor for many, many years at Bantam Books, but I don't think he was there at that point. I think he was at New American Library. Anyway, we sent it off and it was read and ultimately rejected for reasons that are still mysterious to me because clearly it was a better novel than ninety per cent of the novels being published in those days. Maybe it was a little too daring, maybe it was a little too . . . tough, because it was a hard book, sparely written. But not long after the third or fourth rejection, Maurice Girodias arrived in the life of the *Merlin* group and founded his DB line, his dirty book line, and having read *Young Adam* he convinced Alex that with a few . . . careful insertions of sex scenes, he could turn this into a valid dirty book, which Alex was delighted to do. So he did so and the book was published and enjoyed . . . became one of Girodias' top sellers. But the fact remains that with those scenes out, that book to my mind is a major piece of 1950s writing.[4]

How close were you to Trocchi and what ultimately damaged the friendship?
I was as close to Alex, I think, as certainly anybody in the *Merlin* group. I felt great admiration, great friendship, I felt real brotherly affection for Alex and also felt that *Merlin* was a magazine worthy of the best that we could do. When Jane Lougee sort of ran out of money, I took a job outside of Paris and contributed a great deal of my meagre earnings to

keeping the magazine going. That was, in a way, fine but on the other hand I think it was the beginning of the wedge between us, because Alex was increasingly moving towards sexual experimentation and . . . individual rebellion, having nothing to do with the magazine. I think it was the beginning of drugs and the money that I was presumably making and putting in to the magazine, was clearly increasingly not going to the magazine and there came a point where we had . . . a real rift, in 1954, where I said, enough already, I'm not going to give you guys any more money, this is for the magazine, not for your own personal luxurious purposes and Alex took great umbrage at that, claimed that he was up at the crack of dawn every day and working, slaving at the magazine back here while I was out in the boondocks where I would have been much more helpful back in Paris. There was a . . . not a major break, but there was a schism that was taking place because I think his focus was clearly moving away from the magazine towards his own personal fulfilment in . . . in whatever ways that meant.

What was the relationship between Girodias and Trocchi?

The relationship between Girodias and *Merlin* came about because of a mutual need. We, as a group of expatriates in Paris, had no ability to mail our magazine, and other business aspects were constant obstacles to its fulfilment and getting it printed and so forth and so on. Girodias showed up one day because he had heard of us or heard that we were moving in to publishing books. He was concerned that the books we might publish would in some way conflict with his so he made a proposal that he would become the business manager of *Merlin* and as a French citizen he could provide us with all sorts of amenities that would help ease our business life in Paris, both for the publication of the magazine, but also because we were indeed beginning in 1953, as I recall, to publish books, including Beckett's *Watt*, the last book that Beckett wrote in English, which I had discovered and brought to the group as a possible book publication. So Girodias showed up one day and was driving a French Citroën (we were all on foot or on bicycle) and we immediately thought that we had hit . . . a jackpot. A big money daddy. Well, Maurice, it turned out, was totally broke, but we didn't know it. He thought that he had hit a jackpot because here he had all these young aspiring writers who were working away and who could be put to good use to write some books for him and earn some money. So it was a mutual need society. Alex considered that he had Girodias totally under control. Girodias, of course, had Alex totally under control, and it turned out that Girodias was the smarter of the two con men in that he was the source of money and in the con game he who has money and controls the purse strings, does indeed control the game.

I think that both were utterly charming. Alex was a totally charming person, so was Girodias, and they were also total rogues. So I think that in the game between them they each thought that they were in control of the other and . . . and I suspect that when it all shakes out that Maurice really was in the greater control.

Trocchi was writer, translator and editor. What was the breadth of his ability?
Alex had the ability to write with a facility that I've never seen before. He wrote some books for Girodias in a week. I believe *Helen and Desire*, which was a long banned book in the United States and now, ironically, is a selection of the Book of the Month Club in America (which is mainstream middle-class, shows the long way we've come) but *Helen and Desire* was written in seven or eight days. And it depended to some extent on the need. I would suspect that as Alex got deeper in to drugs, his money needs increased and his ability to produce was apparent only when he was on drugs and as soon as he was out of it he would sit down and write for twelve hours and have twenty, thirty pages of absolutely sparkling prose ready for the printer. The funny thing is that the first page of Beckett's masterpiece, *Molloy*, his novel masterpiece, paraphrasing it, the hero is in a lonely room and somebody comes and takes away so many pages and leaves so much money. That really became a symbol for Alex's life, for many years, if the need were there to have money, he would be able to produce enough pages in sufficiently professional form to be paid to go on.

YOUNG ADAM BEFORE

Alex Trocchi

The police sergeant was making notes in a little black notebook, occasionally licking the stub of his pencil, and the other cop was standing with his mouth open watching the stretcher-bearers who seemed to be taking their time. They had laid down the stretcher on the quay and were looking enquiringly at the police sergeant, who went over and looked under the sheet which they had thrown over her when they put her on the stretcher. One of them spat. I glanced away again.

Out of the corner of my eye I saw Ella's legs move.

Four kids from somewhere or other, the kind of kids who hang about vacant lots, funeral processions, or street accidents, stood about five yards away and gaped. They had been there almost since the beginning. Now the other policeman went over to them and told them to go away.

Reluctantly, they moved farther away and lingered. They grinned and whispered to each other. Then they whooped at the gesticulating cop and ran away. But they didn't go far, just round the corner of the shed across the quay, and I could see them poking their heads out round the corner, climbing over each other into sight. I remember one of them had flaming red hair.

The ambulance men had lifted the stretcher again but one of them stumbled. A very naked white leg slipped from under the sheet and trailed along the ground like a parsnip. I glanced at Ella. She was watching it. She was horrified but it seemed to fascinate her. She couldn't tear her eyes away.

'Woah!' the man at the back said.

They lowered the stretcher again and the front man turned round and arranged the leg out of sight. He handled it as though he were ashamed of it.

And then they hoisted the stretcher into the back of the ambulance and slammed the doors. At that moment Jim finished his apple and threw the core at the cat, which was crouched on its belly at the edge of the quay. The cat jumped, ran a bit, and then walked away with its tail in the air. Jim took out a tin whistle and began to play on it.

The sergeant closed his notebook, looped elastic round it, and went over to speak to the driver of the ambulance. Leslie was lighting his pipe.

Leslie had been a big man when he was younger, and he was still big at the time, but his muscles were running to flesh and his face was heavy round the chin so that his head had the appearance of a square pink jube-jube sucked away drastically at the top, and, as he didn't shave very often, the rough pinkness of his cheeks was covered by a colour-less spreading bristle. He had small light blue eyes sunk like buttons in soft wax, and they could be kind or angry. When he was drunk they were pink and threatening. The way he was standing running forwards and outwards from his razor-scraped Adam's apple to the square brass buckle of his belt, you could see he wasn't a young man; in his middle fifties, I suppose.

The ambulance was driving away and the sergeant was going over to talk to Leslie again. I remember it struck me as funny at the time that he should address all his remarks to Leslie. I watched the cat, sniffing at something which looked like the backbone of a herring near the quay wall. It tried to turn it over with its paw. Then I heard Ella yelling at Jim. It seemed she hadn't noticed him before.

'I thought I told you to stay down below! I'll get your father to you!'

And then she turned on me and said I ought to be ashamed of myself for not keeping the boy out of the way. Did I think it was good for him to see a corpse? She said she thought I put the sacks over the body so as not to frighten him. I was about to say he didn't seem very frightened to me – sitting there playing 'Thou art lost and gone forever, oh my darling, Clementine' on his tin whistle – but I could see she wasn't angry. I could see she was in some way trying to get her own back for the long look I had at her backside, and that amused me and I didn't say anything. She turned away, lifted the basin which had contained the wet clothes, and I heard her clump down through the companionway into the cabin. Then, suddenly, I laughed. The kid was looking at me. But I went on laughing.

There was the discussion about suicide or murder. She asked him about it as soon as the police were gone, as soon as the ambulance moved away and the sergeant had finished with Leslie, who with an unlit pipe in his mouth, came back aboard.

'What did the police say?'

I watched her carefully. She was inquisitive but wanted at the same time for us to think that she was above that kind of thing if we weren't.

Leslie said that the sergeant didn't know anything. But there were no marks on the body so Leslie didn't think it could have been murder.

I knew Ella was going to say what she did about its being just like men not to be able to keep their eyes off a woman, especially if she had no clothes on, and I thought the words just suited her standing there as she was in her too tight green cotton dress so that you could see the shape and strength of her thighs. And as she spoke it occurred to me that the line of wet clothes in the background was part of the picture too, of a coarse, sexually frustrated woman calling down the judgement of the Almighty on the sex she despised.

I had the impression at the time that she was talking to me more than Leslie, although it was to him that she spoke. She grudged me the glimpse I'd had of her. She said that we were evil bastards, both of us. Then she turned away.

Leslie winked at me. I noticed there were red specks in the whites of his eyes. He said she had got up the wrong side that morning. He nodded in her direction – she was sweeping near the stern – and he winked at me again.

But I remembered how through the wooden partition between the cabins it was her laughter which had wakened me that morning, and perhaps that was the beginning of it all and not the sight of her as she hung the clothes up. And I thought that perhaps she was angry with me because I knew about the eggs, because she had been caught out at a direct lie.

Leslie said he wondered what the hell was wrong now. I looked up and saw that the ambulance had halted at the other side of the vacant lot which ran directly on to the quayside. The driver was talking out of the window to a man in plain clothes. We watched without saying anything until the man stepped on the running board and the ambulance drove away.

'More to it than meets the eye,' Leslie said.

I shrugged my shoulders.

I said it had nothing to do with us.

'We found the body, didn't we?'

'It might have been anybody.'

'But it wasn't. It was us.' He was reluctant to give up possession.

I didn't feel like arguing with him. I was thinking about Ella, wishing Leslie was to hell out of here so that I could make a play for her. I wanted her.

'Anyway,' I said, turning away, 'it's over now.'

'Maybe,' he said.

There wasn't much to do then until the lorries came with the load. We were leaving in the afternoon with a load of anthracite for Edinburgh and Leith. Ours was a motor barge, so we could move straight from the river to the canal without waiting for a tow. Both of us felt a bit uncomfortable there on deck and doing nothing because Ella never seemed to stop working. She had finished sweeping and now she was doing some vegetables in a wooden bucket. An occasional plopping sound came from it as the potatoes, peeled, white, and shining were dropped in.

MERLIN

Summer / Autumn 1954: volume 2, number 3

EDITORIAL: *Words and War*

In relation to the East–West deadlock today, we find every pronouncement underrun with the stubborn implication that the statements and intentions of the other side are 'wrong' or 'evil'; of course. And each such pronouncement is little more than the deductive unfolding of implications already latent in an unscientific language in terms of which act and intention of the opposing side are to be described. Today, the person idly listening to the news-commentator speaking of 'freedom-loving peoples' is unlikely to be immediately conscious of the implication that the other half of the world is teeming with swarms of 'slavery-loving peoples'. Indeed, he will miss the point by a hemisphere if he is unaware he is tuned into Radio Moscow.

But only in the hands of the Professors do these absurdities take on their grander proportions. Parallel with the political deadlock, and intensifying it, is a cultural one which finds expression in equally absolutist, aesthetic theories. Plainly, these, what gives rise to them, and what they give rise to, are the concern of the writer. In the present historical crisis, and in so far as through the various cultural media they contribute towards it, it is imperative that such theories be countered.

It is our contention that absolutism in the use of words, their hypostatization, is one of the prime progenitors of the present deadlock, for the simple reason that, on a cognitive level, it renders both agreement and disagreement impossible. The frustration aroused by the inability to get to intellectual grips with the opposing power block breeds suspicion and fear. Reason, operating on unverifiable and sometimes conveniently shifting assumptions, contributes illicitly to the moral armament of one block against the other. The literary theories to which we have referred are an extremely subtle and effective type of moral armament. Conflicting attitudes proliferate.

For the world to become sane, it must, among other things, become aware of the foundations and nature of absolutism. Only then is understanding possible. Only then can one know who, if anyone, is one's enemy. At that moment, and only then, can a sane man go to war.

Absolutism arises when empirical verification is treated lightly because propositions so verified can never be more than probable and when *a priori* 'knowledge' is mistakenly treated as though it had factual content, i.e. when it is thought to be synthetic and not analytic or tautological. This confusion leads to the claim that it is possible to frame valid propositions that are neither empirically verifiable nor tautological; specifically, 'metaphysical propositions', whose validity is capable of being apprehended intuitively. In one form or another, that is the main assertion of absolutism and it is one which, following the philosophic analysts, we reject entirely. While not denying that a scientific law may be conceived intuitively (a psychological question), we affirm that it can only be verified empirically (a logical question). The method of empirical verification adumbrated by science is the only method in terms of which man can, with even relative accuracy, determine whether the intellectual structures which he has built for himself have correlation with the world about him. All questions about matters of fact which are not amenable to scientific verification must inevitably be dismissed as mischievous. Man takes a most dangerous step when he endows the categories employed in such metaphysical statements with an inviolable existence of their own.

Besides the method of science, there is at least one other way, more or less imperfect, in which man might be said to attempt to 'verify' his thinking about himself and the world: the way of art. Can we talk of the verifiability of art? Certainly not in the same way we can speak of the verifiability of science. The statements of science and the categories employed in them are neutrally descriptive. The statements of art and the categories employed in them contain an expressive, an emotional element which renders them, in the scientific sense of the word, 'unverifiable'.

In what way, then, can we speak of the 'verifiability' of art? In what correlations does its peculiar validity reside?

We suggest that a work of art is a symbolisation which combines both descriptive and expressive elements; that this complex has contact primarily with the emotional furniture of the individual; that the correlations, by which it is rendered valid or invalid, are with relatively permanent emotional structures in the human make-up. We suggest that it may be useful to distinguish between three correlations:

(a) the correlation between the descriptive–expressive complex as it exists in the artist's mind and his presentation of it in symbolic form (the realised work of art),

(b) the correlation between the exteriorized symbol and the descriptive–expressive complex it excites in the mind of the individual spectator (his experience of the work),

and

(c) the correlation which we may suppose to result between the descriptive–expressive complexes of the two individuals (the communication established between artist and spectator).

At any moment in history, it is within an intricate and interpersonal complex of these correlations that the validity of a work of art will be said to subsist; in short, the so-called 'value' of a work of art is relative and psychological. Art, presenting as it does symbols of emotively significant psychological states, seeking to exteriorize thereby the *affective* potential of the inner experience, does not and cannot at a cognitive level conflict with the neutral descriptions of science.

The hypotheses of science, their propositional elements, and such hypotheses and propositions which can in a like way be verified, constitute the only knowledge we can usefully call 'true'; and even these are only probable and not absolute: they await revision through further experiment and its accessory speculation. We insist on the sanity of the recommendation that the use of the word 'true' in other contexts be recognised as an expression of belief rather than of verifiable fact. It appears to us that this theory (a theory which, like those of science, recommends a tentative linguistic usage) has important implications. Its acceptance, as we shall attempt to demonstrate in the body of this essay, must discourage irresponsible and unfounded speculation, and specifically lead – for we are above all concerned with cultural matters –

to the rejection of certain aesthetic theories which have become widely accredited, and which, in their attempt to impose arbitrary structures on history and on cultural process, past, present, and future, represent an imminent threat, parallel and confederate with the same kind of thinking in politics, to our civilisation . . .

COLLECTION  M E R L I N

1953

is pleased to annouce the publication of

WATT

a novel in English by

SAMUEL BECKETT

The original edition consists of 1,125 copies, the first 25 of which printed on luxury paper signed by the author will be lettered A to Y and will be sold at 2,500 frs, £ 2.10 or $ 7.00. The remaining copies numbered 1 to 1,100 printed on fine paper will be sold at 850 frs, 17/6 or $ 2.50.

Subscription   Form

I, ..., wish

to subscribe to .... copies of

WATT, for which I enclose.. .

Subscriber's address ....

....

Courtesy of Jane Lougee Bryant

GEORGE PLIMPTON

When did you first meet Alex?

I met Alex in 1952 in Paris when a group of Americans were starting the *Paris Review* literary magazine at the time, and Alex was starting or had started *Merlin*. I suppose I met him in one of the cafés. I was immensely struck by him, instantly. He had a very interesting looking face, rather a faun's face with big ears and this wonderful Scottish brogue and a tremendous presence. And of course we were interested in the same things, in literary matters. Paris at that time was flooded with Americans, many on the GI Bill and studying at the Science Politique, others hanging around, some of them writing. It was very inexpensive; you could live for thirty dollars a week very easily. Alex was a great figure in that sort of group of expatriates.

How did he make ends meet?

I don't know how he made ends meet. Of course, he was living with Jane Lougee, who was the publisher of *Merlin*, and who we all thought had a substantial fortune. None of us knew. Alex also made money doing translations for Maurice Girodias of the Olympia Press, writing what were called DBs, dirty books. A lot of the young writers of that time made ends meet by writing dirty books for Maurice Girodias. I even tried one; it was turned down. I think it was the only DB that Maurice Girodias ever turned down . . . too quirky he said. Alex did some very substantial translations. He did the translations of Apollinaire's *Onze Mille Vièrges*, which is a play on words – the eleven thousand whips or the eleven thousand virgins. He'd get up on the table in the Café Bonaparte in St-Germain-des-Prés and read his latest chapter of the *Onze Mille Vièrges* (its English title, presumably devised by Alex, was *The Debauched Hospodar*), surrounded by his acolytes and admirers and it was really something to look forward to. The word would go round the *quartier* that he had a new chapter to read that night.

Was there any competitiveness between the two magazines?

I don't recall there was much sense of rivalry between the *Paris Review* and *Merlin*. I, for example, sat on the *Merlin* board. I think *Merlin* thought we were a bit too commercial, that we used commercial methods to distribute the magazine. We were interested in making the thing viable and read by as many people as possible so we had all sorts of activities to do that. I think *Merlin* was far more ... scholarly would be the wrong word, but they were far more interested in the content of their magazine than they were in mundane matters like distributing the thing. It only ran, I believe, for four issues, *Merlin*, but it was an astonishing magazine. Beckett, of course, I guess was the great star. Trocchi was the driving force behind it, but they had very good editors, a fellow called Austryn Wainhouse, who was extremely brilliant, talented, a Harvard man. Richard Seaver was another, who went on to become one of the great editors in the United States afterwards, bilingual, married a wonderful French woman – Jeanette. They seemed much more involved in the contemporary culture of Paris at that time than the *Paris Review* was. The first issue of the *Paris Review*, for example, had an interview with E. M. Forster. It published very few examples of the French culture whereas *Merlin* was very much more steeped in that than we were.

Was money tight at Merlin?

Well, as for the funding, again, Jane Lougee was the publisher. I don't know how much she spent. It was very inexpensive doing a magazine in Paris at that time. I remember the first issue of the *Paris Review* ran to, I think, ten thousand copies, around that, and it didn't cost much more than five or six hundred dollars. My father gave five hundred dollars, for an example, for me to get started, and I think Peter Matthiessen's father did the same. We didn't have very much. Very early on we got a publisher, Sadruddin Aga Khan, who had an estimable fortune behind him, but we didn't really use up very much of it, say five hundred dollars a year. It was very inexpensive to do. We all lived very cheaply, our expenses were almost zero. The offices of the *Paris Review* were in a tiny little room in a publishing house, and *Merlin*'s, I believe, were in the back of a garage for a while. None of that really made very much difference. I mean, when you start a magazine when you're twenty-four, twenty-five years old, the amenities don't really mean very much.

What about Trocchi and Jane Lougee? How did people see them?

Alex and Jane were really a rather remarkable couple in Paris. They were very striking. Alex was tall, dark, wonderful face and his big ears, and Jane was small and elf-like with dark helmet hair.

I remember we went to the *Quat'z Art* ball once. The whole city is sort of turned over to this bacchanal once a year, in July, and the students of the various *ateliers*, I think there are six of them, and their guests, go to this great dance hall in the Avenue Wagram. They lock the doors. There's a big band that plays way up in the eaves somewhere. The only people who keep order are a group called the *Cadre Noir*, the Black Cadre, and they walk around with these staves, these sticks, and they separate couples if one member of the couple doesn't seem to be enjoying what is going on. Most of the people are naked. We were asked by the *atelier* who had invited us to put on some sort of a spectacle, up on the balustrade of one of these boxes, like in an opera house. Alex and Jane had agreed. One of the other *ateliers* had arranged for their spectacle, a naked girl suspended from the ceiling. She was completely painted in blue. The spotlights went on and illuminated her. She was so beautiful, suspended up there, people began to cry *'La Bleu! La Bleu! La Bleu!'* So Alex and Jane felt that they could do something more spectacular. Jane was to lie on the front of this box and when the lights came on her she'd be completely naked and Alex would then appear from the darkness and couple with her. Even in Paris at that time and at the *Quat'z Art* ball, that was really quite something. Alex was rather nervous about this but he had thought up the idea. He was down drinking when the time came and he rushed up this little stair to get into position and, being a tall man, he knocked his head against a sort of overhang, knocked himself almost unconscious and toppled down so that when the search lights focused on the box, they illuminated Jane lying, naked on the box railings. I was there with a fan, in the background, sort of like an Egyptian scene. But no Alex. She was a very beautiful girl, you could see her lying there, and perhaps they thought that was our show, you know. The lights moved on to something else. Alex was very upset. He thought that one of us should have taken his place . . . which I thought was very gentlemanly of him indeed.

They were a spectacular pair. That was in their heyday. They were both beautiful, young, they were vibrant, they were known everywhere. Considering what happened later, I guess that was their peak.

According to some reports Trocchi was a fairly voracious womaniser. Was that true?

Well Alex, of course, felt that the way to get along in life was to try everything. It was eventually his ruination, of course, but he felt you should try certainly every sexual thing you could think of. I don't know how Jane took this . . . I think too much was made of his voracious appetite. Because when I saw him in Paris they were always together; they were working on the magazine. It may be that many unfortunate things happened later on, but I remember them, at that time, as being very much together.

MERLIN

Spring / Summer 1955: volume 2, number 4

EDITORIAL

In the winter and spring of 1952 international tension reached an extreme pitch. Nowhere was the uneasiness, the feeling of imminent conflict more intense than in Paris. Extraordinary pressures were being exerted upon public opinion – one remembers the repeated meetings of generals, the constant arrivals and departures of prime ministers, the somber tone of the press. One remembers the bitter polemics, the inflating prices, the social disturbances, the riots.

Everywhere, it seemed, a pairing-off of forces was going on, sides were being composed, the world was being definitively divided in two. Attitudes hardened, not only between East and West, but on both sides of the Atlantic. The 'emergency', 'military necessity', 'the common peril' justified any measure, and the pill was sugared with phrases such as 'a community of interests' and 'the fight to save civilisation'. A crusade was afoot.

This review was founded in the spring of 1952, in the thick of this tumult. *MERLIN*'s primary objective was to create a vital meeting-ground for the thought and work of American and English writers on the one hand and Continental writers on the other. With its base in Paris, *MERLIN* was to be international. But it was also to be independent. And it is.

The group of persons – all of them writers or painters – who established *MERLIN* intended to print a neutral review: not one which would declare, explicitly or through omission, an indifference to contemporary realities; but one which would recognise the validity of the greatest range of attitudes existing in a twentieth century penetrated everywhere by relativism, change, and uncertainty.

Accept the proposition that fatally, necessarily, there are two exclusive sides, two irreconcilable camps, that one's choice of doctrine is limited to two systematic alternatives, and one destroys the possibilities of understanding, one destroys the conditions within which thought can exist. To impose that false option is precisely to obliterate what it is the first duty of any thinking person to preserve: that kind of atmosphere, that kind of situation, full of diversities, of contrasts, of new possibilities, in which the creative intelligence can produce its works, in which the critical spirit can live.

The aim of this review is to print *new* writing, *contemporary* writing: not simply the work of younger or less well-known writers, but of those whose achievements, refusing inherited complacencies, are distinguished by an effort to push beyond the tradition which, we consider, is dead, or is dying and which, in any case, is paralyzing our letters – our writers and their readers as well.

Apart from poetry and fiction and criticism – to which it is natural that *MERLIN*, like any other literary review, devote a major share of its space – , we have felt it important to print *reportages, chronicles, documents* and *notes* that record aspects of the present situation and the present temper. While doing our best to maintain the highest literary standards, we have thought it impossible to deny space and consideration to present, often extra-literary problems. We believe that the findings and opinions of historians, of sociologists, of philosophers, of psychologists deserve a place in *MERLIN*. For literature, the most authentic literature, is obligatorily *engagé* in this sense: it is charged with energy and with life only so long as it stems from a critical appreciation of what is real, of what determines its forms and possibilities; and of what, secretly and apparently, concerns and preoccupies the changing men who read it.

The Editors

TERRY SOUTHERN

When did you first meet Trocchi?
I met him one evening at the Café Florian in St Germain and recognised him from having been pointed out to me before but we'd never been introduced. He came over and introduced himself and said that he had read something of mine in the *Paris Review* and wondered if I'd like to contribute to his magazine *Merlin* and he left me a couple of copies of the magazine, a current issue and one previous, and so that was very good. I

was impressed by the magazine. And then he actually dropped by. I was living in this small hotel in the Place de la Concorde, right near the Sorbonne, and he had gotten my address from George Plimpton and he just came by one day, about two o'clock and we talked for a long time. We started seeing each other right away and going out and having a drink, having an aperitif at the Florian or the Deux Magots, and I gradually got to meet his friends, Austryn Wainhouse and Christopher Logue and Jane Lougee and a few others. I think Jonathan Miller came over to Paris about that time. We were introduced.

Were you aware of Trocchi's reputation?

Yes. He was known as a protégé of Beckett's, aside from having this other reputation of being a scholar and having this magazine, which was getting quite a rush at the time. He brought Jane Lougee round and I think the first curious thing that happened was that he had some hashish from someplace and he was quite open in smoking it at the café. He said that he had heard that I was someone who did smoke hashish and wanted to know if I knew a place where he could score, so I took him to an Arab café, the Soleil de Maroc, which was the popular Arab café at the time, with the expatriates, and I introduced him to Mr Hadj, the proprietor, whom I knew very well. In fact I had dedicated *Candy* to Mr Hadj and Mr Zoon, who was the old white-bearded philosopher who hung around the cafés. That was that first meeting and so we got to be quite good friends during the next few months there in Paris.

You've said about him that everything he did was heroic and Wagnerian. What did you mean?

Well, that he did things in a heroic measure, that is to say, if he was going to have a drink of cognac, it would be a big drink, like a large drink, and not something he would sip but he would polish off in a couple of gulps. He was that way. I mean, it seemed he couldn't get enough hashish. One amusing thing I recall was where we had a preference for marijuana instead of hashish, because the hashish was so strong it was almost beyond a recreational drug. It was like, more like opium, sort of immobilising. What we would do would be to try to get Hadj, the Arab café owner and dealer, to agree to let us buy these extraordinary marijuana flowers, instead of converting them to hashish, and smoke it that way. So he would get a kilo and he would divide it in to two. I mean, it would be this gigantic mound on the table, and he would agree to sell us half of it, and then let us choose which half, because he didn't have any kind of scales for it. So Trocchi, who was sort of a renaissance person and prided himself on his ability to calculate densities and things like that, would try to make some kind of geometric equation to figure out which of these piles, these amounts, might be the advantageous one. But meanwhile we're smoking and getting completely deranged so that, you know, our judgements would waver and finally, just . . . Meanwhile the Arab would be advising us, well this is the one, you know, pointing out the right one and of course we would, you know, be overcome with paranoia and think he was trying to influence us to his advantage. I recall Trocchi trying to remember his early education in physics or geometry or whatever and trying to make these calculations and in the end having to rely on the Arab's judgement, you know, getting high enough so that we finally would trust him and take his word for which one to choose. And he enjoyed that very much and he immediately went back to his hotel and wrote a story about it. He showed it to me the next day. I was wondering if it ever got published.

Was Trocchi good company?

Yes, he had the Dylan Thomas quality of entertaining people at a pub by reciting or reading. He had a great memory for Shakespeare, T. S. Eliot, Dylan Thomas and Joyce. He could recite passages of James Joyce, you know, quite abstruse, lengthy passages. The only person I've ever met who could do that. He took me over to Beckett's a couple of times [in Paris]. Beckett would cook a breakfast of kippers. Beckett really loved him, in a fatherly way and considered him a protégé.

What was the relationship between Trocchi and Maurice Girodias?

They were a curious match. Girodias saw in Alex someone who was so prolific and capable of turning out any kind of literature but who had great contempt for the stuff that Girodias was publishing. Alex would do it because he needed money. Girodias would dream up this series of titles and then commission writers to flesh them out, so to speak. I remember a few, *Until She Screams* was one, *Wisdom of the Loins*, *Wisdom of the Lash* . . . During this time, Alex and I and Mason Hoffenberg read Burroughs' *Naked Lunch* in manuscript; he had it at the cafes for a while. We were so impressed, we thought it would be fantastic if we could get Girodias to publish it and showed it to him. But he said, well there's no sex in the book. There's nothing happening . . . well, yes something's happening on page thirty and then it's only a blow job. He didn't consider that true sex. So he said, ask Burroughs, can't you jazz it up a little. He said I'm sure that will happen. Finally we did persuade Girodias to print it and Trocchi was always proud of that happening, having been able to do that.

THE DIRTY *YOUNG ADAM*: AN AFTERWORD

Maurice Girodias

from *The Olympia Reader*

When Alexander Trocchi arrived in Paris he was an eager young Scotsman with a brilliant academic future; he was so misinformed of worldly things that he went to live near the Gare de l'Est – the city's most neutral and forbidding district.

It took him one year to discover the Left Bank and to understand why he had come to Paris. When, at last, he moved to Saint-Germain-des-Prés, he was immediately transformed; he shed his subdued provincial manner to become the big bad literary wolf of his time and day.

Alex was always busy cultivating extreme attitudes, extravagant styles and wild dreams with great gusto and appetite. Sometimes he misunderstood his appetite for ambition, and launched into great projects, very few of which succeeded because there were too many other interests and also too many girls around.

But Alex had a certain amount of electricity buzzing around his shaggy brow, and he naturally became the centre of a very active literary group which formed around his short-lived magazine, *Merlin*.

He was the first of Olympia's all-out literary stallions; his novel, *Helen and Desire*, published under the pen name of Frances Lengel, became a model of the kind. It was the first of a series of Frances Lengel productions, all of them very robust and funny parodies of pornography; and some, as *Young Adam*, of excellent quality.

Although all his books had the honour of being banned by the French authorities, *Helen and Desire* was saved from total annihilation by being reprinted under a different title: *Desire and Helen*. The French police never found out; perhaps now they will.

CENSORSHIP AND VIRTUE

Alex Trocchi

> I myself have heard a birth-control pamphlet condemned as obscene on several grounds one of which was a suggestion that possibly women might enjoy sexual intercourse. *Bertrand Russell*

The proprietors of the *Olympia Press* have the firm conviction that Lord Russell, the eminent British philosopher, is not alone in his contempt for the current laws of censorship in English-speaking countries. While such authors as Chaucer, Boccaccio, Shakespeare, and Congreve are available at least in the metropolis because they are 'classics', each modern work, if it treats of sexual matters – and what serious writer can omit a consideration of them? – is subject at once to the indecent whims and narrow moral codes of the County magistrate. A number of years ago some optimists felt confident that with the final vindication of James Joyce's *Ulysses* an important principle of freedom had been established. Unfortunately, this was not so. No sooner had the enemies of free thought lost on that ground – well-lost, perhaps, since few people had the patience to read *Ulysses* – than they burrowed like the good rabbits they are through each and every book that led man in plain language to look inward at his own sexual nature. The principle established by the legal vindication of *Ulysses* turns out to be a dangerous one. Any book which is courageous and not obscure seems automatically to be branded as obscene without the justification of being of literary value. Mrs Grundy has nothing to fear from the obscure; having given way on that ground she now redoubles her effort in the field of the more outspoken. The book burners are still with us.

In spite of the risk involved, these reasons prompt the *Olympia Press* to place before the general public complete and integral texts of such banned masters as the Marquis de Sade, Frank Harris, Henry Miller, and Guillaume Apollinaire.

But there is another reason: is this censorship of which we have spoken real? We think not. Up till now many of the above books have been available in de luxe editions well beyond the income of the general reader. If they were issued at a popular price, the texts were mutilated and the books abridged. Now, for the first time in history, the works of Sade and

Miller, with full unexpurgated texts, in masterly and exciting translations, are offered at reasonable prices and in handsome book format. We have the courage of our convictions, hoping that in this way many people – the average man as well as the scholar – will be given the opportunity of reading and testing for themselves the greatness of men hitherto condemned to silence by ambiguous laws that have caused our heads to be buried like the ostrich's at the approach of imaginary danger.

Recently there has been much controversy about the Marquis de Sade. Books have been written *about* him by such eminent critics and sociologists as Geoffrey Gorer, Mario Praz, and Simone de Beauvoir. Even under their advanced patronage, his works are confined to a few great libraries. Indeed, the rules of the British Museum demand that the Archbishop of Canterbury be present in the room while his books are being read. Furthermore, they are in French – an added barrier to the circulation of ideas which are dangerous only in their suppression. Writers such as Frank Harris, Henry Miller and Jean Genet are condemned without a hearing. Worse, a more contemporary problem – young writers whose literary efforts include scenes and words, often searching and profound, but offensive to certain ladies and gentlemen *for the most part anonymous*, can find no outlet for their work.

That the position is beginning to be serious is evident from the recent controversy in the British press. One eminent editor is reported to have said: 'It amounts to a reign of terror. There are no hard and fast laws, no way of knowing beforehand. One fine morning one wakens up like K. in Kafka's *The Trial*, and the awesome little gentlemen are there in the shape of a letter. Defence is costly and sometimes impracticable. As any lawyer will tell you, there is no unequivocal law. If one commits a murder one knows roughly speaking where one stands. If, on the other hand, one releases a book in which the author has subjected to searching analysis those areas of human experience which are still considered by the ignorant to be taboo, one has no idea what consequences will follow. Fame, ignominy, even prison – no-one can hazard a guess in advance. The reason for this is not hard to find. The whole subject is shrouded in ignorance. Ignorance defends itself by equivocation. The opponents of free thought cannot state their case in clear and simple terms, for the truth is that their driving force is nothing more or less than a fear of knowledge.'[1]

Is it virtuous to fear knowledge? Is it wise to build walls against it? How many virtuous men will be broken against those walls? We are dealing here with a subject of vital importance. It is a shorter step than commonly supposed between the rigid suppression of eroticism in literature and the creation of a totalitarian nightmare in which tribal unreason erects its black crematoriums for the living dead. There is no virtue in ignorance. We need not go back as far as John Milton to meet with the clear truth of the matter, that *there is no virtue in the Censor*.

YOUNG ADAM AFTER

Alex Trocchi

The police sergeant was making notes in a little black notebook, occasionally licking the stub of his pencil. The other cop was standing with his mouth open watching the stretcher bearers who seemed to be taking their time. They had put the stretcher down on the quay and were looking enquiringly at the police sergeant who went over and looked under the sheet they had thrown over her when they put her on the stretcher. One of them spat. I glanced away again.

Out of the corner of my eye I saw Ella's legs move.

The ambulance men had lifted the stretcher again but one of them stumbled. A very white naked leg slipped from under the sheet and trailed along the ground like a parsnip. I glanced at Ella. She was watching it. She was horrified but it seemed to fascinate her.

'Whoa!' the man at the back said.

They lowered the stretcher again and the front man turned around and arranged the leg out of sight. He handled it as though he were ashamed of it. And they hoisted the stretcher into the back of the ambulance and slammed the doors.

The sergeant closed his notebook, looped elastic round it, and went over to speak to the driver of the ambulance. Les was lighting his pipe.

Leslie undoubtedly was a big man when he was younger, still was, but his muscles were running to flesh and his face was heavy round the chin so that his head had the appearance of a square pink jujube sucked away drastically at the top. As he didn't shave very often, the rough pinkness of his cheeks was covered by a colorless spreading bristle. He had small light blue eyes sunk like buttons in soft wax, and they could be kind or angry. When he was drunk they were pink and threatening. The way he was standing, you could see he wasn't a young man; in his middle fifties, I suppose.

The ambulance was driving away and the sergeant was going over to talk to Les again. I remember it struck me as funny at the time that he should address all his remarks to Leslie. I watched the cat sniffing at something near the quay wall. It tried to turn it over with its paw. Ella lifted the basin that had held the wet clothes and gave me a look somewhere between angry and intimate. She turned away and I could see she was in some way trying to get back at me for the long look I had had at her backside, so I didn't say anything. I heard her clump down through the companionway into the cabin.

Suddenly, I laughed. Les and the sergeant and the cat all stopped to look at me. But I went on laughing.

After the police left there was the discussion about suicide or murder. 'What did the police think?' Ella asked Les as soon as the police were gone, as soon as the ambulance had driven away and he, with an unlit pipe in his mouth, came back aboard.

I watched Ella carefully. She was inquisitive. But, at the same time, she wanted us to think that she was above that kind of thing even if we weren't.

Les said that the sergeant didn't know. But there were no marks on the body so Leslie did not think it could have been murder.

And I knew Ella was going to say just what she did say about it 'being just like men not to be able to keep their eyes off a woman especially if she had no clothes on.' I thought the words just suited her standing there as she was in her too-tight green cotton dress, stretched so far you could the shape and strength of her thighs and the muscles of her belly.

Ah, but if I could have had at her, I'd change her tune. If I could get her without her clothes on she'd know the pleasure of the nakedness she now derided. Just rip that wash-faded cotton rag from her body and expose her to my intimate scrutiny. No need to steal a glance or hurry the moment. Stripped naked I could savour the bodily delights now hidden from my view.

I could enjoy the spread of her broad hips above those sturdy loins. My gaze could explore the quick taper of her waist as it turned above her hips before it rose up and outward again to flesh-covered ribs that showed themselves ever so slightly before the underlying structure was lost in the middle softness distinct to a woman. Her tits were fine for me, I knew. I had glimpsed them from time to time. But to savor the sight of those pendulous hillocks, unfettered. I could teach her to enjoy the viewing as much as I would.

It's all in the seeing, you see. To be seen naked, stripped bare, by appreciative eyes makes all the difference even to one as fearful of the seeing as Ella. I was sure I could convince her. I was equally sure that, despite the view she vocalised there on the deck, she wished to be convinced.

From her breasts my gaze would caress her centerline down the thin track of hair I was certain traced a path between her navel and the fuzz about her sweet slit. Beneath my unflinching eye her excitement would mount and those strong legs would tense and her mons would blossom. Her nether lips would engulf and darken and grow warm and moist, longing for a touch. She would shift and spread her legs apart for better balance and to better expose her sex. But I would not yet grant that touch to her or to my own desire. Just look on appreciatively. And that, in turn, would fuel her passion more.

Her nipples would harden and grow small and dark and tight with anticipation. Her buttocks would tighten and signal their desire to her innermost being. Colour would rise from her shoulders and flush her cheeks with a outward sign of her inward need. And still we would not touch. Only look, a powerful, sensual look. I in the armour of my garments. She in the vulnerability of her flesh. I would move behind her, study her unseen by her. She would quiver at the power of it.

Then, with just enough rustling for her to hear, I would part my clothes, unleash the lance of my manhood, and use it on her. That would change her tune once and for always. But now her voice broke the spell.

I had the impression that she was talking to me more than to Les, although she spoke to him. She grudged me the glimpse I'd had of her. She said that we were bad bastards, both of us. Then she turned away.

Leslie winked at me. I noticed there were red specks in the whites of his eyes. He said she had got up on the wrong side this morning. He nodded in her direction – she was sweeping near the stern – and he winked at me again.

But I remembered how, through the wooden partition between the cabins, it was her soft moans of pleasure that had wakened me that morning. It was such an uncharacteristic noise from that quarter that I raised myself up to peek through the small separation between the boards that afforded me a limited, but adequate, view of Ella's marital bed.

Although coitus had been long abandoned in her relationship with Leslie, Ella's sexual needs were not entirely uncared for. And that morning she was pleasuring herself while the drink-besotted Les snored beside her. Her gentle lowing was reflected by the rhythmic undulation waist-level beneath her blanket. Her shoulders raised and closed forward, the blanket slipped to her waist as her upper arms pressed her breasts together and up to the ceiling. Both her hands moved stealthily about her hips, belly and, clearly, between her legs.

She rocked slowly for a while, both hands secreted. Then one began to move about, coming out from below the blanket, caressing her upper body then returning again to join the other between her legs. Again it moved about, this time her fingertips circling her aureola then tweaking the tips of her upthrusting breasts. Then back below the blanket. Then exploring above again.

Finally, eyes shut against the morning light and the harsh reality of the cabin, she touched her moist and glistening fingers to her lips. She hesitated, then parted her lips slightly. Her tongue moved daintily out to taste. Inevitably her lips parted wider and she put first one finger, then all, in her sucking mouth. Meanwhile the activity beneath the blanket became nearly frantic. Certainly her hidden lips and fingers mimicked the exposed digits and orifice.

I, for my part, had grown excited as her excitement had grown. I grasped my rigid member and matched her action stroke for stroke, one hand flat against the cabin wall steadying my view, the other active as Ella's was active, between my legs. As if the wall did not separate us, I held back my release until I felt certain that Ella too had peaked. My instincts were dead on. As her writhing reached its crescendo so did my tension. I envisioned my rod between those pouting lips above and below the blanket, spurting its seed into the warm willing mouth, filling it to the brim and beyond with the sweet cream Ella only now dreamed of.

Perhaps that, and not the sight of her as she hung the clothes on the line, was the beginning of it all. And I thought that perhaps she was angry with me because I knew about the eggs, because she had been caught in a direct lie.

My reverie was interrupted when Les said he wondered what the hell was wrong now. I looked up and saw that the ambulance had halted at the other side of the vacant lot that ran directly on to the quay side. The driver was talking out of the window to a man in plain clothes. We watched without saying anything until the man stepped on the running board and the ambulance drove away.

'More to it than meets the eye,' Leslie said.

I shrugged my shoulders.

I said it had got nothing to do with us.

'We found the body, didn't we?' observed Les.

I said that it might have been anybody.

'But it wasn't. It was us,' he countered.

I didn't feel like arguing with him. I was thinking about Ella, wishing Leslie was to hell out of there so that I could make a play for her.

'Anyway,' I said, turning away, 'it's over now.'

'Maybe,' he said.

There wasn't much to do then until the lorries came with the load. We were leaving in the afternoon with a load of anthracite for Edinburgh and Leith. Ours was a motor barge, so we could move straight from the river to the canal without waiting for a tow. The idleness left both of us a bit uncomfortable there on deck, doing nothing while Ella never seemed to stop working. She had finished sweeping and she was now doing some vegetables in a wooden bucket. An occasional plopping sound came from it as the potatoes, peeled, white and shining, were dropped in.

JANE LOUGEE

It was disappointing for Alex to have Girodias do the book. Alex would have preferred to have a publishing company of more renown do his first book. That disappointed him, I think, greatly.

Could you explain Girodias' involvement with Trocchi?

Publishing a literary review is a great problem, mostly because you don't have any money. We could not make the magazine pay for itself in terms of advertisements or subscriptions therefore we had to work outside to pay the printer. Girodias came on the scene at this time, after our third edition, I believe, and helped everybody out by hiring writers to write books for him. I think that was the demise of the magazine; it became increasingly difficult to pay the expenses and after the first few books for Girodias, the writers were irritated that they had to be doing this for really very little return and having to put it back into the magazine. It just got to be too much for everybody. Too much.

What effect did churning out DBs for Girodias have on Trocchi?

It was very difficult for Alex as the editor of the magazine (and in a sense, publisher) to do his own writing. He didn't have time. He was pressured right and left, also being in Paris and leading such a café life. It provided very little time for thought and work. I think it annoyed him that he had to do these books in order to make an income to live and not have the time to do things that he much preferred.

How did Trocchi operate within the group at Merlin? *Did he like to be at the centre of things?*

Well, yes, Alex liked to be the centre of attention. At that time he was essentially quite a happy person and very eager, in a sense, to play a clown, but I think that became a bore for him. I think he was distracted in many ways. I think that was one reason he became involved with drugs, because it was a distraction. It was another avenue, another escape, another place to go to find . . . what? I don't know when he really started heroin. I've heard that it happened in Paris, I didn't know. We all had pot and hash. Alex had very much liked the idea of hash and heroin. When he got heroin that took him out into another world altogether, that he really did find an escape. I think Paris was getting to be too much for him.

Why did you give up Merlin *and go back to the States?*

To all effects, I came back to the States to raise money, but everybody knew, and I knew, that I wasn't going to raise any money. Perhaps we considered it time for me to go home. That's what I think I was doing anyway. But I also think, as Alex mentions in the book, that he and I had really decided, although unspokenly, that he was moving away from me and I was moving away from him. But it was supposedly to get money, that's why I came back.

When you left Alex behind in Paris was he still searching for something?

Alex's move from Paris with Midhou or his friends to Greece and to the South of France, to Venice, to all the places that he went, was just this search, this odyssey of his writing, living, thinking . . .[1]

What was it like being with Alex, was there a tension?

Well, being with Alex in Paris, the tensions were worked out by racing from café to café, talking with writers, getting material for the magazine and being in touch with this publisher in London for material or keeping the magazine going. But when that waned and became too much and there were too many people involved and the lack of money ... he needed some big escape. And that's what the drugs afforded him.

WHAT THE HELL AM I DOING HERE

from *Cain's Book*

Alex Trocchi

What the hell am I doing here?

I arrived in London the night before I sailed for America.

I decided not to look anyone up. It would have meant explanations ... just passing through on my way from nowhere to nowhere.

I left the railway station and mingled with the other people on the street. It was the rush hour. Shops were closing. People swarmed in the dusk towards the underground. Men, small bent men, were selling newspapers. As usual I felt myself overcome by the cheerful sense of orderliness Londoners seem to exude. At times it had amused, at times infuriated me, and once or twice during the war, I remember, the sense of solidarity it implied gladdened me. This time, however, leaving France for no good reason, on my way to America for no good reason, with an acute feeling of being an exile wherever I went, I found it oppressive. I was heavy with the sense of my own detachment.

And that had been with me for as long as I could remember, gaining in intensity at each new impertinence of the external world with which I signed no contract when I was ejected bodily from my mother's warm womb. I developed early a horror of all groups, particularly those which without further ado claimed the right to subsume all my acts under certain normative designations in terms of which they would reward or punish me. I could feel no loyalty to anything so abstract as a state or so symbolic as a sovereign. And I could feel nothing but outrage at a system in which, by virtue of my father's name and fortune, I found myself from the beginning so shockingly underprivileged. What shocked me most as I grew up was not the fact that things were as they were, and with a tendency to petrify, but that others had the impertinence to assume that I would forbear to react violently against them.

At that moment I found myself standing in the middle of moving traffic, hesitating, unable to go forward or back, clutching bag and raincoat, until the signal changed. Finally I reached the far side and moved quickly into the crowd on the other pavement. From time to time in just that way my absent-mindedness startled me. Although I was walking quickly I had no idea where I was going. I had thought about it on the boat journey from Calais to Dover, wondering what had moved me to take a ship from Southampton which I could have boarded as easily at Le Havre. For some reason or other I had wanted to spend the last night in London. I had no desire to see anyone in particular. I had been careful to keep the fact of my arrival to myself. I remember feeling a sense of nostalgia for this national metropolis in which I had seldom spent more than a few days. When I first visited it at the age of seventeen I remember thinking I would one day live there, but after years abroad on the Continent I wasn't so sure. Somehow or other I found it difficult to take the English seriously. I had often been appalled by the absurd contrast between what they said and their manner of saying it, between a frequent lack of talent and imagination and the degree of respect they hoped to exact by virtue simply of acquiring a particular accent.

When I say that I loved London I mean it was a place I recognised as one in which it would be possible for a man like me to live, where people in spite of their many absurdities tended to respect an individual's privacy, to a limited degree, to be sure, but more so than in say: Moscow, New York, Peking. (I was feeling already that when I returned from America it would be via London–Paris.) I am not saying that Londoners are not inquisitive. They may be more so than either Russians or Americans for all I know, but they are a conservative people, like most people who are not desperate, and the hard core of constitutional law governing the status of the individual in society is not likely to die overnight. In London policemen do not carry guns in their everyday business.

It had begun to rain. The streets and the grey buildings around Victoria depressed me. I had many memories of Victoria Station. During the war I had arrived and departed from Victoria many times and the streets and buildings round about were quite familiar. I remembered seeing Gill's Stations of the Cross in Westminster Cathedral, refusing a prostitute who offered to masturbate me in one of the air-raid shelters opposite the station, going with a prostitute to one of the streets nearby and thinking she might be older than my mother, the railway bar, the tearooms cloudy with steam from huge tea-urns and coffeepots, and dusty at the same time, and the dry sandwiches under glass, the long tiled lavatories with their shifting men, and the rush of commuters with bowler hats and umbrellas in the early morning.

It was after six o'clock; fifteen hours in London before the boat-train; time to get drunk and sober up, to eat two meals, to go to bed with someone. Plenty of time, and at the same time short, like a bee's visit to a flower, and no commitments.

I took a taxi and told the driver to take me to Piccadilly Circus which was central enough and where I knew I could find a room easily in one of the big hotels which corresponded to the anonymity of my visit . . . no questions, all the necessities, all visitors passing through. Across broad carpets to the lift, silently upwards to the nth floor, along a corridor, realising they had given me a room in the rear which would open on to an airshaft and wishing now I had asked specifically for one which opened on to the street, the key in the lock, the door thrown open and the light switch on, the room looking blankly as it always was and would be, impervious to the stream of human beings who had come and gone, the neatly made bed, the bedlight now being switched off and on by the porter to indicate where it was, vague hotel noises from the airshaft, the smiling face . . . 'All right, sir?' – tipped, gone, the door closed silently behind him. I squashed my cigarette in the ashtray on the glass-topped table beside the bed, protect it against cigarette burns; lay on the bed and looked up at the white ceiling at the centre of which was a small, vaguely noticeable grill. It occurred to me that it might be used to house a camera or a microphone or to inject a poison pellet to fill the room with gas.

When I had taken a shower I left the hotel again and made my way on foot into Soho where I dined at a small French restaurant. Walking down Charing Cross Road afterwards I experienced a pleasant glow from the wine I had drunk. At Leicester Square I hesitated. I wondered whether after all I should have contacted someone. What to do now? For the moment I didn't feel like drinking any more and it was still relatively early. I was vaguely regretting having come to London instead of going directly to Le Havre. If I had done so I would already have been aboard. The ship had probably docked by this time at Southampton. But what the hell, what did it matter? A man should be able to waste time without being seized with anxiety . . .

I had travelled so often and in so many directions that I was bored at the mere thought of it. Moreover, this particular voyage had a more than usually sinister aspect; not only was I unable to produce for myself a convincing reason for going to the United States, I was tolerably certain there wasn't one; no reason, that is, other than the fact that neither could I find one for remaining in Paris, nor for going anywhere else. On previous voyages I had at least gone through the motions of satisfying myself that I should go here or there, even if the journey were for its own sake like a trip to Spain for the bullfights; but in this instance I had no means of knowing what my experience would be. And as a man was not a piece of litmus paper to register this or that property of the objective world – even as litmus paper was finally expended with too much immersion – I was sceptical of the value of going to another new place and facing an entirely new set of objective conditions. I would notice them effectively or I wouldn't. If I did, I might widen my experience without deepening it. In travel, as in all things, there is a law of diminishing returns. And if I didn't, my experience might be drastically short.

During the last year in Paris I had drifted away from my former acquaintances. I could no longer share a common purpose with them. I had spent most of that year in a small room in Montparnasse, going from it to play pinball or to distract myself with a woman. This room had three sides and one large studio window which looked out over the projecting roof of basement studios on to a high wall which cut off all view of the sky and of the summer sun. It was like living in the box in the kitchen in Glasgow when I was a child. I spent more and more time in the room. I can remember lying on my back on the bed, staring at the ceiling, thinking of Beckett, and saying aloud for my own edification: 'Why go out when you have a bed and a floor and a sink and a window and a table and a chair and many other things here in this very room? After all, you're not a collector . . .'

It was in that room I had begun to write *Cain's Book*, the notes for which took up a disproportionate amount of space in my only suitcase, and which I was carrying to America with me.

'Another drink, sir?' The waitress was speaking to me. The commercial travellers were getting up from their table.

'Yes please.'

'That was Scotch and water, wasn't it?'

'Yes, it was.'

At a certain age, looking back over the past, I began to wonder how much, except in a purely negative way when they presented themselves as limits, objective conditions really affected me. Certainly, for as long as I could remember, I had been selective of what was external to me, and not merely, I think, in the sense that all perception is selective; sometimes, and unconsciously, I had excluded 'facts' with which every one of my immediate acquaintance was familiar, facts which I should consciously have judged to be vital to my own well-being if I had been aware of them. For example, in the two instances in which I had lived with women in a full-hearted way, it was a friend who drew my attention to the fact that my wife had deserted me six months ago. I remembered saying: 'No, you're wrong, man. She's coming back,' and then suddenly realising that she wasn't, couldn't come back, because in a dimly conscious way I had been organising my life to exclude her, from the moment she had left me. And yet I was not quite wrong, because what was left out of the present situation as described by my friend was my own will, which, it startled me to see, he left quite out of account. And then I realised that in presenting myself as up till that time unconscious of my wife's desertion of me I had all the time demanded of him that he should ignore my will, which he saw very well, as something external to him, and fairly predictable. My momentary annoyance that he should think of me as predictable he perhaps excused in me as my friend, at the same time excusing himself, no doubt, for excusing me who he knew stood in no dire need of excuse, since nothing is predictable which is not externalised.

Sitting there in the deserted lounge reminded me of the smokeroom in downtown Glasgow where my father used to sit and while away the long hours of the afternoon. I thought that my father would be alone now, that he would have turned on the light in his room . . . it was nearly midnight . . . and would be alone. The last time I had seen him was at the funeral of my uncle who, running after a tramcar, was suddenly on his knees, arms akimbo as his heart burst.

NEW YORK

1956 30TH APRIL. Trocchi arrives in United States of America. In the autumn he takes a job as a scow captain with the New York Trap Rock Corporation.

1957 13TH AUGUST. Trocchi marries Marilyn Rose Hicks in Tijuana, Mexico. They spend the winter in Venice West, California.

1958 APRIL. The Trocchis move briefly to Las Vegas, before returning to New York in August.

1958 2ND OCTOBER. Mark Alexander Trocchi born in New York Hospital, Manhattan.

1959 26TH MARCH. Trocchi signs a contract with Grove Press for the publication of *Cain's Book* for an initial payment of $550, with $200 more to be paid on publication.

1960 25TH APRIL. Grove Press, New York announce the publication of *Cain's Book*.

1961 APRIL. Trocchi is charged with supplying drugs to a minor. He flees America and returns via Canada to Britain.

JANE LOUGEE

Why did Trocchi eventually choose to go to New York?
Alex expresses himself very well in *Cain's Book* when he touches on this.
He speaks of being in London and not really knowing that he wants to
go to the States. Why does he want to go to the States? Why does he
want to go anywhere any more? Because there really isn't any answer.
Or is there an answer? You know, what am I doing here? It's his search
and so I don't think there's any transition period anywhere. I think this is
Alex's life. It was looking for the room, the box, the hiding place, the
place to play where it was safe. I don't know whether this is the time to
say it, but the combination of Beckett and Alex – Beckett the older man
and Alex the younger – Beckett learned and knew how to be alone and
knew how to play, but Alex was searching. The undoing of Alex the
writer . . . As an eight year old he was left, and this affected him in everything he subsequently did. Alex feared very much being alone. He couldn't
be alone. He speaks of not being able to laugh alone. He can't play alone.
I think his mother left him alone when she died and he never found her
again in any of his searches. There was a security that he obviously had
with his mother in his unfortunate rooming house life that he never found
anywhere else in his wanderings.

How affected was Trocchi by the death of his mother?
It affected him very greatly because he had loved his mother and had
very close contact with her. His father had been the one who didn't really
like working and his mother really bore the hardships of having to support the family by having a rooming house. She died of tainted salmon.[1]
I think he was only eight at the time that it happened and his father then
took over the boys. It was very difficult.

How did you feel when Alex came to New York?
I had left an Alex in Paris that was really on the beginnings of further
search. He wasn't the joyous person that I'd first known. When he came,
I think I had to sign papers that allowed him to come in on a short term
visa. There was always the feeling that, oh well, Alex is coming to New
York and . . . it's more of his trip. I felt a little concerned really, because
he speaks in *Cain's Book* of my treating him as a child but I think I did
feel that way.

When he took work on the scows did you ever visit him there?

I think some of the best writing in *Cain's Book* is the description of life on the barge and the hardships and his search for himself. The odyssey of the barge. It was a hard life. I did go out on one of these trips up the Hudson. On the barge he could have his heroin experience that took him off on other odysseys, removed from the barge, removed from New York. He could go, he could try something, try to find some answer on these trips.

When did Trocchi meet his second wife, Lyn?

The first fall of Alex being in New York, he was taken to parties, through friends and Dick and a few of the other writers. It wasn't like France at all, but at one of these parties he met Lyn, who was, I believe, doing some editing at one of the women's magazines, perhaps *Mademoiselle*. She was a girl who had graduated from Smith, extremely interested in poetry and obviously immediately attracted to Alex and he to her. Very attractive girl, an only child. Her parents lived in New York State somewhere. Then they were married very shortly after meeting, I think six weeks or a couple of months later, and I believe they went to the West Coast. After having introduced Lyn to drugs, I don't know what happened after they went out of New York, but when they came back a year or so later, she was very damaged by the taking of drugs, and she had a child. It was a very difficult period. Very difficult period.

When Lyn was put out on the streets, was there concern that things had gone too far?

Alex would refute his being an addict but he was an addict and she became addicted too. You have to pay for it and in order to pay for it Lyn went out on the streets and it horrified everybody. Everybody was outraged that Alex should have permitted that. But Alex felt that, well, this was just part of a junkie's life. And all junkies had to go out on the street to get their fixes and that's the way it was. There was sadness about his addiction. I didn't condemn him, it was just sadness. I look back on Alex in New York with sadness.

Did you see Alex writing in New York at all? How did this compare with the man you'd seen at work in Paris?

That's an interesting combination, or change. In Paris it was one who sat comfortably and confidently on an old chair at a table. I could go to sleep and the next morning there would be a whole chapter of *Young Adam*. Perfect. No changes necessary, just outstanding. It was all in his head; he sat down, it just poured out, it just came out ... The sentences, the structure, the thoughts, there were no ambiguities, the right word, the right sentence, the right chapter. In New York, it was work, it was terrible. You know, trying to make changes, write, get the thing down on paper to get to Dick to get paid to get a fix.

After Cain's Book, *it seemed that Alex couldn't write ...*

I feel, personally, that Alex had expressed it all, all he could find in his searches, all he could find to answer any of those questions that were always in his head. He says this in *Cain's Book*. He says I may not go on, you know, the end is the beginning, is the circle. He went full circle and went back to England where he could live and that was it.

When Trocchi gave you a copy of Cain's Book, *he wrote a dedication that made reference to posture. What did he mean by 'posture'? Why did it matter to him?*

Alex was a person whose life was, in a sense, acting. It was part of going out of himself. Part of him wanted to be the entertainer, part of him distrusted the entertainer because the entertainer is false and he wanted basically always to be true and honest. Posture speaks of what one is. Posture is that which is put before the public. Posture also means you can pose and be a poseur, you know? But he didn't dedicate the book to me. He told me he couldn't do that, that he had to dedicate it to Lyn.

Trocchi was always testing himself, other people, boundaries – why?

Come on. Alex was testing people. He was testing life. He was testing this, he was testing that, in this search to find himself, in his search to touch the infinite, to touch that which is here, there and everywhere.

You've suggested that something had happened to Trocchi's sense of fun in New York. Could you explain that?

Alex liked to entertain, he was an entertainer and he liked to have fun. He lost that just before I left Paris. When he came to New York, this wasn't going to be fun and he felt it. I felt it and people who knew him felt it and it wasn't. I don't know that Alex ever inspired fun, either for himself or for other people when he returned to England. I saw him only one other time after he returned. In 1970, I believe, I had inherited a part-ownership of a house in Deià, Mallorca, and I got in touch with Alex, thinking that it would be great fun to go down to Deià. I think at that point an anniversary of the magazine would be coming up and it might be fun for us all to go. Alex agreed and we were to meet in Paris. He came but he was four days late and we went on our way, driving down to Barcelona. But he was so strung out not being able to have his fixes all the time that it was a horrible trip. It was just terrible and by the time we got to Barcelona he had to come right back. So that sense of fun and play was gone.

TERRY SOUTHERN

You worked on an anthology with Trocchi and Richard Seaver called Writers In Revolt. *What did that revolt consist of? What attitudes did you share with Trocchi?*

Well, the original title of this book, this anthology, was to be *Beyond the Beat*. The publisher decided on the *Writers In Revolt* title, but the idea was that there was a timeless literature that is forever contemporary. See, this is the period when books by Kerouac and his protégés were very popular and so Alex felt that the literature that he knew of, that is to say of Celine and Malaparte and Jean Genet, and a few others, was much more important so he wanted to have an anthology that he felt superseded the present vogue and it just happened that our tastes seemed to be very similar. It was easy to agree on some contemporary classics. We involved Dick Seaver. Alex said, well now, the key to this undertaking is Richard H. Seaver because he has access to all the great contemporary authors, having worked at Grove Press for several years. So that's how that got started.

How did Trocchi feel about literary convention?

He was conscious of literature that existed quite apart from the avant-garde. It had to do with multi-level meanings and he often used the analogy that musicologists couldn't agree on certain passages of Bach, whether they were celebrating joy or sorrow and he liked that notion. He felt that the best story a person could write would be one that was able to be published in *Reader's Digest* but it had in fact been written for *Weird Tales*. It was written so artfully that it would satisfy the readers of both disciplines.

Did Trocchi consciously set out to rebel, to pioneer new territories?

Well, he wasn't consciously a pioneer. It was just that his faith and perceptions were so extreme and so rarified and highly developed that it took him into those areas which were unexplored by others. He was . . . you know, the quintessential bohemian. He seemed to have no grasp on conventional reality or what was expected, or indeed, demanded of someone in terms of obeying laws and so on and he tried to live as though there were no restraints and he seemed determined to experience everything possible. Regardless of the risks.

How did Trocchi get the job on the scows in New York?

A friend of mine, Mel Sabre – a wonderful talented guy, a writer, who just didn't bother to publish and had a bit of a drug problem – he and Alex met once when they were both trying to score some heroin. Mel Sabre already had a job on the barge so he introduced Alex to the person who was head of the barges, or head of the hiring, whose name was Scotty. He was, you know, Scottish . . . Alex explained to me how with every generation they have these jobs which are favoured by writers because of the almost total absence of demands of the job, such as night clerk at the hotel and nightwatchman, that sort of thing, and that he had discovered such a job for our time, which was to be on one of these barges which were towed up and down the Hudson and the East River, round and round the islands actually and then upstate. He said, I'll put in a word for you with Scotty and sure enough he did. As you know, that's where he wrote *Cain's Book*, while he was on the barge.

Did you visit him on the barge?

It was totally isolated and deserted. I mean there was nothing on the barge except this cargo of rock on the deck and the small cabin. In the summer, the weather being fine, you could sit outside and it was an ideal place to work. All you had to do was to catch the huge ropes, hawsers they were called, from the tugs which would come by. You just put it on the post, the capstan, and then they would start towing you. So there was nothing, no real duties except to keep the scow pumped out if it was going to fill up, as it would occasionally.

Was Cain's Book *autobiographical? Did you recognise any of the characters in it?*

Yeah, I suppose Mel Sabre's wife was in it . . . There were a number of characters whom we both knew and he included in *Cain's Book*, undisguised, but I don't think anyone was ever embarrassed about being in it. Except there was one incident where some zealous narcotics officer found passages which he felt were incriminating and warranted an investigation. So they did come aboard a couple of times but they didn't pursue it, you know.

It seemed that in the early days writing came easy to Trocchi. Did you think that because of that he didn't value it?

It depended entirely on what he was working on. He had the marvellous facility of writing in a kind of stream of consciousness manner, which was very easy for him, but then he would painstakingly rewrite. He could knock off these Girodias things just as fast as he could write, but of course he considered that a waste of time really. Although occasionally he would show me some passages that he had written in one of the Girodias books just because he thought it was so absurd. Which was where his humour came in. But his *Cain's Book* type writing was very serious indeed. I mean, very painstakingly done . . . took a lot out of him.

HALF AN HOUR AGO I GAVE MYSELF A FIX:

from *Cain's Book*

Alex Trocchi

My scow is tied up in the canal at Flushing, N.Y., alongside the landing stage of the Mac Asphalt and Construction Corporation. It is now just after five in the afternoon. Today at this time it is still afternoon, and the sun, striking the cinderblocks of the main building of the works, has turned them pink. The motor cranes and the decks of the other scows tied up round about are deserted.

Half an hour ago I gave myself a fix.

I stood the needle and the eye-dropper in a glass of cold water and lay down on the bunk. I felt giddy almost at once. It's good shit, not like some of the stuff we've been getting lately. I had to be careful. Two of the workmen in wide blue dungarees and wearing baseball caps were still hanging about. From time to time they crossed my catwalk. They were inquisitive. They had heard the noise of the typewriter during the afternoon and that was sufficient to arouse their curiosity. It's not usual for a scow captain to carry a typewriter. They lingered for a while, talking, just outside the cabin. Then, a few minutes before five, I heard them climb back on to the dock and walk away.

Lying on the bunk, alert to the sudden silence that has come over the canal, I hear the buzz of a fly and notice it is worrying the dry corpse of another fly which is half-gouged into the plank of the wall. I wonder about it and then my attention wanders. A few minutes have passed. I hear it buzz again and see that it is still at its work, whatever it is, settled on the rigid jutting legs of the corpse. The legs grow out of the black spot like a minute sprout of eyelashes. The live fly is busy. I wonder if it is blood it wants, if flies like wolves or rats will eat off their own kind.

– Cain at his orisons, Narcissus at his mirror.

The mind under heroin evades perception as it does ordinarily; one is aware only of contents. But that whole way of posing the question, of dividing the mind from what it's aware of, is fruitless. Nor is it that the objects of perception are intrusive in an electric way as they are under mescalin or lysergic acid, nor that things strike one with more intensity or in a more enchanted or detailed way as I have sometimes experienced under marijuana; it is that the perceiving turns inward, the eyelids droop, the blood is aware of itself, a slow phosphorescence in all the fabric of flesh and nerve and bone; it is that the organism has a sense of being intact and unbrittle, and, above all, inviolable. For the attitude born of this sense of inviolability some Americans have used the word 'cool'.

It is evening now, the temperature has fallen, objects are growing together in the dim light of the cabin. In a few moments I shall get up and light my kerosene lamps.

NED POLSKY

When did you first meet Trocchi?

I had gone to a town called Ajijic in Mexico on Lake Chapala; that was late May of 1958. It had a community of American expatriates, a number of whom had been writers and painters but they had been driven out, largely because a lot of them were marijuana users. The American alcoholics had driven them out, complaining to the police. So when I got there, there was a kind of underground of about seven or eight marijuana users, and of course we sniffed each other out. Alex and Lyn were already there, and we had to be very furtive, not because of the Mexicans, they didn't care, but because of the American alcoholics putting on the pressure. I got to know Alex who lived up the block from me. He and Lyn had rented a house, like mine, which consisted of a whole block that was a small house and then a large walled-in garden and Alex at that time was writing very well, I think every day. He'd gotten an advance from Grove Press and was working on *Cain's Book*. Very heavily into drugs but able to work quite well, I thought. First of all he had no difficulty obtaining drugs there so he was able to devote his time more to his writing.

Did you know Lyn?

I knew Lyn only slightly. I never really had much of a chance to talk with her because I always saw her in the context of Alex. She was very nice, very pleasant, seemed kind of witty. My impression basically though is that she was totally dominated by Alex, but totally. Whatever Alex would say she did.

How was he writing? What was your impression of his creativity at that stage?

He was working very well on *Cain's Book*. We would get high in the evenings on marijuana (he was smoking marijuana as I was). He was also very heavily into hard drugs and surprisingly enough he was still able to get high on marijuana, because usually the hard drugs obliterate that pretty quickly but not . . . not with Alex. At least not then. And I would say he worked very well then on the book because he had no difficulty obtaining drugs. When he got back to the States, of course, like any junkie his whole life got oriented around activity to get money for drugs and that's of course when he was unable to get much writing done.

What were your impressions of Trocchi, simply as a person? Was he an attractive person?

Oh yeah, he was marvellous. He was a very outgoing, generous person, very encouraging. Also we shared a lot of literary tastes. That summer, for instance, Beckett's *Krapp's Last Tape* had just been published and we both agreed that was one of Beckett's masterpieces. And I'd written some stuff about James Joyce that Alex was impressed with. We had very similar literary tastes.

When Alex left to go back to the States he gave me a sports jacket of his that I had admired; it didn't fit me well – he was taller and broad-shouldered – but I was very pleased to have it.

When did Trocchi return to New York City?

I stayed on until February of '59 . . . yeah, but Alex had gone back several months earlier. I think in August of '58, something like that, maybe September. Essentially, as he told me, he didn't want to go back but he was running out of money and he thought the only way to get more money out of Barney Rosset at Grove Press was to go back there and, you know, plead his case in person so that's . . . that's when he went back. In the fall of 1958.

RICHARD SEAVER

How did Cain's Book *come in to being and what was your involvement?*
I left Paris in the mid-Fifties and came back to the United States. Alex stayed on for several more years, a couple at least, and then I was out of the United States but not in Paris for a couple of years after that. When I came back I joined Grove Press and learned that Alex was now in the United States. He was living on a scow, plying the trade up and down the Hudson River. He was actually the captain of a scow which is one of those barges which brought merchandise up or garbage or whatever it was and it provided him with room and sufficient money to keep body and soul alive. He was deeply into drugs at that point. When I met him I found him quite unchanged, actually. Still utterly charming, tall, hawk-like, bright, but slightly ravaged in the face, and he brought to us at Grove, probably through my connection, he brought this portion of a novel called *Cain's Book*, which was the story of life on a barge and the drug scene in New York and I would suspect that he brought us thirty to forty pages. The publisher at Grove Press was a man named Barney Rosset and I brought these pages to Barney and I said this man is extremely talented and this is the best writing about drugs I've seen since . . . since William Burroughs. To make a long story short, we signed up the book for a very modest advance and we got Trocchi a contract and a first payment. The second payment was due only upon completion of the book.

I think, if memory serves, it took another two years before we actually got the completed book. Alex would come in with five, ten, eight, four pages at a time and hope to get fifty bucks or fifty dollars or seventy-five dollars or thirty dollars or whatever the exchequer would bear, clearly to support his drug habit but it made the novel inchingly slow and more and more formless so my job was to try and stitch this together, because many of the pages were superb but where they fit and how they fit and to get Alex to sit down and make them fit was . . . was a painful job, so I can't say that there was any real close relationship, although I was his editor at that point, the relationship, the close relationship that had existed between us in Paris, was almost totally, if not totally gone.

Cain's Book took a long time between inception and completion. Over two years as I recall. Maybe longer. But it was in stark contrast to Alex's earlier facility to turn out a book, even *Young Adam*, I suspect, was written in a month, maybe six weeks, and it came out sparkling. Here pages came out sparkling but it was painful to see that his ability to produce had been . . . had been condensed so that he couldn't write more than a page or two a week. But my job was to try and say Alex, what we need now is a scene about *this*. Joe Necchi, who was clearly an autobiographical character, based on Trocchi's New York and earlier life, was a fascinating protagonist, in that the drug scene in the 1960s in New York was a very important scene. Drugs were, for the first time in America, or the first time certainly since World War II, a major concern and a major factor and Alex was writing about that scene like nobody else. It was also an enormously introspective book. Much more so than *Young Adam* and Necchi's reflections about himself and about his earlier life and about where he was going and what he was doing, what he was involved in, both his life as a drug addict and the total immersion in the drug scene was . . . absolutely mesmerising and absolutely . . . authentic.

Did he make claims that he was writing something new?

He did claim that he was writing a new kind of novel. *Cain's Book* was a radical book, even in the context of the Sixties where a great deal of radical writing was going on. I think it was partly because Alex was not able to function the way he had before. The facility was gone, the . . . the scintillating intelligence – because Alex was extraordinarily bright and his mind was like a steel trap. It was clearly affected by the drugs and the continuity was affected by the drugs. So *Cain's Book* is a book of discontinuity. It's small scenes stitched together, so that it really comes off as a novel, but it was hard to do and I think he made claims for the discontinuity as a new kind of literature, or a new departure for himself, but I think its essence was . . . the fact was, that was all he could do, so it was easier to justify it as a new kind of literature. It was clearly the end of his writing as well. Because it was . . . it was a train slowing down. The later portions of the book were much slower to come into being than the earlier portions of the book.

What happened to Trocchi the writer?

I think that if Alex were here he'd say that he stopped writing because he had nothing further to say. I think the fact of the matter was he was incapable of writing because of drugs. Period, end of sentence. He took in later life, as you know, to doing miniature paintings which would take him months to produce and I believe are not wonderful art. He had dried up and the focus was all inward and self-destructive. Alex was an enormously self-destructive person. Even in the early days one saw that. He would do things to alienate Jane who was his sustenance and his great love and then try and get her back but having done his best to alienate her. He did that with his friends and acquaintances. And ultimately he did it to *Merlin* which was nonetheless his vehicle into the world of literature, politics, writing.

What was the root of that self-destructiveness?

Alex was a sincere and total rebel against the establishment, however you want to define the establishment, whether it's the Scottish establishment, whether it's the French establishment, the English establishment, the American establishment. The establishment for him was anathema and to be brought down at all costs. I think that many rebels in France – Artaud, a great poet, a great rebel – ultimately do themselves in by the force of their rebellion. There's only so much energy against the whole establishment that you can expend without trying to call on other resources. In Artaud's case, and in Trocchi's, it was drugs, and in both instances I think that the drugs took control. Alex was a man very much in control of himself and his environment when he was younger. When he was deeply into drugs, drugs were in control of Alex.

Do you think he genuinely saw the taking of drugs as a legitimate move of some kind?

My strong suspicion is that being into drugs, you then have to find the justification for being in drugs and therefore you find whatever premise suits your purposes. He did form a kind of magnificent empty political movement, based on rebelling against everything, to justify his stance on drugs or the fact that he was stilled by drugs. I wrote an introduction to a reissue of *Cain's Book* about ten years ago, slightly longer because Alex was still alive, and I sent it to him and it's really quite a laudatory introduction in my view. Kind, but I did deplore the fact that Alex's great talent . . . in my view, he did himself in because he deprived, I think, the English language of maybe a masterpiece but certainly several good books. Alex wrote me a scathing letter back saying who was I to judge? Was I God to judge his life? If he took drugs it was because he planned to take drugs and needed to take drugs and that was his fulfilment and drugs brought him to the illumination that he was looking for in life which he had not had without them so buzz off already, Buster. I mean it was, I think I still have that letter, but it was . . . it was . . . I think it was the last communication between us.

How was Cain's Book *greeted, particularly in America? People such as Mailer spoke highly of it.*[1]

Cain's Book had a number of very good reviews, including a review in the *New York Times*. It did not sell massively well but it sold respectably. I would suspect that in the hardcover edition it sold between ten and fifteen thousand copies, which is certainly not bad and in subsequent paperback editions it has probably sold another fifty to sixty thousand copies and it remained in print almost without exception for most of the next twenty years. So . . . Trocchi was a name known in America. He was known from Paris, he was known from *Merlin*, so he did get about, despite his stint on the scow. He was a figure, he lived for a year or so in 14th Street up here in a huge loft, and his writing appeared in the *Evergreen Review*, excerpts of *Cain's Book* were greeted with enthusiasm when they appeared at least in two issues of the *Evergreen Review*. So that he was not totally unknown by the time *Cain's Book* appeared. There was a literary ripple and . . . and Mailer among others, touted it very highly. Burroughs certainly touted it highly and a number of other literary figures called *Cain's Book* one of the major books of that year.

Trocchi lost thousands of dollars through bootleggers, which is still going on today. How did that come about?

In the 1960s, the books that Alex had written for Girodias were not available here but there were a number of censorship battles fought in the United States. The first of which was *Lady Chatterley* in 1959–60, the second was Henry Miller in the early Sixties, followed by the battle over *Naked Lunch*. All these were lengthy legal battles but once those legal battles were won, which they were, and Maurice Girodias moved to the United States, he began to reissue some of his earlier Paris Olympia Press editions in New York and most, if not all of those, were out of copyright because he had not properly copyrighted them when they were first published. That's a Catch 22 because you weren't allowed to copyright dirty books and then you were penalised because, since they were out of copy-right, you could not protect them in any way, but some of those Girodias books, including Alex's, were indeed pirated by a number of other pub-lishers on the West Coast. Some here in New York, who simply took them and reset them and never paid a penny to Alex or to Girodias. Girodias made some effort – as did Grove Press, because some of the Grove Press books were equally pirated – made efforts to stop the pi-rates or to get money from them, but these were people who would pop up at a post office address and print fifty thousand copies and then disap-pear into the night so there was never any way you could really track them down and nab them. So Alex, yes, lost, if royalties had been paid on the books that he wrote, he would have been a relatively wealthy man.

You've said that Trocchi was not contrite. What did you mean by that?

Alex had a lot to atone for, I would think. Again, I'm not playing God but . . . if one looks at the history of those he cheated, start with George Plimpton, who lent him considerable sums of money, got him out on bail, posted bail for him and Alex fled into Canada, leaving George hold-ing the bag for, I would suspect, a couple of thousand dollars which, in those days, was a lot of money for anybody. And his family. Lyn, his wife, whom he got into drugs and who died as a result of it; his children. It's a pretty sad spectacle and yet Alex, in my correspondence with him or talking with him, never felt the least responsible for any of that, and certainly not the least contrite. He still felt that he was a major figure, a major talent, and that . . . the end of that justified whatever means, in-cluding his personal life, which was, I would say, a disaster.

What was Lyn Trocchi like?

Lyn was a very pretty, very young girl from a middle-class Long Island family. I don't remember how they met but they were living together and . . . my first memory of them as a couple was in the loft up on 14th Street when I went up to gather a few pages of *Cain's Book* one afternoon and the first time I had gone up to the loft was mid-afternoon and the place was in a total shambles. Needles all over the place, beds unmade, both Lyn and Alex sitting in a chair looking as though they were staring into space for ever and I realised that . . . that Lyn already was, you know, was a lost soul. So I really didn't know her except as Alex's very pretty girlfriend and subsequent wife but someone who, while she was still in her teens, was completely drugged out.

Can you trace any of the story of Trocchi's departure from the States?
Cain's Book really is the book of a pursued person, a man who is increasingly going underground because the Feds are after him, whether it was the FBI or the drug enforcement folk or whoever it was. I suspect it was the FBI because, although he always denied it, Alex was certainly dealing in drugs and that is where you got into real trouble. Using drugs was a problem enough but dealing in drugs could get you into real trouble and many years in prison, especially in those days, probably today still. But as I recall Alex was being pursued and he was dodging the Feds and he and Lyn knew that people were after him. Lyn lived on Long Island and had gone back to see her parents and I think they both had actually gone back when they realised that the FBI or whoever the Feds were, were really moving in to arrest them.

Alex, as I recall, jumped on a train somewhere out on mid-Long Island, leaving Lyn behind, and literally escaped. Now there's where George Plimpton can fill you in because George was involved. As I recall Alex left the country wearing two of George's suits . . . but he really left the country to avoid going to jail. He would have been arrested, he would have been in jail had he not really run for the border at that point.

Looking back, what were your feelings about the man and his work?
Alex was, as I said, a brother to me in Paris. We were extremely close, we shared thoughts, hopes, aspirations, writing ambitions, we had a common cause which was the magazine, which we both very strongly believed in as did the others around us, Christopher [Logue] and Austryn Wainhouse, Patrick [Bowles] . . . but I think Alex and I were more focussed on it than the others and believed in it . . . believed in it more. Alex was a great charmer, a great friend to be with. Scintillating conversationalist, someone who provoked you to think sharper yourself. He was close to brilliant and in the two year span we were extreme . . . as close as I have probably been to any other male person in my life, aside from my children, but that translated not into I think the work of which Alex was clearly fully capable. I think his work is secondary, I think *Cain's Book* remains an interesting . . . I think it will last in a minor way. I think some of his other writing may, when culled, be of interest to future literary historians but I don't think he wrote the major works of which he was capable.

GEORGE PLIMPTON

NEW YORK

Alex met and married Lyn. I don't remember where Lyn came from, but I do remember that she was an absolutely startling beauty. She had one of those fragile faces, sort of childlike. What made it so tragic was that she married Alex at a time when Alex had begun this descent caused by drugs. I remember Alex used to come to my door and ask for money to pay for his drugs. Lyn was working in the streets as a prostitute to make money for Alex's habit, and indeed her habit. She told me this extraordinary thing once; she said that very often when a man would pick her up, they would take her to these hotels and then they would find themselves unable to make love to her because there was something so touching and fragile about her. They would simply sit there and talk and then after a while they would hand over, whatever it was, fifty bucks. That would immediately go. John Marquand was a great friend of theirs. Because Alex would go from friend to friend to friend borrowing money, he suggested that we put all our money into a big vat and boil it into a sort of paste and then put this paste into a big syringe and then pump that into Alex. It was a black joke but that's what a lot of us felt that we were doing. We were all enablers. But he was a man who was very hard to refuse.

He tried to get me hooked on heroin once. He said, George, you've done everything. You've played football, basketball, all these things, with the pros . . . and now you've got to try this . . . So I was stupid enough to go with him to this sort of underground cellar. The place had quite a few people in there, one of them a man with one leg, I remember, lying on a mattress, I remember a girl was sick in a basin as soon as I walked in so it was not really the most appealing place to find out what this great thing was all about. What saved me, I think, was that Alex was so . . . so anxious for a big hit that he diluted whatever he was going to give me to such an extent that it had absolutely no effect whatsoever. I remember sitting there reading a comic book waiting for the effect to take place. Nothing. But I must say Alex was very good with a needle. It was one of the best, least painful, shots I think I've ever received in my life in various clinics, but thank goodness it didn't work.

What had happened to Alex Trocchi the writer in New York?
I don't remember Alex ever being pessimistic about things. I don't ever

remember any despair. I think he always felt that he was going to be recognised somehow. He was going to turn the corner and everything was going to be all right and his books were going to be accepted.

He lived, for a while, in the back room of the *Paris Review* office, which we had on 82nd Street. I don't know what went on back there. There was a burlap bag that hung as a curtain. Alex had no other place to stay. Part of the time he stayed on a barge, what they called a stake barge, way out there beyond the Statue of Liberty, where the other barges come and tie up to and then the tug boats come and they move them into the docks and the wharves and it must be one of the most melancholy places in the world . . . because you look and you see the skyline of New York but you can't get there. You're alone out there in the stake boat. There's not a row boat or anything you can row across. You just have to stay there until finally a tug boat comes and you can get on that. That must have been terrible for him but what a wonderful place to write. I don't know what he wrote out there but there was nothing else really you could do. Anyway he hated that so much he finally came and lived in the *Paris Review* offices, behind this burlap bag. I used to look in there every once in a while, terrible scene of disarray, but Alex was always cheerful about wherever he was. At least I'll remember him as such. A lot of laughter. Even the most awful . . . I remember another terrible story. He got picked up once for drugs and he had his dime, in those days it was a dime, and you could make one phone call from the police station, and he called his wife Lyn and said he was sure that the police were going to come and search their apartment where they had a lot of drug equipment and maybe even drugs and to get rid of it. Peter Matthiessen and I went down to pick Lyn up to go up to the Court House to bail him out. Lyn was with us in the car. She was very proud of herself because she didn't want to throw away the syringe; it meant an awful lot to them this syringe. So she stuck it into a baby's turd which was floating in the toilet. She didn't think the police would ever find it there. So we bailed out Alex. Things got worse and worse for him and finally, of course, he had to leave the country. Good old Alex. He knew he couldn't take any baggage with him, so he took two of my suits . . . Brooks Brothers suits. I still remember them, a blue pinstripe and a white and a grey pinstripe, very fond of these two suits. I mean I only had, you know, three suits, and these were my two favourite suits and he took quite a lot of shirts and a bit of underwear and he put them all on, you know? Four layers of underwear. Four shirts one over the other and my two suits . . . He probably had a little handbag or something like that, reckoning if he had a big suitcase they'd catch him. So that's how he got out of the country. With all my suits. I think he may have written me a letter about the suits and apologised and said he'd give them back to me but I never saw them again. I was very angry for a while but . . . and of course in a funny way I suppose I aided and abetted this man's departure from the United States.

Why did Trocchi have to leave the country?

I can't remember the exact circumstances. I think there was an arrest out for him to appear in court because of the drug violations and I think maybe even selling drugs. I don't know, when he finally left the *Paris Review* office, I didn't really see very much of him, so I don't know what he was involved in. But anyway he had to appear in court and he didn't . . . didn't feel he should, and so he left the country. Crossed over the border into Canada, wearing all the suits.

What do you think of him as a writer?

Well, I haven't read Alex's books for – what? – thirty years now, so . . . But I remember his writing as being very powerful, very clear, sure sense of dialogue, sure sense of drama. I mean the Glasgow street-gangs, about which I know nothing, I can still remember in reading *Cain's Book* some of the puissance, some of the atmosphere that he was able to create about that particular part of the world. We all thought in Paris that, judging our contemporaries, he was way up there. I mean people like Bill Styron came through Paris, Peter Matthiessen, of course, Jimmy Baldwin, all these people were there and I remember thinking, wow, Trocchi. He seemed much older than all these people. I've never really known how old Alex actually was but he'd had so many adventures that fed him huge volumes of material to work with. The great sadness about him was that the worlds that he'd been in were full of interest and possibilities, that he wasn't able ever to put those things down on paper after a while. The fuel wasn't there.

How does the man you knew in Paris compare to the man you knew in New York?

In Paris he was a man of enormous . . . presence. Walk into a cafe and people would say, there's Alex Trocchi, he's the head of *Merlin*. In New York he became pathetic. He was like a homeless man. What he did to

Lyn turned an awful lot of people against him. I mean, to send your wife out into the street . . . Then they had this child, of course, which made it even more poignant. So you weighed all these things when he would appear at your door and ask for money for milk for the child. Of course you'd empty your wallet but you knew darn well it wasn't going to the child. He became an utterly tragic, weak . . . and hopeless and you didn't want to really answer the door when you heard a knock. He'd come very late at night and you'd say, oh God it's Alex, and sure enough it would be and your heart bled for him but it was such a terrible shame.

I would like to say that the Alex I would remember would be the Alex of Paris, this dynamic figure, but alas, it isn't. It's the tragic figure that would turn up at the door and ask for money to feed his child and you knew that was very unlikely because he was hooked and it's sad to think that that's the Alex that I will remember, but . . . I try not to. I try to remember the other one. The other one was joyous, a great man, a great writer.

FROM *CAIN'S BOOK*, VOLUME 2

Alex Trocchi

Thoughts on Bill Burroughs, Hashish, Hitler, as a Prolegomenon to a New Beginning of Unspeakable Memories, with a Spontaneous Discourse on Oblomov and the Long Sanity of Proust in a Padded Room.

'Now it is a game I am going to play,' rules dimly intuited, not yet verbally articulated: I am lying. This book is written to kill.

Titles have been a kind of diarrhoea with me, or the very opposite, with difficulty evicted out of great constipation. I would look at a title for a minute or an hour or a day, seeking in it the Absolute Title beyond which there would be no more to be said. I passed some beautiful bright titles in the long years of dying, complex, with point and counterpoint, black-backed with white underbellies, smooth as sharks, and stood them up, each separate as penguins on the ice-floes of my anaesthetized imagination. — *Bob's Gumrot and the Gaitered Crab,* by Pantagruel, *Lie Down in Arsemess, The Naked and the Feds, Marjorie Warningdear,* and *The Inmost Beef,* reviewed for posterity by Alexander Pope become unheroic as he drops as another turd another identity.

As for characters, I never met a character but he vaporized when you applied the torch to his little pink ringpiece. Atomized they all were by the simplest detergents. And as for their interaction, there is implicit in this cute notion of Victorian optimism at least one most obdurate misconception, viz.: that characters interact. I take it as part of the given that the monads have no windows.

The barbecue was executed at 4.45 p.m. on a late August afternoon in a dark chamber given over for the purpose. It was supervised by Dr Hare Q. Kildare, prominent ovary researcher, who headed the disciplinary board at the hospital and who, at a recent general meeting of the A.M.A., was highly commended for a speech entitled: 'The Health of the People under Free Enterprise' in which he stressed the importance in a free society for a man to pay his own medical bills, at the same time calling for a strict international ban on narcotics as a must for democracy. In their various official and unofficial capacities the following ladies and gentlemen were present: the Rev. Filing Delinquent of Llareggub, Prof. Horst Wesel, Dr Mengele of Auschwitz Sanatorium, Lord Jeremy Stoppit, Mrs Remember Gomorrha, and the Countess Dracula, sophisticated wife of the Enemanian Ambassador, who is herself a student of the science and who studied under our own Commissioner Manslayer.

The jolt, or 'charge', was what is considered average for the particular situation, Rev. Filing Delinquent said afterwards, slightly more than is ordinarily employed in European practice, considerably less than that recommended in Ambassador Dracula's country, 263,400 XGH-volts (Methodist) in parallel field action with no special electrodes, – 'Enough', the Noble Prizewinner continued, 'to atomize neural tissue without causing body odour.' Mrs Remember Gomorrha spoke afterwards, calling for the stimulation of public interest in the various modes of electrocution. 'That boy,' she said, referring to the electrocuted catatonic, 'is now healed.' She ended by calling for the immediate segregation of that portion of the population which was infected. In this she was eagerly seconded by Dr Mengele who placed his sanatorium at the disposal of the committee. His engineers, he averred, were already studying the feasibility of chain treatment.

At the third jolt the patient's torso was seen to shudder like a tall jelly, a reaction referred to in technical nomenclature as 'reintegration'. The patient reintegrated slowly, the shuddering (except for a muscular twitch at the lower jaw which, in the opinion of Dr Kildare, may unfortunately, if the patient lives, prove to be permanent) subsiding gradually over a period of two-and-a-half hours after which the patient was returned to the ward.

It was the practice, Dr Kildare pointed out to those present, to wait three days before attempting to estimate what he called the 'moto-total effect' of the operation, since further changes not unlike those of terrestrial subsidence (earthquakes, volcanic eruptions, etc.) were often met with during the period up to forty-eight hours after the barbecue. The patient's eyeballs, which had been driven out of their sockets by the electric shock, had a 'cooked' look which made the eminent ovarist reluctant to predict success or failure at the present time.

'Purely marginal, purely marginal,' Prof. Horst Wesel was heard to mutter as the committee left the ward.

New York, 1960. The date implying a certain continuity. Cf. 'sordid story of a drug addict in poor taste', described by a little fart from Atlanta, Ga., as a journal of my 'sordid half-existence'. Onward.

Each time I sit down again and take up where I left off I am in a certain mood whose symptoms I recognise . . . a quickening of the pulse, a shortness of breath, a tingling at the abdomen. Nevertheless, I know it was not the same sordid half-existence who sat down early this morning and took a fix. *Que suis-je?* A pseudo-entity out of inertia, with a thirst to be. A swift fix makes nonsense of whatever definition, rings an epistemological bell. Nevertheless, that is the kind of question that interests me, the illegitimate question, the meaningless one, the one in which is involved a host of ambiguities, a morass of symbols, a swarm of bees, words chasing sense, sense chasing words, and out of which suddenly as a ship out of fog an image, a crisis, a sound. On. Again. Along a road. There is still a road, the same road, blank and categorical like a state highway in the desert, and friends as old as lizards with their stone grimaces . . . how swiftly they scuttle when surprised! That isn't what I meant to say, not at the beginning when I sat myself down. It's the same road, different, bare of particulars, unfolding itself towards the red suppuration of sun at the long blue horizon, which might be volcanic, or a burning man. At the road's edge, a few scrub oaks, stones of many colors, quartz, feldspar, fluorite, garnet, gold. A world is soon furnished, peopled, in the desert. In the desert emotions take on a nakedness which might be offensive in the salon. There was as I remember dust clinging to the woman's thighs which had been wet and weren't any longer and it clung there as wet sand clings forming a ridge against her white flesh, a glinting leaf-edge against the soft northern city-protected loins of a city woman who kept on her nylons and her garterbelt for ye oulde prospector who sprinkled her wet melonbelly with the gold-dust of his strike, Goldenballs Gannon from Ioway died a year later in Las Vegas, Nev. in the stroke of his passion. . . . 'Jesus Christ, the old fart's croaked!' . . . and her, her first thought for insects that crawled, before she was persuaded, because she remembered the day just off the highway between Nogales and Guaymas, and the exhilaration at having escaped at last across the border, and the climb down over the embankment at the side of the road to the small bridge under which we lay with our naked legs intertwined, when suddenly she felt the red ants and saw them move like a minute river of blood over her shin. There is nothing that is not in some way or other ambiguous, dialectical, in time. It was along the road those moments at which I was out of time, at which the world was like a perfection at my senses, whether it was a woman or a stone, it was those moments which provided me with a hieroglyphics out of which I was able to construct it again; and it is so even now again as I go on. I chose the desert to begin with because of its relative emptiness, because, especially in remembering, I didn't wish to be at once overcome with a profusion of things, much as I suppose Descartes chose his *cogito,* to have an apodeictic posture from which to be going on. Perhaps I am as deluded as he was (though that is hard to believe), even in my indirection. – Darling, there's nothing like gold for correct friction.

New York, 1960. A man lying on a bed, naked except for underpants, becomes a man in pants and a singlet with a dressing gown over, wearing socks in whose knit sawdust clings. The sawdust comes from the wooden boxes I am making. Coffins for my enemies. 2.30 a.m. It has been raining all day. Catatonia has threatened since late morning. The image of a grey man lying motionless on a white stretcher. Not a flick of muscle on his face. It is rigid. The eyes are inflexibly closed; the nose like a dumb finger pointing; jaws clenched. He neither speaks nor reacts to the spoken word. Would you? He doesn't react to pinpricks and other irritations. If food is put in his mouth it decays there.

New York, 1960. The hero as junkie, confounder of conformities, sinker of moral ducks, alone with his twilight detergent, in every shuddering act, in his original posture, he resists the times. With the bad fiction of international politics he wipes his pile-encrusted arse. Can't buy vaseline these days without a prescription. Where would the Empire City be without its junkies, the blue geek with his sliding walk, slobbering hymns with his liver-loose lips at the sanitation squad sent to dispose of him? Where he lay on the stoop a hoarfrost of his peculiar perspiration, snail-glint, and five cigarette ends left over from a previous work of fiction lying extinguished in their own long ash. It got dark a short while ago a long while ago and the fog and the night wrap themselves up in each other until suddenly under the pale yellow cone of light from the lamppost, transparent parvenu amongst my sensations, is me. That brings me back to my first concern, my proper study, my improper gesture. It is the tilted town of St Tropez and night has fallen and I am awake abroad among the pissoirs. The procurer draped a ten thousand franc note like a modest flag or fabulous winding sheet across my erection. – 'I want you to meet the Existential,' he snickered triumphantly as I zipped my fly fast and furtive to contain my *pourboire*. I didn't like the look in his eye, his narrow squint, nor the way his long thumb and forefinger closed damp and hard about my left wrist like a miniature boa constrictor, and I was kind of doubtful when with his other hand he retrieved the sodden hunk of bread from the urinal in front of me and shook it nicely like a leaky fountain pen to rid it of excess moisture. – 'For whom the calories?' I enquired, preparing there and then to do him in in the black of night. – *'Ta gueule!'* he said rudely, and before I had time to react he was moving fast as a bicycle along the street with me in one hand and the holy bread in the other towards the villa where his employer waited darkly, like a long cocoon. I must admit it took me aback. The guy was a basket case after the war and they put him out of sight in a dark attic in a hospital cut off from the nearest village by miles of green fir trees and the few conversations I had with him before his wife drowned him were an inspiration to me. His pension because of his high rank and the extent of his physical injuries was considerable and as he was at first anyway more or less confined to his basket he soon had a sizable capital with which he was able to indulge in his passion for the stock market. Unlike the Button, another inmate and close friend whose nickname derived from the fact that half of one thigh was miraculously left to him when the explosion of a landmine removed the rest of his limbs and sight, he was highly successful and soon possessed two Cadillacs and the said villa in St Tropez where for two months each year he lived incognito under the pseudonym of the Existential. Jackie Salamander had left Athens and me about two weeks before and I was alone with Midhou now, Midhou the expatriate Algerian who to give himself a sense of direction in the bloody drains of history consulted a newspaper one fine morning until he came on an appropriate headline: FOUR REBELS POT-ROASTED IN ALGIERS. COLONS CALL FOR MORE POTS. – *'Sales poules!* I go to Algiers. Why don't you come with me?' – 'You're mad. *Au moment que tu te tournes le dos tes amis vont me rôtir les couilles, sʒʒʒ!* Besides, like here in Athens, everything that doesn't walk on wheels will soon be a soldier over there.' All around us, everywhere, like the dust, were the modern guardians of Greek democracy. The unemployed. Groups of them in ill-fitting uniforms, making an uneasy barracks of the town. Whose democracy? – *'Ce n'est pas la même chose. Ici ils sont les cons, mais ils sont grècques; petits cons du civil foutus par les petits cons de l'armée foutus par les petits cons du civil, mais grècques la ronde entière, n'est-ce pas? Mais en Algérie il nous faut les détruire, les soldats-moʒʒerfokèrsʒ!'* He brandished his fist and his metal teeth glinted dully in the intense yellow sunlight. *'Moi, je vais semer le désordre, un désordre affreux. Et puis il nous faut frapper au ventre, soudain, un coup de poing au paralytique!'* – *'Et aprés?'* –*'Aprés!'* . . . he pulled himself to attention like a soldier and spoke up towards a non-existent flag . . . *'Aprés il y aura l'Algérie pour les algériens!'* – *'L'Algérie pour les punaises,'* I said to him. – *'Ha!* . . . *si. Si tu veux, Josef!'* *'L'Algérie pour les mouches,'* I said. *'T'as encore raison, Josef!'* *'L'Algérie pour les fourmis!'* – *'Bien sûr, pour les fourmis aussi!'* – *'Je te vendrai l'Algérie pour dix francs, le hashish pas inclus. Tu la prends, Midhou?'* We were walking and we came to the meat market. Vast sheds. Carcasses. Armies of them. Hung, split, neatly butchered on marble slabs. Attacked by ravenous bluebottles. Armies of them. Glinting blue. Transparent wings beating madly like the arms of drowning men. They hovered and struck in droves. An insectal

Armageddon. *'Quel désordre!'* Midhou gloated. *'La destruction du biftek!'* 'Algeria for the bluebottles,' I said. *– 'Oui! for de bleubottls!' – 'Alors, Midhou, tu es un bleu-bottle? Algérie! Pourquoi pas y aller à cette époque? Tu n'es ni insecte ni cadavre . . . .'* Midhou lifted the two ears and the tail of a pig from one of the slabs and thrust them at me. He did this so quickly that I was forced to take them in my hands. – *'Pour ta logique, matador,'* he said with the smile and bow of a maitre d'hôtel. – 'If I accept them you won't go back to Algeria?' There was sadness in his next gesture. A slight shrug. *'Tout de même j'y vais,'* he said. – 'But why, Midhou?' – *'C'est peut-être pour le hashish,'* he said. So while Midhou sailed from Marseilles for whatever reason I betook myself to St Tropez where in a pissoir on the Promenade de Grands Néants I was procured for the Existential's lust.

'Here he is, General,' the procurer said.

'Bring 'im over to the light where I can see him!'

The voice came from a coffin-shaped box tilted at about seventy-five degrees from the horizontal and lined with white quilt. Strapped there, laid against the quilt like a piece of super-fine candy, was the Existential, all there was of him, that is; a head attached to a limbless torso by a short and powerful neck. It gazed at me with two angry watery blue eyes. Hair and scalp had been removed by a flame-thrower so that just above the level of the albino-white eyebrows and where the forehead should have been all violet and soft with scars like raisins in it the head sloped gently earless upwards and away. It appeared to be quite without bone for an expanse of four or five inches so that between the ridge of eyebrows and the sudden sharp top of his cranium I saw his brains move with the thought of me like nudging insects beneath the graft.

The possibility of such a man was something I had never before had occasion to contemplate and I must have registered my surprise in a physical way because the first words that the Existential addressed to me directly were: 'You think I'm handicapped, do you?' And for the first time for a long time I couldn't find words to reply.

New York 1960 . . . certainly I am making a great demand upon you, asking you to follow the inconsequential convolutions of unconscious memory held briefly in the prism of present awareness. Nevertheless, it is for me the only way; what I write will carry the mark of my own pose and posture and it will be haunted by the delirium of the moment at which

I confront you to whom I address myself. The other night I found confirmation in Artaud: 'If there is one hellish, truly accursed thing in our time, it is our artistic dallying with forms, instead of being like victims burnt at the stake, signaling through the flames.' The image of Fay, who by the way has been seen in none of her usual haunts for nearly a year now, and of the 'day of wrath' I invented for her, comes crowding into my mind. The emotion crystallizes into an image, not yet possessed, which has to be seized by the creative imagination at the same time as it is truant to violent seizure, tenuous, fragible, something not to be *taken* but more precisely *inhabited*, until the mind which creates is momentarily contained within the created crystal as electricity is contained in a clear glass bulb, the man and his creation being one at the instant at which the thing is created, lived in, overcome.

Meanwhile, when Dr Hare ('Rabbit' to his friends) Kildare returns to his study with the other members of the committee, the long grey gink on the stretcher is left alone. Poor sod is contained within the thin clear bubble of his isolation. Up, down, North, South, East, West, from all sides bounces back his own dirty reflection. – 'Trouble was,' Kildare extemporized before his captive audience, 'He failed to distinguish between two kinds of perspiration, the physical kind and the mental kind. Science shows that in the glands of the mature male and in the glands of the mature female perspiration caused for example by anxiety emits an offensive odour. For two thousand years man has sought to avert this embarrassment. Poor Cleopatra had to spend twelve hours a day in milk baths and having oils and expensive elixirs rubbed into her skin to avoid what we in this country very bluntly call B.O. With our modern techniques, in this instance electric shock therapy, we have found ways to abolish all thought and thus, Ladies and Gentlemen, all offensive odour.' This brief address is followed by a round of enthusiastic clapping.

People are walking about in long rooms. His own silence intensifies, becomes suffocating, is not, for being a lack, nothing . . . he almost imagines it to have weight, and yet it is invisible, an invisible wall sustained by himself against the others. He is still lying on the stretcher in this hospital. All the time people are coming in and out of doors. They don't exactly use the word 'it' of him but sometimes their behaviour towards him seems to imply that their commerce is with a thing, to be moved here or there, up in an elevator, along a green corridor, the sheet stripped away, the two men in white coats, one wearing a stethoscope, the woman in white . . . The woman in white was in one of his daydreams. She wears a white smock with white stockings and white shoes and a white cap on her head; pink hot body beneath. Big buttocks and thighs slabs of white cod. His response to her existed almost entirely as an infinitesimal weight at his nostrils. Today as she comes into the ward beside the consultant and the interne (it is he who wears the stethoscope) she passes four fingers of her right hand across the sleek gold hair at her temple as though to relieve it of sweat. He is thinking she has fucked since he last saw her. Shirley Temple with her Mona Lisa look. As they stand close he can smell rather than see her, pink, with a bloom as virtuous as a five-day deodorant pad. — 'No response to any of the tests?' He knows that when the interne has answered the consultant's question in the negative the consultant will lean over him smelling of disinfectant and lift with his warm thumb the eyelid of his left eye and they will look at one another through the invisible wall. He holds the patient's lid open, tilts his chin on which he wears a fashionable Van Dyck, and peers. Closer. His left hand hovers nearby with a small pencil-shaped flashlight. He shakes his head. — 'Guess we'll have to barbecue this one,' he says.

— 'What time, Doctor?'

This last from the Pink Lady, cool, coming across space-years from the planet Venus, and he began to think of her pubic hairs, like a close blonde beard at the nob of her body, out of sight. Her voice is efficient and professional. She is perhaps exaggerating to impress the senior doctor, remaking an emotion that came originally as dismay. The horizontal man smiled without moving his lips. Nothing dismayed the Pink Lady. On one occasion he had heard her say: 'I wish Dr Van Dyck would prescribe a good jolt. It would do this one a world of good.'

What the flame-thrower had done for the Existential. The Pink Lady in fact reminded him of the Existential's wife.

— 'Did you say something, Nurse?'

– 'Do you wish to make an appointment for the barbecue, Doctor? We have to reserve the theatre at least twenty-four hours in advance except in case of an emergency.'

– 'Oh yes, no. We'll give it another day or two. He might come around. You never know . . . . Anyway, Dr Kildare should be consulted. There's an electricity shortage since the last atomic attack.' He hums a tune vaguely and bending over the patient again pretends to look into the treacly pool of his eye. He is not actually looking in. The horizontal man knows that because it is his eye. He sets himself up at a distance from it and poses.

The nurse and the interne exchange a glance. 'You think I should scramble his brains at once, Nurse?' the consultant said sideways, at her, with a leer.

'I don't think anything, Doctor. I merely wish to know if you want to make an appointment.' Her notebook and pencil at pause, English, her heavy pink smell coming through the starched linen like the wind of blown roses.

With a gesture of impatience the consultant leaves the room.

The nurse looks at the interne. 'I *loathe* that man! Why don't you say something when he insults me like that?'

The interne looks at the nurse. 'Let's get the stiff back on ice.'

He crosses the room to her quickly, thrusts one hairy arm with its gold identity bracelet under her skirt.

Beyond the clear plastic sphere they tilt like kites. Whispering. Rapid breathing. Huskily: 'Do you think he hears us?' She is crooked back on the leather couch, her floft flies utterly out, a rigid hinge of female, hard and wide as a coathanger to take his prick. Later, as she rearranges herself, she says: 'Do you think he heard us?'

'Why don't you go down on him and see?' The voice of the interne. 'Squat on him and let himself bite off a piece.'

'I think you're disgusting!'

'What about him? . . . a charity case . . . found him naked on a white horse . . . wandering along 42nd Street . . . thought he was Lady Godiva . . . no identity . . . not a scrap of paper on him . . . no money . . . not a filling in his head . . . just caries . . . better get him out of here now . . . put him where you got him . . . .'

Wheeling along clinical-smelling corridors, down in a lift, forward on a rectangular tray. A warm thumb. The smell of the palm of her hand. Her broad pink face, squarish teeth, small blue eyes. Blackness. Receding steps. Silence. At the point at which his senses come in contact with the external world he stops abruptly, as a wheel is stopped by running an iron bar between its spokes. He feels a sense of loss.

A FIFTEEN-YEAR-OLD CHICK AND A DOUBLE BASS

Trocchi in conversation with
Allen Ginsberg and Peter Orlovsky

ALEX TROCCHI: Jim Cobb . . . he's still alive?

ALLEN GINSBERG: No. He's dead.

AT: Gayton?

AG: I think he's dead too . . .

AT: OK . . . They were taking a lot of heavy speed then?

AG: They were in my house in 1964.

PETER ORLOVSKY: Did you take a lot of speed?

AT: Oh sure.

AG: He had this methedrine scene.

AT: You know that we actually made this score. We went into a chemist. We got a pound of it. We pretended that it was for a horse! We entered a chemist, a bloody old chemist, somewhere down in the Village, I don't remember where it was, and he had a whole load of it, bottles of amphetamine.

And we said that we knew that it was a protein, and that we were feeding it to our horses because the protein would build the horses' muscles, and this man believed us! He gave us one pound, one pound of protein . . . of amphetamine . . . I think it cost us about three dollars, something like that!

AG: Crystal?

AT: Crystal yes . . . it was a powder, you know, like a powder.

AG: Amphetamine or methamphetamine? There was something called methamphetamine in those days that Heine used to take around and put in little vials in the freezer of the ice-box, remember that?

AT: Yeah.

AG: Is that the same stuff?

AT: Well, it no doubt came from the same place, because Heine was one of us. We got all this stuff from the same source. I forgot the name of the bugger who got it for us. He was a chemist and he saved my life, this chemist, by the way . . . Not exactly, but that's another story . . .

PO: I remember a young girl that was there . . . there was one young girl that had funny lipstick who was . . .

AG: Walking on bags? Walking along on burlap bags?

PO: She had lipstick that was never really on her lips, it was always like all over her face.

AT: Yeah, I can't quite remember the lady's name, but it sounds familiar.

AG: Could you have written about that anywhere?

AT: I haven't written about anything, Allen!

AG: You really ought to do it, in the form of just a simple account of what you can remember . . .

AT: I shall, I shall. Don't worry, I'm not dying yet!

AG: You know why? I think that particular period was very outrageous.

AT: It was outrageous in Paris too actually and I haven't written about that either.

PO: It happened in Paris? The same amphetamine thing?

AT: Not amphetamine, not amphetamine but. . . . Do you remember Mel Sabre?

AG: The name I remember.

AT: He had this one-legged girl? Beautiful! That's the one-legged girl I refer to in *Cain's Book*.

AG: Ah ha.

AT: Oh, she was beautiful. I fell in love with her, you know. But, shit, we went to bed and I couldn't get a fuckin' hard-on! Now if I had got a hard-on that night, my whole life maybe would have been changed, and so would hers. But not being able to get it up? I suppose I couldn't because I felt like I was betraying Mel. And then about six months later she was dead.

AG: Of what?

AT: Overdose. And six months later Mel gave himself an overdose in the bath, Brooklyn, his mother's flat.

AG: Suicide?

AT: Yeah. Mel did it absolutely consciously. I loved that lady . . . that was before I married Lyn, you know.

PO: And who were you with on Avenue C?

AT: Lyn was around then.

PO: Did she take amphetamine too?

AT: Oh she took everything.

AG: See, I didn't realise that.

AT: One time she also almost OD'd. I had to bring her back to life. We were talking about Bill Heine, right? Bill Heine's girl was with a double-bass player – you were living around the corner at the time, Allen – and the double-bass player, he died. That night, a couple of spades came in with some very powerful heroin and we were going to take some over to this girl, who eventually became Bill Heine's girl – she's the one who got busted and got me exiled, made me run away – anyway, her boyfriend at the time was this guy, a beautiful person, who played the double bass, and these two spades just murdered him! They wanted his girl . . . they wanted to put her on the street – like, you know, they wanted to fuck her first, and then put her to work.

And they tried to do the same to Lyn, you see. I wasn't there at the beginning. They gave her some heroin and it was very strong, much stronger than the stuff that we had. I turn up and find Bill Heine blue and Lyn blue.

AG: Blue?

AT: Blue, yeah, blue, blue in the face, you know, so, like, I shoot them up with speed. I get Lyn back, dash back to Bill Heine, get him back, but then, you know, like, I was concerned for Lyn – and for the other girl . . .

AG: Where were they?

AT: Well they were still in the can. It was an accident, you understand. No-one was trying to do anyone in. It was just one of these accidents that happen. The other chick had been with them – this was the little chick that subsequently became Bill Heine's girl – and before I left I said, well, he's all right now isn't he? – and he was all right, he was up, you know, and I said, well you can look after him now, you know, because I wanted to take Lyn home, like she'd almost died et cetera, and – oh boy, as I remember it, it comes back – OK, so unfortunately Bill Heine didn't come back far enough evidently, or something happened after I left, because next morning the guy was dead.

AG: Which guy?

AT: The bass player.

AG: Who was that?

AT: I don't remember his name. Dead in the bloody apartment where I'd left him.

AG: The Avenue C place?

AT: Yes . . . not my place.

AG: Oh I see, near our place.

AT: Well, just round the corner. I think it was nearer your place than mine but, anyway, it was all in the neighbourhood. You see, Lyn, the girl and he went off – at that time I had my bottle of Demerol, you know and I'd been cooling it a bit so I didn't necessarily pay too much mind – but they went off together, the three of them. And when I got there Lyn and this boy were blue, and first of all I was just looking at him and then I asked where Lyn was and they said, 'Oh she's next door, she's all right' . . . I dashed next door to have a look at her and she was blue, you know, absolutely blue . . . so I had to bring her back. I brought her back, finally, got her on her feet, came back, and meanwhile the amphetamine and stuff that I'd shot into this cat had woken him and the young girl was with him and . . . everything looked all right. I went away with Lyn and next day I found out this guy had died. I mean they killed them, there's no question about it. They wanted her, you know, for their business or something.

PO: You must know a lot of funny stories.

AT: Oh shit . . . like thousands, thousands you know – and I ought to get them down before I croak.

AG: I can't remember much anymore, you know. I find my head's very fragmented.

AT: Oh my memory is terrible too, Allen, you know, really terrible. I mean, I can't remember names but then, you know, eventually someone says something to me and I remember the name, I can fill it in. You know that day was an unforgettable one. Well, it was a horrible night, and I remember, the next bloody day, I'm walking down the street with the double-bass that belongs to this cat who has died and the kid, the chick – this is a fifteen-year-old chick I should point out – and we go and see someone else . . . someone else, you know – this was '59 or something like that, '59 or '60.

We're walking down the road, like a dirge or something with this bloody old thing and we go up to a pad, and we're only in there a minute, when boom, we're all arrested . . . went down to the Tombs you know and I'm . . . at that time, I'm in for two days or thereabouts. I lost a bit of a tooth when I tried to get an extra drink of milk. A big bloody old black man with a fucking stick, hit me over the face with it.

PO: In jail? A guard, you mean?

AT: Yeah a guard . . . I wanted a little more milk, you know, and the trustee said I could have the milk and I was just putting it in my mouth and the trustee was watching, that is the guard was watching it all, and he came over and banged me and broke my tooth!

It's all coming back . . . a bit. I think we were actually taking some bottles to get the ten cents or five cents you get back on bottles you know, but, anyway, the police came in while we were collecting the bottles and busted us.

AG: For what? How did they know?

AT: Well, they found some amphetamine or something you know, something was there, there was no question that something was there. And I nearly walked out of that place, you know. I went upstairs for a pee, walked down, and suddenly I saw that I could walk out, because no-one was paying any attention. I started walking towards the door, and I was actually out of the fuckin door when someone jumped on my bloody back and dragged me back up. A policeman dragged me back in. Well, I was out a couple of days later because Grove Press got me out, put up the bail and all the rest of it, but I had about three or four charges going on at that point. That's why, when finally I ran, I really had to run, because if your bloody mother-in-law is going to say that you've turned her daughter into a prostitute, turned her into a junkie and all the rest of it, and meanwhile your own prescription has got stopped . . . presented by a fifteen-year-old chick . . . I mean I was a natural for the first test case.[1]

I've got to write it down, I really have.

NED POLSKY

What impression did you have of his life in New York at that stage?
When I came back it was to take a job running the college text book

department at St Martin's Press. Our office was in the Flatiron Building on 23rd Street and Alex and Lyn, it turned out, were living just around the corner practically, on 23rd Street. His life then . . . he'd gotten much more deeply into hard drugs, particularly heroin, and his life was oriented around doing the things that junkies had to do in order to get money for the next fix. I had to bar him from my office at one point because of some of that stuff. It was difficult. For example my boss, the president of St Martin's Press, was a Scotsman named Ian Mackenzie, and when I introduced him to Alex almost the first thing that Alex did, as one Scotsman to another, was to con Ian out of some money.

Was Cain's Book *the first thing you read by him?*

No, the first book I read by him was in Mexico, he had a copy with him. This was one of the books that he had done for Girodias. The one that he was proudest of, called *Young Adam*, and he, I gathered, had either written it completely or mostly before doing pornography for Girodias and at Girodias' request added a lot of sex to it to make it a dirty book. But Alex, you know, thought of it as an important literary . . . and I was very impressed with it and then *Cain's Book*, of course, I read later on.

What was your opinion of him as a writer?

Well, that's important not to lose sight of, because it's always easy – certainly with anyone who knew Alex during the last twenty, twenty-five years of his life – one immediately starts talking about drugs because those provide the most dramatic episodes. But really why we're interested in Alex now is his importance as a writer. Let's not lose sight of that with all the stuff about drugs.

Like any real writer he knew how to push the language around, you know? Great precision and concision, great insight, I think as much insight certainly into the drug addict's world as Burroughs, and I think a better writer, a better stylist.

Do you think that Trocchi still has some significance as a writer and if so why?

Oh sure, I think Alex, first of all, represents one of the important people in the Fifties who were trying to extend the range of literature and of course trying to shock the older, more conservative . . . You know every generation has to do this, has to have some people who set out to shock and in that sense I think Alex was somebody who was always testing the limits. If it hadn't been heroin it would have been something else. A very anarchistic, existentialist, kind of character who reminds me very much of the Marquis de Sade in that respect. I think Alex was compelled to test the limits of what the bourgeoisie would tolerate. But beyond that, Alex was not simply a shocker. I saw, for instance, most of the Beats as *simply* that, without much literary talent, but Alex I thought, and still think, he's a master of words. I think he's a much better stylist than Burroughs; structurally *Cain's Book* is not as daring perhaps as *Naked Lunch* but it's much better written, much better written.

What kind of life was Trocchi leading in New York City? I've heard he was doing these painted 'futiques' (or future antiques) as he called them . . .

Well, there's an old junkie proverb, 'junk treats everybody the same'. That's what happened to Alex, as strong as he was. He was involved in one scheme after another to get money for the next fix of heroin and one of them was, he and Lyn had brought back with them, from Las Vegas, little bits of petrified wood that they'd gotten in the desert or someplace, and they were painting them bright enamel colours and Alex thought that they would be able to sell these to gift shops as some interesting objects. I don't know what ever happened with that scheme but that was one of his ideas for raising money.

This is where, I think, Richard Seaver did something of genius and why I think *Cain's Book* finally got finished. Seaver did the most intelligent thing under the circumstances. He made the writing of *Cain's Book* one of the things that Alex could do to get money for the next fix. Seaver said to him, every time you turn in x number of pages you will get x amount of dollars, and so for Alex this became simply one more way of raising money to get heroin. And that's how the book finally got done.

What were the events leading up to Trocchi's hasty departure from the States? Had he been under some kind of surveillance by the FBI?

I don't know anything at all about FBI surveillance but I'd been seeing Alex fairly often, which was surprising because I had given him some money a couple of times for drugs but then I said no more. I've got my own expenses, I can't keep helping feed your habit. You know, usually a junkie then doesn't have much time for anybody who's not going to help him, but Alex and I did still see each other. One day he told me he had gone to get heroin from his supplier, which I think was up in Harlem, and as he emerged he walked into a police stake-out and the police grabbed him. As Alex told it to me they caught him with the heroin on him, of course, so there was no question about that. They booked him on a charge of possession with intent to sell which was a very serious felony offence and he told them, well, you know, I'm just a sorry junkie and they said, we know that. We want you to turn State's evidence against your supplier. That's a very common police tactic and he refused to do it. They said that if he did that they would reduce it to a simple possession charge, a misdemeanour charge, and he refused to do that so the original, more serious charge stuck. Then he was out on bail and I saw him during that period once in a while.

About a week before his trial was to start his lawyer, who knew I knew Alex, called me up. He'd lost contact with Alex. Alex had disappeared, he was hiding out in the Phoenix Bookshop, down on Cornelia Street, and the lawyer said, I've got to get hold of Alex, do you know where he is and how can I get hold of him? I knew but I wasn't about to tell the lawyer without first clearing it with Alex. The lawyer said to me, if you see Alex, please tell him that he must show up for the start of the trial, that, yes, the odds are that he will be convicted, maybe not, but probably yes. However, because of all the testimonials from big shots and prominent people in the literary world, I'm sure I can get him probation. He won't actually have to do any prison time. So then, what turned out to be the night before Alex actually fled, the night before his trial was to start, I got a call from Alex to come over to the bookshop on Cornelia Street and I went over there and I sat up with him for the remainder of the night and Diane, the poet Diane Di Prima, came over at one point. She stayed quite a while too and I relayed this message from the lawyer to Alex. Alex was debating whether or not to show up for the trial or to flee, but actually his mind had been pretty made up that he was going to flee. But I relayed this message from the lawyer and Alex said, well, what the lawyer doesn't know is that while Lyn and I have been staying with her parents, out in Port Chester, I've been forging a lot of prescriptions and there are warrants out for me on fourteen separate charges of forging Demerol prescriptions and if I show up in Court tomorrow there's sure to be somebody there to arrest me on those additional charges and I *will* have to do some prison time. I'm not about to do that, you know, because of these insane narcotics laws. So there was no point trying to argue further that he might go to trial. His plan was to go to Canada, because he still had his British passport, and from there get a ship to England. After he was back in England we corresponded.

What was Trocchi's state of mind on that last night in the States?

He was of course very upset but determined not to go to prison for these absurd drug laws. For instance at one point while we were discussing this I pointed out to him that if he did flee they would have this additional charge on him of being a fugitive from justice and he could never come back. Of course, they wouldn't extradite him from England on such a charge, but still he could never come back. Nevertheless he was determined to go because, from what he said – and I believed him – he probably would have had to do some prison time.

You said he was hiding out in a bookstore . . .

Well, it was on Cornelia Street, called the Phoenix Bookshop; it was owned by a man named Larry Walrich. This would be sometime in late 1960. It was a good literary bookstore, a secondhand bookstore, and Larry Walrich had a small backroom. There was some kind of cot there where Alex had been sleeping. Just a very tiny, grimy little backroom for storage of books. Plus storage of Alex.

HANDS OFF ALEXANDER TROCCHI

Guy Debord, Jacqueline de Jong, Asger Jorn

For several months the British writer Alexander Trocchi has been kept in prison in New York.[1]

He is the former director of the revue *Merlin*, and now he participates in experimental art research in collaboration with artists from several countries, who were regrouped on September 28th in London in the Institute of Contemporary Arts (17 Dover Street). On that occasion they unanimously expressed in public their solidarity with Alexander Trocchi, and their absolute certainty of the value of his comportment.

Alexander Trocchi, whose case is due to be tried in October, is, in effect, accused of having experimented in drugs.

Quite apart from any attitude on the use of drugs and its repression on the scale of society, we recall that it is notorious that a very great many doctors, psychologists and also artists have studied the effects of drugs without anyone thinking of imprisoning them. The poet Henri

Michaux has hardly been spoken of in recent years except on the successive publications of his books announced everywhere as written under the influence of mescalin.

Indeed we consider that the British intellectuals and artists should be the first to join with us in denouncing this menacing lack of culture on the part of the American police, and to demand the liberation and immediate repatriation of Alexander Trocchi.

Since it is generally recognised that the work of a scientist or an artist implies certain small rights, even in the U.S.A., the main question is to bear witness to the fact that Alexander Trocchi is effectively an artist of the first order. This could be basely contested *for the sole reason that he is a new type of artist*; pioneer of a new culture and a new comportment (the question of drugs being in his own eyes minor and negligible).

All the artists and intellectuals who knew Alexander Trocchi in Paris or London ought to bear witness without fail to his authentic artistic status, to enable the authorities in Great Britain to take the necessary steps in the U.S.A. in favour of a British subject. Those who would refuse to do this now will be judged guilty themselves when the judgment of the history of ideas will no longer allow one to question the importance of the artistic innovation of which Trocchi has been to a great extent responsible.

We ask everyone of good faith whom this appeal reaches, to sign it, and to make it known as widely as possible.

October 7th, 1960
Guy Debord, Jacqueline de Jong, Asger Jorn.
Address : 32, *rue de la Montagne-Sainte-Genevieve, Paris-5ᵉ*

LEONARD COHEN

What was your first meeting with Trocchi?
I don't remember too much about it. The impression of the man is very strong and clear because he was a . . . he was a very impressive figure. A noble figure, I think. Not that I remember anything too clearly but he had a certain presence and a certain hard edge that was memorable.

I believe I knew about him before I met him because he had published a book – I believe it was *Cain's Book* – Grove Press had published the book and that [he] was part of this group of writers and publishers in New York City which, to the provincials in Montreal (where I was at the time) represented the cutting edge of the whole literary scene. So his work was known to me and his messianic view of drugs was familiar to me. That was not unique in his case. There were a number of writers and thinkers and philosophers in those days who seemed to feel that, through drugs, this shabby reality could be pierced and a more authentic existence could be seized and embraced and lived. I think that experiment had disastrous consequences, but a few people saw a few things and I guess purposes were served somewhere along the line.

Now, I understand that Alex had written a couple of bogus prescriptions in New York City. I don't know what he was after. Maybe amphetamine, not sure, but anyways he'd been nailed and he'd been chased and I'm not sure whether I had anything to do in the actual Scarlet Pimpernel operation with which he got across the border but I seem to remember that he came across through Niagara Falls and I met him at the bus station in Montreal.

Well, you know, I guess if you live long enough you meet a lot of people at bus stations and when you meet people you don't know, you're given some kind of description. So I imagine the description I was given was, you know, a tall, thin, wild looking Scot, with very unhealthy grey skin, who would be holding a paper bag. I think his possessions were in a paper bag at the time. So I guess I spotted him using that description.

I took him up to my little apartment on Mountain Street in Montreal where he stayed for a few days. I understand it was only four or five days. In retrospect it seems like three or four months, or even years, because you couldn't escape the guy. He was . . . he was very clear about his life. Very unambiguous about what he thought and how he conducted himself. In a certain sense he saw himself as the General Secretary of some new subversive worldwide movement which would overthrow the old sensibility and establish a new one, nearer and dearer and closer to the heart than the one we were all forced to live in and indeed are still living.

Anyhow, we got to my apartment and he immediately took out a . . . a chunk of opium and he asked me if I had a little pot to cook it in and I did – that's about all I did have – and he tried to melt it into some water and he didn't succeed in melting too much of it in to the water. A lot of it was left in a rim around the bottom of the pot. He shot himself up with this very mild solution of tap water and opium and he said to me, a novice in the matter, would you like to lick the pot? So I said, you know, is it okay? I mean, you know . . . he said, oh there's enough, you'll feel it. I had no idea about amounts of opium that one could safely ingest. So I scraped the bottom of the pot and ate it. Now I know exactly how much I had taken. It was . . . it was a very large and dangerous amount and we were on our way down to a Chinese restaurant, near the corner of Peel and St Catherine in Montreal, that's one of the busiest intersections, and crossing that intersection I went blind and that was a rather panicky moment because it was in the midst of traffic, and then I went down, fainted or passed out. So that was my social introduction to Alexander Trocchi. He'd overdosed me on opium and I had, you know, fallen on the street in the middle of Montreal night-time traffic and they got me back to my apartment and it was nothing. I suppose I was a few grams or degrees away from anything really dangerous but I did understand that his company had some risks at that point and I think that's everybody's impression of him.

He had a vision and he had the charisma and the conviction to manifest that vision at almost any . . . any given moment. He believed in himself and he believed in what he was doing and he believed in the world he wanted to bring to birth and the one he wanted to overthrow. He knew what he was doing.

Can you recall how you assisted his departure back to Britain?

Yeah, well . . . let me see. I remember bringing him up to the house of Irving Leighton who is a national treasure in Canada. He's probably our most prolific and our greatest poet. He's a man in his eighties now and I guess Leighton and me were really two Jewish moralists. Certainly in comparison with this . . . revolutionary. So we were fascinated and appalled when he offered us a demonstration. He had heroin by this time. I don't know where he connected and he, you know, dug around for some veins in his poor abused arm and shot up and Irving wrote a poem about it and I think a very beautiful poem. I'm sorry I don't have it here. I'd say it was more insightful and more mature than my own. I was celebrating his bravado and his plunge into his own dark stream, but Irving's is a little more considered and a little more savvy about what the consequences about this kind of writer, this kind of man, would be on himself and on his culture.

We spent the evening with him, shop-talking as poets did in those days. They didn't discuss royalties in those days, they didn't discuss publishers, you know, they actually discussed poetry. So it was a good evening, I remember, and then we kind of led that quiet Montreal life for, you know, a few days.

Well, after that night up at Irving Leighton's house, both of us were very very touched by the man, by his . . . his madness, his bent for destruction, his sense of self-sacrifice, his self-characterisation as a . . . as a messianic figure, as a suffering servant, as the one appointed and anointed to reveal a new truth, and also on the human side about this guy. Because I remember now, looking at this poem, that his skin was grey. I remember that both Leighton and myself remarked to each other afterwards that his skin was grey. We'd never seen skin quite that shade of grey. So there was something . . . poignant, foolish, noble . . . a touching figure. Because when someone touches you it . . . it's beyond any description you can give of that episode. There was something deeply serious about the guy. Most people are not willing to put their lives on the line – and most people shouldn't and most people don't have anything to put their lives on the line about – and it's probably better that way. But he was one of those men who would put his life on the line for one reason or another. They seemed like . . . they seemed like bad reasons at the time. It didn't really seem like the way to bring anything about, to let anything happen but we recognise that these figures arise and somehow they open the heart in a little way, they soften the walls of cruelty and resistance and somehow they play a part that maybe is bigger and deeper than anyone knows. So that was Alexander Trocchi to us and I remember I went home and began a poem, Irving began one too. Mine starts this way . . . forgive these glasses, they're prescription, I didn't bring my other specs up . . .

Alexander Trocchi, public junkie, prié pour nous . . .

Who is purer
more simple than you?
Priests play poker with the burghers,
police in underwear
leave Crime at the office,
our poets work bankers' hours

retire to wives and fame-reports.
The spike flashes in your blood
permanent as a silver lighthouse . . .

Well, that's the first few lines of a long poem, praising this man's . . .
absurd conviction in his own mission.

I remember there was some question of a passport and a photo . . .
there was some scam we had to arrange and pull off to get him out of the
country, which we did, or people we knew did and he left and I never saw
him in Montreal again. I think I did visit him a few times in London.

What kind of state was Trocchi in? Some accounts suggest it was appalling.
I didn't get that impression. He was thin, you know that he didn't eat a
lot, but he was probably on the edge of a junkie's collapse. But he had
one of those constitutions. You know there are certain people who have
the constitution for alcohol and drugs. People like Winston Churchill.
You know, mortals like us would be finished in an afternoon. I had a
friend who . . . who really used to drink a bottle of Scotch with his
breakfast. So, we really can't judge it by any standards except that these
Olympians have their own criteria. So he was probably on the edge of
his collapse but I would reckon that his collapse took a long time. When
I knew him he seemed healthy, he seemed vigorous and as I say he had a
noble presence. He had a square jaw, he had a hawk of a nose and he . . .
he leaned into the conversation, into his life. There was a deliberateness,
there was a certainty and a confidence that was impressive.

We were, in those days, I think, cultivating a kind of ambiguity as the
prevailing style . . . you know, the obligation to look at every side of all
questions. So his style was very, very much in opposition to the one that
we were cultivating in the cafes in Montreal. He was a very impressive
figure to all of us.

*Did you get the impression that he really did consider himself a revolutionary
on the front line? How much of that was his ego?*
Well, I don't know, and I don't know how much in human enterprise you
can separate that thrust from the ego. I think first of all, as Irving Leighton
often pointed out, he had the qualities necessary for a young poet, which
were arrogance and inexperience. Leighton was fond of pointing out that
a poet has to have a very, very strong ego, a very strong self-image because there's so many voices saying sit down and shut up, you know, that

unless you have a very strong, almost demented, exaggeration of your own importance, you're not going to make it. You are going to listen to those voices and you are going to keep quiet. So he had those qualities in spades. I think he was stoned most of the time, so he was able to cultivate these projects with a fevered intelligence. So he was not unlike William Burroughs or Allen Ginsberg or a number of drug philosophers of the day, who believed that we would have to alter our perception of reality in a very radical way. These are ideas that have been explored, you know, in England for a long time. Since De Quincey and, in France, Celine and Rimbaud; these were very popular ideas among poets in those days.

Did you remain in contact in any way with Trocchi?

I don't remember. I think we had some mutual friends in that we'd, you know, exchange regards. We exchanged regards over the years and then the revolution that he was prophesying started to materialise. That's probably when he lost interest in it and it certainly was when I lost interest in it. It became the movement that we all know about, which was more or less preempted by the merchants and the cultural salesmen and, you know, the whole project called the Sixties was defined and merchandised.

We sent each other regards over the years. I kind of lost touch with a lot of folks over the years, our lives took different turns. So I . . . I really hadn't heard much about him for quite some time until I bumped into his nephew at the bar of the Mayflower Hotel in New York City a couple of years ago and he told me a little . . . a little bit about Alex's last days. So I really hadn't heard about him or of him for some time.

When Cain's Book *was published it seemed that here was somebody on their way to some kind of significant career. When he got back to Britain that seemed to dwindle. What were your feelings about Trocchi, looking back?*

It's hard to say. I haven't looked at that book for a long, long time and it's . . . it's impossible to say anything about a man's work, because each new generation revises their estimation of the importance of its writers and its artists so . . . As we see now, there's some interest in Alex, which had really dwindled to nothing for a number of years. So, you know, who is to say that *Cain's Book* won't be considered the seminal book that, you know, produced or engendered a whole school of writing that had some significance in America? Maybe still does to a lot of people.

I think that anybody who wants to do anything in their life – and I don't mean anything that's going to attract renown – but anybody that wants to fashion their life or take a stab at it anyways, is going to have to have some of those qualities. They may not manifest them in exactly the same terms, they might not come out that way, but somehow you have to cross some line and somehow you have to flip out a little bit to do the things you really want to do. I'm not talking about art, I'm not talking about fame, I'm more or less talking about love and friendship and keeping the heart open. Sometimes you have to take some drastic measures — or what appear to be drastic measures, or radical measures — and without that kind of activity, the human heart seems to close little by little, by imperceptible degrees until you forget that you were really alive.

Was Trocchi really of the counter-culture? What were his ideas aimed against?
Well, I guess sociologists or cultural historians would certainly describe him that way. You know, I think he was one of the guys who would say, with the former Minister of Propaganda of the Nazi regime, Joseph Goebbels, he'd say, when I hear the word culture I reach for my revolver. I think he saw culture as the enemy — although he was an eminent cultural figure. Because you can't escape your own culture. Even if you take the most radical position in regard to your culture, you're in your culture. Your culture embraces you and you can't get away from it. So, in a sense, he was a very well-defined cultural figure, but he himself deeply resented the culture of his time, I would say.

ALEXANDER TROCCHI, PUBLIC JUNKIE, PRIÉ POUR NOUS

Leonard Cohen

Who is purer
more simple than you?
Priests play poker with the burghers,
police in underwear
leave Crime at the office,
our poets work bankers' hours
retire to wives and fame-reports.
The spike flashes in your blood
permanent as a silver lighthouse.

I'm apt to loaf
in a coma of newspapers,
avoid the second-hand bodies
which cry to be catalogued.
I dream I'm
a divine right Prime Minister,
I abandon plans for bloodshed in Canada,
I accept an O.B.E.

Under hard lights
with doctors' instruments
you are at work
In the bathrooms of the City,
changing The Law.

I tend to get distracted
by hydrogen bombs,
by Uncle's disapproval
of my treachery
to the men's clothing industry.
I find myself
believing public clocks,
taking advice
from the Dachau generation.

The spike hunts
constant as a compass.
You smile like a Navajo
discovering American oil on his official slum wilderness,
a surprise every half hour,

I'm afraid I sometimes forget
my lady's pretty little blonde package
is an amateur time-bomb
set to fizzle in my middle-age.
I forget the Ice Cap, the pea-minds,
the heaps of expensive teeth.

You don a false nose
line up twice for the Demerol dole;
you step out of a tourist group
shoot yourself on the steps of the White House,
you try to shoot the big arms
of the Lincoln Memorial;
through a flaw in their lead houses
you spy on scientists,
stumble on a cure for scabies;
you drop pamphlets from a stolen jet:
'The Truth about Junk';
you pirate a national tv commercial
shove your face against
the window of the living-room
insist that healthy skin is grey.

A little blood in the sink
Red cog-wheels
shaken from your arm
punctures inflamed
like a road map showing cities
over 10,000 pop.

Your arms tell me
you have been reaching into the coke machine
for strawberries,
you have been humping the thorny crucifix
you have been piloting Mickey Mouse balloons
through the briar patch,
you have been digging for grins in the tooth-pile.

Bonnie Queen Alex Eludes Montreal Hounds
Famous Local Love Scribe Implicated

Your purity drives me to work.
I must get back to lust and microscopes,

experiments in enbalming,
resume the census of my address book.

You leave behind you a fanatic
to answer RCMP questions.

NED POLSKY

What about Trocchi the drug proselytiser?
That was the bad part. In one sense, Alex was an evil man, because he made junkies out of people. Alex begged me, on more than one occasion, to try heroin . . . he gave up, but there were plenty of weak-willed people, including some of the women he was involved with, whom he turned into junkies. That was a terrible thing. Given the lives that junkies had to lead then, and still do, it was condemning them to a terrible life and I felt that was an evil thing. Heroin became the focus of all his objections, all his anarchistic existentialist objections to the powers that be and anything he could do to promote it, he did.

Are you able to tell us anything about what happened to Lyn?
After Alex had gotten back to England, he and I corresponded. He was sending letters to me at my office, St Martin's Press. He told me that Lyn was being held virtual prisoner by her parents and they were of course guarding her against communications from Alex. She was off heroin at last, because she couldn't get any. Alex asked me would I mind passing some letters from him on to Lyn, which I did a couple of times. Then he did something which ended our friendship. One day at St Martin's Press I got a package, an oversized kind of letter, from Alex with a covering note to Lyn which was open, which I could read. The part I remember was that it said to Lyn, remember how we were planning that literary magazine to be called *The Four Horsemen of the Apocalypse*? The word 'horse' was underlined – a slang term for heroin. He said, enclosed are some samples of what I think would make an excellent stock for the cover, what do you think? And underneath it were several fairly large squares of white blotting paper. First of all, I tore the stuff up and flushed it down the toilet and I wrote to Alex an angry letter saying first of all, Lyn is off heroin, maybe involuntarily, but let her stay off, maybe it will stick. And secondly, you son of a bitch, what do you mean, not even warning

me, much less asking my permission, sending heroin to me at my office, putting me in that kind of jeopardy? I said to him look, it's a lucky thing that the Customs didn't open that package, the dumbest Customs agent in the world would realise you were sending me blotting paper soaked in heroin.

So he wrote me back an angry letter, the kind of letter that Dick Seaver mentions having received in that introduction to the reissue of *Cain's Book*; you know, how dare you judge me. You're capitulating to these bourgeois standards, you agree with me that the narcotics laws are insane and our duty is to oppose them in every way we can, and so on . . . So I wrote him an angry note back and then that ended it. That was the end of my communication with Alex.

Your impressions of Trocchi the radical – did you see him as a genuine radical? Or was he just self-indulgent?

No, I don't think it was being self-indulgent. I mean it was partly that, of course, but Alex really reminds me more of the Marquis de Sade than anyone else, because his concern was to expose bourgeois hypocrisies, to widen areas of personal freedom – in a way that I think is essentially unproductive, that turns out in the end to be self-indulgent mostly, because it seems to me much more fruitful to be active in some radical political party. But of course Alex didn't want to be part of any political party. He wanted to be the star of the show. I would say anarchist-hyphen-existentialist describes Alex's attitude . . .

For all his shrewdness about lots of things, Alex was politically naive. I think he may truly have believed that if you could turn enough people into junkies, you would bring down the system, overthrow the established order of things. It was his version of anarchist terrorism, a 'functional equivalent' as the sociologists say.

LONDON

1961. Heinemann publish a clean version of *Young Adam*.

1962 AUGUST. At a Writers' Conference during the Edinburgh Festival, Trocchi clashes with Hugh MacDiarmid.

1963 27TH FEBRUARY. Calder Books, London publish *Cain's Book*.

1964 14TH APRIL. *Cain's Book* is tried for obscenity at Sheffield Magistrate's Court and found obscene. The resulting ban never had any effect outside Sheffield City Boundaries.

1964. Trocchi publishes his essay 'Invisible Insurrection of a Million Minds', announcing the foundation of sigma. In the three years following, thirty-nine pamphlets are produced and circulated.

1965 11TH JUNE. Trocchi comperes 'Wholly Communion', a poetry reading at the Albert Hall. Five thousand people attend to see Allen Ginsberg, Harry Fainlight, Adrian Mitchell, Michael Horovitz, Christopher Logue, Gregory Corso and other figures from the underground perform their work. The event is filmed by Peter Whitehead.

1966. New English Library publish the 'definitive' version of *Young Adam*.

1966 NOVEMBER. Calder Books announce the publication of *The Long Book* by Alexander Trocchi. It is never completed.

1966 28TH DECEMBER. Nicolas Adam Trocchi born in Westminster Hospital, London.

1970. Trocchi obtains a writer's grant of £500 from the Arts Council.

1972. Calder and Boyars publish *Man at Leisure*, a collection of Trocchi's poetry.

1972 9TH NOVEMBER. Lyn Trocchi dies in Guy's Hospital of chronic active hepatitis with complications.

1973. The race rights activist Michael X is imprisoned in Port of Spain, Trinidad on three charges of murder. Trocchi campaigns vigorously for his release.

1977 21ST MAY. Mark Trocchi dies. Earlier that week, Trocchi was introduced to Sally Child by the poet Robert Creeley.

1984 15TH APRIL. Trocchi dies of lobar pneumonia.

1984 DECEMBER. Nicolas Trocchi commits suicide by jumping from the roof of his father's burnt-out apartment in Kensington.

RESPECTABLE YET SINISTER

Interview for *Scope*, BBC Radio Scotland

Leonard Maguire and Alexander Trocchi

LEONARD MAGUIRE: We had traced him to an address in Glasgow, and to the other end of a telephone. Yes, said the voice, he would be prepared to speak to us. No, he wouldn't mind answering personal questions. When? As soon as possible, we said. He came on the next diesel.

Alexander Trocchi is halfway through the fourth decade of his life, which is another way of saying he is thirty-six. He was born in Glasgow, educated in Glasgow and took an Arts Degree at Glasgow University. He took the name Trocchi from his Italian grandfather.

There was something very respectable about his long, black overcoat, his hand-stitched black gloves, hand-stitched black shoes, chalk stripe suit, and ivory cigarette holder. Respectable yet sinister.

Particularly the bulging brown briefcase. His black hair, cropped short, upholstered his skull like a wall-to-wall carpet. His long fingers were fat at the end like toes. And somebody else's nose, his grandfather's presumably, a strong Roman nose, that made his large eyes seem too close together. A good face. A fascinating face. The sort of face you might expect to see in a spoon.

We knew that Trocchi had written a couple of novels, and that these novels were being turned into films. But at one time, he was editor of *Merlin*, a literary magazine, published in Paris, perhaps the best of its kind in the world. He published people like Sartre, Genet, Ionesco, Adamov, and Beckett in English.

Sometimes for the first time. Of course, their future fame was apparent even then . . .

ALEXANDER TROCCHI: . . . to me, yes, but of course Beckett couldn't get published in English at all. The novel which we brought out first was one called *Watt* which had actually been written in Paris during the Occupation. He had sent it to twenty-two English publishers, and had been rejected. And as a matter of fact, when I first asked him for a manuscript he gave me a . . . a really extreme piece which included passages like 'He walked from the door to the window, from the window to the door, from the door to the mantelpiece, from the mantelpiece to the wardrobe . . .'

and this went on for pages. And I think it was a kind of test. If I published this, the treasure trove was open so, of course, I went ahead and ... made no comment and published this kind of ridiculous piece, with the result that he, from there on, he opened his hoard of manuscripts to me and I could choose what I liked.

Of course there were great complaints that day ... this piece appearing but, well, anyone with any intelligence anyway, wouldn't read it. One would see what he was at and jump four pages and go on.

LM: Alexander Trocchi, a young Scot with Italian blood in his veins, who wanted to write. Did he pitch his tent deliberately on the Left Bank?

AT: I was always interested in the avant-garde literary world. But, I have found in life that I don't consciously set out to become this or that, it is more a question of tactics, once one discovers where one is. Looking back I feel it couldn't have been much ... much different but I didn't really know where it was taking me. I didn't, for example, know that it was going to take me on a ... six years in Paris, and five years in New York and returning twelve years later, still unpublished in my own country. I don't know what I would have thought had I known that at the beginning.

LM: In fact he has lived only half of his life in Scotland so we didn't bother going into all that ... We wondered however, if he was home to stay.

AT: I don't ... anticipate that I am going to stay in Scotland very long, at the moment. I haven't got anything against ... visiting or staying for even protracted periods in Scotland but there is not sufficient intellectual excitement for me in Scotland. I don't know, I don't want to criticise Edinburgh, I don't know Edinburgh. I know that it is difficult to find an intellectual milieu in which the problems which I feel are significant and contemporary, are being constantly with great passion, being discussed. There is no such place in Glasgow. One ... feels too, that some of the problems that seem to ... involve the emotions of ... the Scots, are ... well, kind of provincial. They are not the kind of problem that is important on the international stage.

LM: Yes ... so far so good. But polite? Hmm? Almost too polite? Surely this wasn't the Alexander Trocchi who took the Lallans poets apart in a newspaper article? And accused them of inventing a 'plastic vocabulary'?

AT: I think ... when a word is so meaningful, in everyday parlance, that it tends to force its way into literary vocabulary by all means, it should be taken right in and used. But, for an intellectual to look over old texts and discover that 'coge' meant something, I don't suppose that is a word, and therefore to try to foist it on me and give me a vocabulary to go along with it, I think that is an imposition and I don't think it is important . . . I think it is kind of silly. I could never understand why otherwise intelligent men would want to do it. Another thing that I really disliked about my Scots contemporaries while I was at university, was the fact that they announced the Scottish Renaissance and the Renaissance, well, Renaissance as a word, or as a term, is something which should be applied by a historian and not something which can be foreseen in advance. One can feel that one belongs to a movement and flatter one's self, but really to forecast a Scottish Renaissance and then when asked to produce it, to produce a . . . plastic vocabulary, well, it strikes me as kind of pitiful.

LM: Something in the man's eyes made us come to the point. Certainly, we were interested in the editor of *Merlin*, of course we wanted to hear his views as a Scottish writer, but there was something else.

AT: I had started taking drugs in Paris early in 1951, '52, I . . . had the same prejudices against drugs as . . . most people. Until such time as I . . . realised that the greatest poem in the English language was written under opium. You knew that of course 'Kubla Khan' by Coleridge was written under opium and also, the greatest work in criticism ever written, was written by a man who was an opiate addict all his life.

LM: Did he think that later, or was it a conscious thought from the beginning?

AT: Oh, indeed, it was . . . it was something that I thought about at university quite a lot. I thought about because also the . . . the particular . . . artistic and literary renaissance that excited me, was the end of the century, the post-impressionists. Both in . . . painting and in writing. And amongst these people, practically every one of them at one time or another, used drugs, and many of them all the time. Baudelaire, Rimbaud, Picasso, Jean Cocteau . . . of course I am now coming into more modern times but . . . also, by the way, at the same time, Aldous Huxley had begun to take an interest in drugs like mescaline. And it struck me that . . . it was a terrible prejudice, to think that a drug introduced in the form of a liquid into the mouth like alcohol was . . . not a drug and that something taken in pill form was a drug. Or something injected was a drug.

LM: Which explains in part, why so many addicts belong to the medical profession. Apart from having access to drugs, knowledge, and experience, have dissipated the normal fears of admitting poison to the body.

AT: The reason why I started taking drugs was because . . . well, I can't give you one reason, but that is one reason. Now, that is, shall we say, the rationalisation that went along with the reason. Of course, one never acts rationally, one chooses to do and then one rationalises afterwards. No, I . . . I found myself drinking very heavily, and I found many of my contemporaries drinking themselves to death. Especially the more talented ones amongst them. And I knew that . . . alcohol wasn't good for me so I thought to . . . perhaps I should vary my poisons. Now, this too, is a . . . a rationalisation. But it's another one . . . with a certain emotional content. Now, a further one was that . . . I wanted, of course, to escape. Now . . . the word escape . . . well, we all must escape. We all do escape. My mother-in-law imbibes much more poison in two hours, in a morning, at church, in a . . . in a . . . little church in Connecticut and comes back entranced and ready for a week's evil after two hours in . . . in this kirk. Well, I take a much more quick drug. It doesn't take me two hours!

LM: If drugs stopped him drinking, they had no effect on the smoking. Never was an interview punctuated by the spurt of so many matches. He took a long pull from the ivory holder, and launched into a defence of drugs.

AT: I, like every other sensitive human organism today, need artificial methods of relaxation. And the man in the street needn't turn round to me and say that he doesn't. He is gaping over television, hours and hours and if that isn't an artificial form of relaxation, I don't know what is. Of course it would be great if I could without introducing any . . . foreign chemical into my body, although I don't have a prejudice against that, as a matter of fact, I don't see any reason why we should not discover a chemical for example that wouldn't in the end give us longevity or something like that. But if I could manage to bring about the states of mind, which drugs induce in me, without those drugs, then by all means I wouldn't use the drugs. But there is a problem. If I have never known the state of mind which is induced by this or that drug, how will I ever know if I can induce it? Therefore it seems to me that I as a . . . one of the . . . discoverers in the realm of human emotions have a bounden duty to go out and to experiment with strange and unknown states of mind.

LM: And what was the effect of these 'unknown states of mind' on his work?

AT: There are many famous doctors, lawyers, painters, writers, all . . . all types of people who function very well, under the opiates shall we say. I am going to say the opiates rather than heroin or morphine or anything in particular because we have a great deal of evidence, about opium from the Chinese, now, did you read André Malraux's book, *Man's Fate?* Well, if you remember, that the most interesting character in that, or one of the most interesting characters, was the father of the protagonist. Now, this man was a Professor of Philosophy at, I think, Peking University, and he was an opium smoker. Every evening he disappeared as it were, into the world of himself, under opium and all the wisdom in that book is contained in the utterances of this opium addict. How do you account for that? How do you account for the fact that the greatest work in literary criticism in the English language was written by a man who was habituated? How do you account for the fact that Picasso paints under opium? How do you account for the fact that Cocteau writes under opium? How do you account for the fact that I write under opium and how do you account for the fact that I am talking now and articulately under opium?

LM: Morphine, heroin and laudanum are all derivatives of opium which is in turn derived from the juice of the white poppy. The flower that caused the war between Britain and China in 1839. The flower that brought vast prosperity to the East India Company and today, the most banished flower in the world. It wasn't difficult to fashion our prejudice against opium into an image. We saw a little yellow man, in a sordid room, lying on his side, smoking a pipe. His dreams were his own. But by all accounts, they should have been green and red and devilled by dragons.

AT: Shall I describe what I feel heroin, for example, does for me, or has done for me? Or sometimes does for me? I find, being a very conscious man . . . and very sensitive to . . . things that are going on in the world that, sometimes I am inundated by anxieties and worries – from the atom bomb to what is going on outside in the street. If I want to get on effectively with any particular problem I have got to have a rather Jesuitical attitude towards states of mind in general. I happen to treat them as very important. I have got to be able to say, well, I am going to forget all that, and put it aside and attend to the problem in hand because otherwise I will get nothing done. One thing that heroin does for me, is I am immediately transported into a world where I am immune from all these worries that besiege me. I can then, without the least diminution in the sharpness of my intellect, apply my whole intellectual . . . and emotional organism to whatever problem is at hand. At the same time, experiencing a tremendous, artificial if you like, but a tremendous elation, and an inviolability. Things that come from the outside don't worry me. I see them as not important to the problem in hand. And, therefore, I am able to . . . with this very good feeling inside me, to get on with the job . . . and that is precisely why I have found that to use . . . use it in my case, has been a Godsend. It has also caused me to . . . leave off drinking and using alcohol at all, except for social reasons. I never drink alone.

LM: We wondered if the physical effects were also pleasant?

AT: Well, it is difficult to separate physical and mental, as you know. It . . . it relaxes the tensions of the body as well as the tensions of the mind. And, in this way, I think, too, it has a wonderful healing effect.

LM: De Quincey said that the slave to opium was more abject than Caliban to Prospero. How was the twentieth-century state of slavery affected by the worldwide rigidity of drugs' regulations?

AT: It is possible . . . to obtain supplies if you can prove that you have been . . . a user for many years, and that it would cause therefore a great deal of discomfort to discontinue. I wouldn't dream of trying to obtain it illegally . . . I . . . you see, I got into a great deal of trouble in America . . . one can only obtain it illegally in America, and frankly, that was my main reason for leaving America just when I did. Although I may have left it before, had I not got into trouble. I was . . . constantly going backwards and forwards to court and prison in America and . . . that of course prevented my return to Europe. I didn't spend any long periods of time incarcerated but I had to be there. I was out on bail a great deal of the time and this, in the end, got to be completely intolerable. On the one hand, I was . . . at one of the most creative periods of my life, as a writer and as a painter. And on the other hand, I was gradually becoming looked upon as a habitual criminal and I was dead scared that I was going to be seized and incarcerated for twenty years as many of my friends are, at the moment, in America. So I am naturally very concerned with this problem and I am going to do everything in my power to try and bring a more liberal attitude into existence in the United States. And to see that the liberal attitude that is present in this country, at the moment, doesn't through the ignorance of . . . people concerned, disappear.

LM: Heroin is usually administered to kill severe pain. Well, why does it have an analgesic effect on some and act as a stimulant to others?

AT: Heroin . . . the opiates in general, are . . . have an anaesthetic effect. They have that on me too. But I require a larger dose. Every time I take the stuff I no doubt am anaesthetised to a certain degree but of course once one becomes habituated . . . The anaesthetisation is . . . is with the amounts that I take, is negligible . . . I mean, if you prick me with a pin I will feel it.

LM: But, even that, we suggested, would be a pleasant sensation compared to the discomfort of withdrawal symptoms.

AT: If you suddenly leave off taking it after . . . taking regular doses, then you . . . will have all sorts of rather extreme physical reactions. Like, stomach cramps. Sweating. Cold periods say . . . watering of the nose and of the eyes. And very, very unpleasant withdrawal symptoms. But these withdrawal symptoms last only for about seventy-two hours. After which time, there are no more physiological symptoms.

LM: Drugs, and their effects on one man became the subject of Trocchi's second novel, *Cain's Book*. It received rave reviews in the United States. It will come up for judgement in Britain in March. We asked him what the book was trying to say.

AT: I was . . . giving my subjective reactions and I felt that, in a way, I . . . I was a guinea pig and a symptomatic character here. It is written in the first person and the 'I' of the book of course is not absolutely coincident with myself. But nevertheless, there is a great deal of me in it. I was giving my subjective reactions to the kind of nightmare world of . . . repression and revolt, in modern New York.

LM: Some people will undoubtedly say that *Cain's Book* is obscene. Its publication in this country seemed to involve a certain risk?

AT: I feel that if the publisher will take the gamble I will certainly go along with them. It was published in America without . . . I think it passed unnoticed in the general . . .

LM: Very well reviewed . . .

AT: Yes. Of course it was . . . but the fact is that if there is any objection on the part of the establishment, they are certainly going to have to contend with the big critical guns from all over Europe if it comes to an open trial. And, while I don't have any ambition to make a stand in court, I certainly will if it is necessary. I have got more important things to do than to fight this battle. This battle seems to me to be well, it's almost like no longer a contemporary problem. It . . . unfortunately it is, but damn it, it's a shame that it is. Because we have got so much more important things to do.

LM: Alexander Trocchi's next stop is London where he hopes to set up a spontaneous university.

AT: This is not a home for drug fiends, I'll have you know. Shall we say, it's a university in the same lines as Summerhill is a . . . school for infants, children . . . there are no degrees. Well, we are going to form a limited liability company, and we are going to . . . make the university pay in the sense that those who are attached to it, will be . . . using another part of their university as their agents . . . as their literary and artistic agents. With the result that, as we always seem to be able to recognise the coming people ten years before the professionals, the professionals are going to have a pretty lean time in a few years time. Like they have had their last! And all the money that comes in from this will be contributed towards this . . . the theories of education and the research that goes on in the establishment. It will grow, I think, with an astounding speed. It certainly did in New York. For the few brief months that we were in existence.

LM: And how can one matriculate?

AT: Anyone who can come in and feel comfortable will be welcome to remain. I think anyone who is not in place will leave. It always has happened in the past. We shan't have any specific teaching courses, it will be more like being the old painters in Renaissance Italy. Where the master is there, working in his studio, and he has apprentices. And . . . we always say, well, there is no professor . . . he who speaks is the professor. And if anyone has anything to say, they will say it.

LM: And finally, a plea.

AT: If people will leave me alone to get on with my work then I . . . I am the happiest man in the world. I . . . am full of joy.

LM: Leave me alone. The plea of the peasant who wants none of your chrome and coffee bars, the plea of the dufflecoat in a society of grey flannel suits . . . the plea of the outsider. Many artists are outsiders and some are further out than others. Alexander Trocchi has put himself out on the perimeter with De Quincey, and Picasso, Coleridge and Cocteau, Baudelaire, Rousseau, which doesn't mean that he claims parity with them, or that we are claiming it for him. We have tried to be as honest with ourselves as Trocchi has been with us. Take away his eccentricity as a heroin addict and he becomes just a Scots novelist without honour in his own country and there is nothing remarkable about that. So, we are left with the image of a human being who has set himself apart from ninety-nine per cent of his fellows, by being weak enough, or strong enough, to seek a new consciousness under a drug. It is like meeting a man who has cut off his ears, or . . . a mother who has given away a child. Such is the power of prejudice. Perhaps like André Gide, Trocchi would appeal, 'Do not understand me too quickly.'

We have tried also to assemble some opinions and facts about drugs. For instance, a standard text book on the pharmacology of drugs says that the heroin addict almost always suffers from some serious deficiency of personality and that he cannot be relied upon to tell the truth about his dosage. A general book of reference says that some authorities see the opium habit as a major vice. Others say that in moderation, it is no more harmful than smoking. De Quincey took eight thousand drops of laudanum a day, three hundred times the normal therapeutic dose. And he lived to the ripe old age of seventy-four. Coleridge was an opium addict from the age of thirty, until he died, at sixty-one. In Britain, 150 years ago, opium was the aspirin of the day, it didn't become proscribed by law until 1920. And we are the only country in the western world which allows confirmed heroin addicts legally to obtain supplies. It even provides them with a ration of the drug under the National Health Service.

Well, so much for statistics, you must make of them what you will and come to such moral judgements as you want to come to for yourselves.

In all that we have read and heard, about drugs, in the last few days, nothing impresses more than the words of Norman Mailer. Another novelist. Another outsider. Mailer used marijuana. He used it, like Trocchi, to escape and when at last he got away from it, he said, 'In the end, you pay for what you get. If you get something big, the cost will equal it. There is a moral economy to one's vice, but you learn that last of all.

Good night.'

JOHN CALDER

What were your impressions of Trocchi when you first met him?
I first met him in London after he came back from the States via tramp steamer to Aberdeen and was trying to settle and to earn a little bit of money. I knew about him from his American publisher. I had read *Cain's Book*, I had a general intention to publish it one day if I could, but in those days it was still very dangerous to publish anything that had four-letter words in it and that had any sexual descriptions and so on. The Penguin trial of *Lady Chatterley's Lover* was in 1961, I think, and it was about that time that I met Trocchi. He was of course very broke, looking for some kind of literary work, but immensely self-confident, believed everything would go his way very quickly.

In 1962 I was able to persuade the Director of the Edinburgh Festival, Lord Harewood, to let me organise a big conference of writers. I invited quite a number of people who were banned writers, Henry Miller being the most notorious. Trocchi was totally unknown in Britain of course but I'd brought him mainly as a Scottish writer to put him into a Scottish day. He was very unlike every other Scottish writer. He'd had years in America and Paris, had been part of the most avant-garde writing scenes everywhere and was in touch with the new Beat writers who were then not really heard of in Britain but were beginning to be read by students and more adventurous readers. He put forward a point of view, on the Scottish day, of an international culture that was classless, that was bohemian, that was sexually in no way inhibited, that was not prejudiced against things like homosexuality – which was an unmentionable word in Scotland at the time. And he was attacked by MacDiarmid, who was really on his side of the fence and was also a bohemian, a left-winger, a man opposed to establishment values, but who was rather puritanical and all that MacDiarmid picked up, in fact, was the free-living side of Trocchi. MacDiarmid called Trocchi cosmopolitan scum, and Trocchi replied that practically all the good Scottish writing of the last twenty years had been done by himself. He really believed it. In fact, Trocchi had not written all that much except two conventional novels and half-a-dozen pornographic novels for Olympia Press, as well as a lot of odd journalism of one kind or another and articles and pieces for his own magazine. But he thought of himself as having a brilliant career in front of him that had only just started. Now, he might have been one of the great novelists of his time. Unfortunately, he got involved with the Jean Cocteau circle in Paris – he wanted to get involved in every literary circle, particularly if it was influential, particularly if it was in the news and particularly if it had some money connected with it – they were all experimenting with drugs, but they were a little more sophisticated than he was in that they knew how dangerous drugs could be. Trocchi believed that he was so powerful, both in his mind and his body, that he could resist anything, and of course he got hooked very quickly and was never able to get off it for the rest of his life. It stopped his ability to write. His ideas were always there. He was a great talker, right up to the end, but the ability to actually sit down and face the white paper disappeared.

The argument between the two of them took over that day and got on to the front pages of most of the British press the next morning. *The Scotsman* made great play of it. After that Trocchi was a personality. People were totally unaccustomed to hearing intellectually frank talk with no holds barred in public. The McEwan Hall seated 2,200 people, and we were sold out. So that week the conference carried off all the publicity of the Edinburgh Festival. It enabled people like Trocchi and Burroughs to come to prominence. Their names became known. Trocchi appeared every day. Always had something to say. I know that he would go off to the loo every so often to give himself an injection to keep his energy level at the top, but he made a great impression on everybody. Even on the last day of the Conference, a Yugoslav writer got a girl in to a room and there was a misunderstanding; he thought she was saying please, please, and she said no, she was shouting Police, Police, but Trocchi broke down the door and saved the girl. There was that knight errant side to him as well.

He always appeared eminently reasonable in conversation. He would make statements that might seem extremely shocking, but always had a very calm reasoned tone of voice. He had great energy, he had great bounce, he had great success with ladies, as a result of which he made a few enemies, but he had an internationalist point of view at a time when the Scottish Renaissance in literature was not making too many waves outside Scotland and was very much rooted in Scotland itself, trying to invent a new language, trying to find a new point of view. Trocchi would have nothing to do with that. He was an internationalist, he said, look, a writer is a good writer, it doesn't matter if he's Scottish, French, comes from Timbuktu, anywhere else. The important thing is he's got to be good and he's got to say something new. He reproached other Scottish writers for their nostalgia for the past and their unwillingness to look at anything new, particularly if it came from outside Scotland, and of course MacDiarmid and Sidney Goodsir-Smith and Douglas Young, who were the leaders of the Scottish Renaissance, were very inward looking in that sort of way. Trocchi made them look at the outside world and he got their respect and it was the beginning of his career in Britain.

When was Trocchi's heyday?

Well . . . he was a success in three ways. First of all in Paris, when he was the acknowledged powerhouse of a group of talented young writers trying to make great new literature, and they were associated with Beckett, whose career was just starting. They were connected with the French new novel, where reality is largely interpreted by the person who reads the book instead of the law being laid down by the writer. He was involved in the middle of all that . . . he was in the middle of a circle that everybody admired. He was of course very broke, money came his way from time to time but he spent it very quickly and he was always having to raise money for his magazine and to pay for his lifestyle which was never overly modest.

Then he had a success when *Cain's Book* came out in America, it was a reasonable bestseller, and that continued when I published it in Britain . . . it came out the same year as the *Tropic of Cancer* and it benefited from that. There was the new freedom and he had extremely good reviews and at that point I was much more a publisher in the fashion than I am now — everything I did that was new received a great deal of press attention. So he was then accepted as a writer, even at a time when most of his writing was behind him.

Then he had a third period of success as a sort of radio and television personality, always being interviewed about his opinions, about drugs, about literature. He was always very articulate and drugs, of course, were one of the great discussion points of the Sixties and the Seventies. There were very few drug addicts, nearly all registered, but the effects that drugs can have on opening your general awareness were very much under debate. So every time the BBC or some other television or radio channel was looking for a spokesman to put the drugs point of view, they would pick on Trocchi. Sometimes if Burroughs happened to be in England then the two of them together.[1]

THE EDINBURGH WRITERS' CONFERENCE, 1962

Tuesday, 21st August: The Scottish Writers' Day

DAVID DAICHES: This question, is Scottish literature provincial, or parochial, I wonder what Alexander Trocchi has to say about that. He has probably seen more of the world having lived in France and America, than the rest of us.

ALEXANDER TROCCHI: I notice by the way, Dr Daiches, that I come in last. Well, perhaps that is in deference to my youth, though I don't feel very young any longer. I felt about last when I left Scotland, and from what I have heard so far this afternoon apart from a couple of words made by the junior lecturers, I don't think I was mistaken in leaving. The whole atmosphere seems to me turgid, petty, provincial, the stale-porridge, bible-class nonsense. It makes me ashamed to sit here in front of my collaborators in this conference, those writers who have come from other parts of the world, and to consider the level of this debate. This debate which was supposed to be something more vivacious than what went on yesterday. I would like to ignore all that has been said today except by the last two speakers, and the lady on my right. I think it is a lot of rubbish, with all deference to Mr MacDiarmid whom I have a certain love and respect for – I think he is an old fossil.

I think yesterday Angus Wilson just spread before us the social pretensions of Angus Wilson and described the English novel in terms of it. I didn't know what he was talking about. I have never thought in terms of the English novel except when some professor or other forced me to write an essay on it. I spoke in terms of wisdom, and creative expression. I no longer think in terms of the novel either – Mr MacDiarmid's rather old-fashioned and rather, by now, hatred of the novel is just too crummy to be commented upon. Most of the great poetry of the last century has come from novelists. Joyce, Millar, Beckett and many others, and I am sorry if I have missed anyone out.[1] I would like very much sometimes to have a sense of identity with Scotland. But this whole problem came to me when I was going through the university in Glasgow. On the one hand those people with whom I could talk, were writing Lallans, and they seemed to me to be chasing a red herring. It was pathetic. And they would have this stock response against Englishmen, and English in general. I had to get away. It was Mr Millar's books which helped me over the Scots sabbaths, seven days a week normally. And I went to join him in Paris, but unfortunately he had left. But I found other people there. And I hoped when I came back to this conference we would have something really vivid to talk about. I don't want to be too hard on our superiors, but I think frankly that of what is interesting in lust [the last], say twenty years of Scottish writing, I have written it all.

HUGH MACDIARMID: The point of view of Mr Trocchi, and one or two of the other speakers who preceded him, seems to be that it is absolutely necessary to keep up with the Joneses. Because America has gone absolutely rotten in the bulk of its production and so on, we must do the same too. Because, as J. B. Priestley has pointed out, English literature today is at a lower ebb than at any time since the fourteenth century, we must consent if we are not to become too provincial in Scotland here by sticking to our own traditions, we must also descend to the depths English literature has descended to. Mr Trocchi seems to imagine that the burning questions in the world today are lesbianism, homosexuality and matters of that kind. I don't think so at all. I am a Communist, and a Scottish nationalist and I ask Mr Trocchi and others, where in any of the literature they are referring to us . . . us to, are [as] less provincial than our own, and so on, are the crucial burning issues of the day being dealt with, as they have been dealt with in Scottish literature, if you knew enough about it. And apart from that, in comparison with the English, we have had the reputation for centuries of being far more internationalist than they are, and even at the present time, you have a whole sequence of European writers who have most influenced European thought and you would find that first translations of them were done in Scotland and by Scots. This is an absolute fact. I question very much whether Mr Trocchi is not so blinded by his American prepossessions that he doesn't know anything at all about what has actually been happening, and is of value, in Scottish literature today. I think we can rest assured that we have got a world acceptance today for the very small amount of real work that is being done in Scotland that will lead us to develop on the basis of our own tradition in a way that will enable us to challenge the point of view of modernity, in point of view of crucial interest, anything that is being done in any country of the world today.

AT: Mr MacDiarmid, you began by saying who wants to keep up with the neighbours and you ended up by saying, doing some Scotch work which will enable us to keep up with the Joneses.

HM: There is no distinction. There is no contradiction there. By Joneses, by keeping up with the Joneses I was using a phrase meant to cover what you said about our being relegated to a provinciality in comparison with the work that is being done in America.

AT: May I say . . . I would like first to say that I am not . . . I am sorry if it has been taken as an attack personally on you, because as a matter of fact you are one of the few writers I would exclude from this kind of provinciality, except for the fact that you have a few rather old-fashioned quaintnesses that are not of my generation, and I am sorry if you took it as against yourself personally. But everything else stands.

DD: May I interrupt a moment. I have just heard from the floor that many people did not get Alexander Trocchi's name. The man who has just finished speaking, who's flighting [fighting] with [Hugh MacDiarmid] now. Alexander Trocchi, Glasgow-born, I think, but widely travelled. Sorry.

AT: I would like to really have an opportunity to sat [say] something in view of that tremendous torrent that poured from Mr MacDiarmid just now. I would like to say in the first place that I had to escape from America across the Canadian border with false papers. And therefore, if he is going to accuse me of being pro-American he is wrong. But, I am pro-some-American. I am pro the American criminal, the American writer . . . I don't know what to say, I think that there is no doubt about it that the most vital questions today are being discussed by young American writers, and young French writers. The question of identity for example. Now, I don't think so, I don't think so . . . we are not going to get very far. I think perhaps we should meet together one evening and have that sort of thing.

HM: I didn't take any of your remarks personally. I will be delighted to meet you any evening that is convenient to you and to me, but I don't think that we will get any further, even in a private conversation, because the things that you are expected to accept and so on is a . . . as a Calvinistic, Communistic Scot I have no use for at all.

AT: I am only interested in lesbianism and sodomy.

HM: I resent the preponderance of paper and ink that is wasted on issues that seem to me peripheral and undesirable.

AT: I think the question of human identity is the only central question and it is a question of man alone and I don't give a damn if he's a Scotsman, or an American, or anything else. It is high time we transcended nationalistic barriers.

HM: No . . . no . . . here . . . here . . . I want no uniformity.

AT: I want no uniformity either, not even a kilt.

HM: I want to get a great diversity in unity.

DD: There is a clear difference of opinion here as to whether nationalism is a good thing or a bad thing, but I am not sure whether people are using the word with the same sense. Both speakers are against uniformity, and in favour of diversity, humanity, the multifarious difference between individuals, and it is a question, I suppose, of the ways in which that variety and diversity of human identity reveals itself in literature. We can't go further into this teasing and really, I think, rather sandy [?] question of how far nationalism is necessary to literature. Whenever you got to the stage of talking about nationalism something has gone wrong with it. I wonder perhaps, if one of our European, or English observers would like to comment.

HM: Surely we don't need to call on another writer for the Scots' day? If he has anything to say let him get up on his shanks and say it.

DD: Just a moment, I am the chairman here, I decide who speaks.

?HM: That is the trouble with Scotland. There is always a bloody chairman.[2]

DD: My head is bloody but unbowed.

?HM: If you want me out of here, you will have to throw me out.

AT: I am sorry I didn't mean that Dr Daiches. I have a great respect.

DD: I thought you didn't mean it. If I felt you meant it I would have thrown you out.

TROCCHI'S SPEECH
TO THE 1962 WRITERS' CONFERENCE

Edinburgh Festival, August 1962

THE FUTURE OF THE NOVEL

Categories die hard. Born of experience, invented to fit experience, to give form to our knowledge, they tend nevertheless to outlive their usefulness, to lose relevance. Such categories – scientific, economic, aesthetic – become armour against experience, a barrier between the mind and new understanding.

I believe the 'novel' to be such a category. I think the 'painting' – in the sense of a picture painted on canvas – is another. And I think it's enlightening to look at them together. There is an interesting [parallel], and an historically necessary and understandable one, between the disintegration of both.

When I say the novel and the painted canvas are no longer in themselves significant, I am not saying they won't continue to be written. I am saying that – something profoundly important which during the nineteenth [century] could be best expressed within these forms can no longer fitly be expressed in them. The problem is not to play yet another variation of the tune. It is to accept the fact that it is necessary to jettison the tune itself.

The novel and the painting on canvas were born of the middle classes which were born of the industrial revolution. Middle class culture demanded a work of art that was transportable – frescoes were for palaces – the epic was for palaces (for reading aloud) – so the novel form and the picture came out of an economic necessity. They flourished up until the end of the nineteenth [century] at which time most vital writers and painters began to feel them as *limits* rather than as inspiration.

Ergo, the spate of experimentation at the beginning of the twentieth [century] – examples.

The anti-novel.

Finally, what I call the destruction of the object – in painting, non-objective expression – in writing, the 'anti-novel'. The vital poetic substance that once flowed naturally into these forms finally burst out and could no longer be contained.

All art can be considered as man's expressive reaction to his state of being in the world. If this is understood it's not difficult to understand why modern art should be as it is. The modern artist – sensitive to the findings of modern science as well as the religious and political disorders of his time – reflects and expresses the need for new forms, new categories. Modern art begins with the destruction of the object. All vital creation is at the other side of nihilism: it begins after Nietzsche, after Dada. The appropriate attitude is tentative, intuitive, a creative passion, a spontaneity leading to what André Breton called 'the found object'.

A 'found object' is at the other end of the scale from the conventional object. To free themselves from the conventional object and thus to pass freely beyond known categories, the twentieth-century artist finally destroyed the object entirely. The future of the novel *per se* is insignificant.[1]

WILLIAM BURROUGHS

What was the first occasion that you met Trocchi and what were your impressions of him?

I met Alex on a plane, going to the literary conference in Edinburgh in 1962. That was a conference organised by John Calder, who came over to Paris and persuaded me to go. We both got there and they handed us some money, you know, sort of spending money. I'd read Alex's *Cain's Book*, which was one of the early books about heroin addiction, and so we had a lot in common immediately. He was sort of an ally at the conference. Hugh MacDiarmid was stalking around in his kilt with his knobby blue knees saying that Burroughs and Trocchi belong in jail, not on a lecture platform, old jerk. Yeah, it was kind of a lively conference. Another guy got up and read in his native language, which was Swahili or something that nobody could understand, and Norman Mailer was more or less the master of ceremonies. It was a very lively conference I would say. Lady Rebecca West, or Dame Rebecca West, disapproved of us very much. Well, it was no . . . my impressions of him were, well, what I expected.

And what did you expect?

A knowledgeable person and knowledgeable about addiction and intelligent.

There was an argument at the conference when MacDiarmid denounced Trocchi and yourself as cosmopolitan scum . . .

Well, they were arguing. I wasn't present at that particular occasion. But yeah, MacDiarmid was very much in evidence, and also, well not to get on to the subject of myself but Mary McCarthy gave me a boost at the conference. Myself and Nabokov, and it helped me a lot.

You saw Trocchi on frequent occasions after that. In what way were you like-minded?

Well, I was on heroin too. Later, when I met him in London, he used to help me shoot up. See, my veins were gone in my arms. Old Alex could find a vein in a mummy. Marianne Faithfull mentions that when she'd get her heroin pill she'd go to Alex to get shot up.[1] Alex had a lot of trouble with the police for saying that heroin should be legalised and also he would let people in to his apartment that he shouldn't let in, you know, people with stolen goods, stuff like that. I remember when John Calder and myself went down to court for him and the Judge said, well, people like Calder and Burroughs . . . I guess, you know? Okay, so he got off with it. The story was that a guest had some stolen stuff. It's known as guilty knowledge but he should have known that this material was stolen. Not receiving, but . . . it's a lesser form of receiving stolen goods 'cause he didn't buy them. So there were a number of occasions like that when Alex was in trouble.

Trocchi liked to see himself as an outsider. Did you share that idea about being an outsider?

Well, I don't know. Alex, of course, had a terrible writer's block. He'd almost rather do anything than write and he had something called *The Long Book* that he was working on. He stuck a number of publishers by getting an advance on this book that he hadn't written and which was never going to get written. I didn't know him in Paris when he was editing that magazine *Merlin* with Dick Seaver. I think Christopher Logue was in on that too and someone named Roundhouse or something like that.[2] I met him at the conference then and quite a bit later in London.

Did you share the same philosophy about drugs as Trocchi?

Oh, I don't think there's any philosophy about drugs particularly. I don't think of it in philosophic terms.

Trocchi decided to take heroin for a particular reason. Did he ever speak to you about why he took it?

Well, usually, most people like it when they take it and they go on taking it. They become addicted and then they have to have it. It's a pretty simple proposition really, you don't need any elaborate justifications, particularly, once you're hooked.

When Trocchi had writer's block, were the drugs an excuse for not writing?

I don't think so. It wasn't the drug, because he wrote *Cain's Book* when he was on heroin in the States and that was certainly almost the only thing that he did write. He was one of the early writers on addiction, one of the first writers on addiction. It was published by Grove Press and was sort of classic, is still more or less a classic.

What particularly impressed you about Cain's Book*?*

It was just a very good book, a very accurate book about addiction. The whole experience of addiction, what he got from it and the feeling of self-sufficiency, impregnability. Yeah ... it was a very good book on the subject, one of the best.

You described him as being 'a pivotal figure in the literary world of the 1950s and '60s'. What did you base that upon?

Well, I ... (*telephone rings, conversation ensues*) ... Okay, Patti. Well, I'll have to sign off now ... I hope to see you. Thank you for your call. Bye. ...

Patti Smith, to say that he was one of her favourite writers. She also said ... she didn't know he was dead, for Christ's sakes. She was waiting for another book. I said, you could wait a long time, even if he were alive.

You described him as a pivotal writer ...

A pivotal writer in that he was one of the early writers on addiction, which became an increasingly important, pivotal subject. . . . Incidentally, Alex Trocchi, I remember at the literary conference, said that he was an astronaut of inner space, that phrase ... it's rather ... not in a rocket but in inner space.

You were one of the first people Trocchi wanted to get involved with his international organisation ...

I wasn't ever involved with it really and it never went anywhere at all. He introduced me to Ronnie Laing,[3] that was way back, and to Michael X.[4] I think in many ways it was just an excuse not to write. Subsequently I heard that he made a living by stamps ... selling stamps and antique books. As far as I know he never wrote a book after *Cain's Book*.

What was your understanding of sigma?

Well, it was a big idea of getting all sorts of pivotal people together, like Ronnie Laing and, I don't know, others. He was also affiliated, to some extent, with the French Situationists, whatever a Situationist is, I have never quite figured that out, something like the Existentialist, you know? The situation immediately in front of you. As I say, it never got off the ground, sigma never got off the ground, really. He also knew Feliks Topolski,[5] quite a few people.

People have described Trocchi as being charismatic, what was your impression of him?

Mmm . . . always . . . nice to talk to, intelligent. As I say, Marianne Faithfull in her autobiography mentions that she went to Alex to help her shoot up.

Trocchi had a small part along with you in the experimental Towers Open Fire.[6] *What were your intentions in the film?*

Anthony Balch was the director and photographer. It was just done on a shoestring. We used cut-up techniques and it seemed to have an effect. Now, the manager of the theatre [where it was shown in London, 1963] said he'd never had so many people come and say that they'd enjoyed the film or that they hated it and they wanted their money back. They'd never seen so many things left behind in the theatre, so it did unsettle people, discombobulate them by using cut-up techniques.

Did you and Trocchi share ideas about mainstream society in any way?

I don't remember anything. Well, he always saw himself as on the other side of course because the police were always bothering him, coming around searching his place. Although he got his heroin on prescription from the noted Lady Frankau. A lot of junkies came from America to avail themselves of her services. She died, then he got another doctor.

Does it strike you as ironic that somebody who was preaching some kind of revolution ends up on the National Health Service getting drugs?

Well, no, it was the only way he could get them. There was pressure on the English to stop prescribing for addicts which they did, more or less. So there were the same problems of people OD-ing in public toilets and a large black market, mostly Chinese White from Hong Kong, so the number of addicts increased geometrically. See, at the time, when I knew Alex, that was in the Sixties, there were only about 600 addicts in the whole U.K. After the Brain Commission got through, there were thousands. Still are I imagine. I don't know.

In Trocchi's essay 'The Invisible Insurrection of a Million Minds' he gave the idea of being radically opposed to society. Did he ever discuss this with you or did you find it a bit far-fetched?

I think that it is indeed far-fetched but he possibly had some idea there's enough minds that would. . . . Different ideas would of course make a change in society and that's not without foundation. It's the way changes come about.

Do you think in the Sixties Trocchi effected much change?

Hard to say.

Were his ideas respected?

Mmm. Respected by the people that agreed with him, yes, but . . . He was one of the literary figures, certainly. As I say, I met Feliks Topolski, Ronnie Laing, Michael X, through him. I'm trying to think. He didn't seem to know the Francis Bacon, Sonia Orwell circuit very well.

Can you recall the last time that you saw Trocchi face to face? What kind of state was he in?

Not too much different. I do remember the last time; it was at a party at John Calder's and I was in London, I don't remember for exactly what occasion. This was . . . oh, it must have been in the Seventies, shortly before his death. He looked a little the worse for wear but otherwise, not bad. He'd gotten kind of corpulent, as I remember. Unusual for junkies.

One of the last occasions you saw Trocchi was at the Phun City pop festival in England. What was that?[7]

Oh, it was one of those outdoor things with booze and stuff and there were some people there policing the event with sticks they'd cut off with leaves on them, like neanderthal men. It was not a particularly pleasant occasion as I remember, but Alex was there. He was always there for things like that.

When you look back on Trocchi, how do you think of him?

Oh . . . he wrote one good book, *Cain's Book*. It still is good and it remains as a classic of addiction, like De Quincey. That was his big accomplishment I would say.

Have you ever read any of his pornographic books, the DB's?

I thought they were mostly very dull. Girodias in Paris had a number of addicts on his string for writing these books for immediate cash. They'd pawn their typewriters, he had some difficulties with them, obviously. I forget which one of those books published in the *Traveller's Companion* Series by Maurice Girodias — he's dead too you know, fairly recently — which ones Alex wrote. Wait a minute . . . he also wrote a book called *Young Adam*, or something like that. That was his first book I believe, besides these pornographic . . . was one *Helen and Desire*? I think so, yes . . . no I couldn't read those . . . just too dull.

Did he write them to outrage? Or just for money?

Oh money, money, of course. That's what it was for. No, I don't think he was interested in outraging people at all. They were paid very little but it was money.

There was one occasion on which yourself and Trocchi had talked about doing a book together, maybe an anthology on drug writing and he actually came to Tangiers with the possibility of collaborating. Did that come to nothing?

It very much did. I remember I went to a publisher once and . . . He was trying to get an advance on his *Long Book*, I forget the name of the publisher, Heinemann I think, but we never did anything together, never wrote anything together. It was someone named Jeff Nuttall who published something called *My Own Mag*, he was saying something about a possible collaboration between Alex and myself in his magazine, but it never came to anything.

Is there anything about Trocchi that lingers in your memory?

He was an individual . . . that's it. They don't make 'em like that any more.

INVISIBLE INSURRECTION OF A MILLION MINDS

Alex Trocchi

And if there is still one hellish, truly accursed thing in our time, it is our artistic dallying with forms, instead of being like victims burnt at the stake, signalling through the flames. *Antonin Artaud*[1]

Revolt is understandably unpopular. As soon as it is defined it has provoked the measures for its containment. The prudent man will avoid his definition which is in effect his death-sentence. Besides, it is a limit.

We are concerned not with the *coup-d'état* of Trotsky and Lenin, but with the *coup-du-monde*, a transition of necessity more complex, more diffuse than the other, and so more gradual, less spectacular. Our methods will vary with the empirical facts pertaining here and now, there and then.

Political revolt is and must be ineffectual precisely because it must come to grips at the prevailing level of political process. Beyond the backwaters of civilisation it is an anachronism. Meanwhile, with the world at the edge of extinction, we cannot afford to wait for the mass. Nor to brawl with it.

The *coup-du-monde* must be in the broad sense cultural. With his thousand technicians Trotsky seized the viaducts and the bridges and the telephone exchanges and the power stations. The police, victims of convention, contributed to the brilliant enterprise by guarding the old men in the Kremlin. The leaders hadn't the elasticity of mind to grasp that their own presence there at the traditional seat of government was irrelevant. History outflanked them. Trotsky had the railway stations and the powerhouses, and the 'government' was effectively locked out of history by its own guards.

So cultural revolt must seize the grids of expression and the power-houses of the mind. Intelligence must become self-conscious, realise its own power, and, on a global scale, transcending functions that are no longer appropriate, dare to exercise it. History will not overthrow national governments: it will outflank them. The cultural revolt is the necessary underpinning, the passionate substructure of a new order of things.

What is to be seized has no physical dimensions nor relevant temporal colour. It is not an arsenal, nor a capital city, nor an island, nor an isthmus visible from a peak in Darien. Finally, it is all these things too, of course, all that there is, but only by the way, and inevitably. What is to be seized — and I address that one million (say) here and there who are capable of perceiving at once just what it is I am about, a million potential 'technicians' — is ourselves. What must occur, now, today, tomorrow, in those widely dispersed but vital centres of experience, is a revelation. At the present time, in what is often thought of as the age of the mass, we tend to fall into the habit of regarding history and evolution as something which goes relentlessly on, quite outwith our control. The individual has a profound sense of his own impotence as he realises the immensity of the forces involved. We, the creative ones everywhere, must discard this paralytic posture and seize control of the human process by assuming control of ourselves. We must reject the conventional fiction of 'unchanging human nature'. There is in fact no such permanence anywhere. There is only *becoming*.[2]

Organisation, control, revolution: each of the million individuals to whom I speak will be wary of such concepts, will find it all but impossible with a quiet conscience to identify himself with any group whatsoever, no matter what it calls itself. That is as it should be. But it is at the same time the reason for the impotence of intelligence everywhere in the face of events, for which no one in particular can be said to be responsible, a yawning tide of bloody disasters, the natural outcome of that complex of processes, for the most part unconscious and uncontrolled, which constitute the history of man. Without organisation concerted action is impossible; the energy of individuals and small groups is dissipated in a hundred and one unconnected little acts of protest . . . a manifesto here, a hunger strike there. Such protests, moreover, are commonly based on the assumption that social behaviour is intelligent; the hallmark of their futility. If change is to be purposive, men must somehow function together in the social situation. And it is our contention that there already exists a nucleus of men who, if they will set themselves gradually and tentatively to the task, are capable of imposing a new and seminal idea: the world waits for them to show their hand.

We have already rejected any idea of a frontal attack. Mind cannot withstand matter (brute force) in open battle. It is rather a question of perceiving clearly and without prejudice what are the forces that are at work in the world and out of whose interaction tomorrow *must* come to be; and then, calmly, without indignation, by a kind of mental ju-jitsu that is ours by virtue of intelligence, of modifying, correcting, polluting, deflecting, corrupting, eroding, outflanking . . . inspiring what we might call *the invisible insurrection*. It will come on the mass of men, if it comes at all, not as something they have voted for, struck for, fought for, but like the changing seasons; they will find themselves in and stimulated by the *situation* consciously at last to recreate it within and without as their own.

Clearly, there is in principle no problem of production in the modern world. The urgent problem of the future is that of distribution which is presently (dis)ordered in terms of the economic system prevailing in this or that area. This problem on a global scale is an administrative one and it will not finally be solved until existing political and economic rivalries are outgrown. Nevertheless, it is becoming widely recognised that distributive problems are most efficiently and economically handled on a global scale by an international organisation like the United Nations (food, medicine, etc.) and this organisation has already relieved the various national governments of some of their functions. No great imagination is required to see in this kind of transference the beginning of the end for the nation-state. We should at all times do everything in our power to speed up the process.

Meanwhile, our anonymous million can focus their attention on the problem of 'leisure'. A great deal of what is pompously called 'juvenile delinquency' is the inarticulate response of youth incapable of coming to terms with leisure. The violence associated with it is a direct consequence of the alienation of man from himself brought about by the Industrial Revolution. Man has forgotten how to play. And if one thinks of the soulless tasks accorded each man in the industrial milieu, of the fact that education has become increasingly technological, and for the ordinary man no more than a means of fitting him for a 'job', one can hardly be surprised that man is lost. He is almost afraid of more leisure. He demands 'overtime' and has a latent hostility towards automation. His creativity stunted, he is orientated outwards entirely. He has to be amused. The forms that dominate his working life are carried over into leisure which becomes more and more mechanised; thus he is equipped with machines to contend with leisure which machines have accorded him. And to offset all this, to alleviate the psychological wear and tear of our technological age, there is, in a word, ENTERTAINMENT.

When our man after the day's work comes twitching, tired, off the assembly-line into what are called without a shred of irony his 'leisure hours,' with what is he confronted? In the bus on the way home he reads a newspaper which is identical to yesterday's newspaper, in the sense that it is a reshake of identical elements . . . four murders, thirteen disasters, two revolutions, and 'something approaching a rape' . . . which in turn is identical to the newspaper of the day before that . . . three murders, nineteen disasters, one counter-revolution, and something approaching an abomination . . . and unless he is a very exceptional man, one of our million potential technicians, the vicarious pleasure he derives from paddling in all this violence and disorder obscures from him the fact that there is nothing new in all this 'news' and that his daily perusal of it leads not to a widening of his consciousness of reality but to a dangerous contraction of consciousness, to a species of mental process that has more in common with the salivations of Pavlov's dogs than with the subtleties of human intelligence.

Contemporary man expects to be entertained. His active participation is almost non-existent. Art, whatever it is, is something of which the majority seldom thinks, something almost derisible towards which it is sometimes even proud to flaunt an attitude of invincible ignorance. This sorry state of affairs is consciously sanctioned by the stubborn philistinism of our cultural institutions. Museums have approximately the same hours of business as churches, the same sanctimonious odours and silences, and a snobbish presumption in direct spiritual opposition to the vital men whose works are closeted there. What have those silent corridors to do with Rembrandt and the 'no smoking' signs to do with Van Gogh? Beyond the museum, the man in the street is effectively cut off from art's naturally tonic influence by the fashionable brokerage system which, incidentally, but of economic necessity, has more to do with the emergence and establishment of so-called 'art-forms' than is generally realised. Art can have no existential significance for a civilisation which draws a line between life and art and collects artifacts like ancestral bones for reverence. Art must inform the living; we envisage a situation in which life is continually renewed by art, a situation imaginatively and passionately constructed to inspire each individual to respond creatively, to bring to whatever act a creative comportment. We envisage . . . But it is we, now, who must create it. *For it does not exist.*

The actual situation could not be in sharper contrast. Art anaesthetises the living; we witness a situation in which life is continually devitalised by art, a situation sensationally and venally misrepresented to inspire each individual to respond in a stock and passive way, to bring to whatever act a banal and automatic consent. For the average man, dispirited, restless, with no power of concentration, a work of art to be noticed at all must compete at the level of spectacle. It must contain nothing that is in principle unfamiliar or surprising; the audience must be able easily and without reservation to identify with the protagonist, to plant itself firmly in the 'driving-seat' of the emotional rollercoaster and switch over to remote control. What takes place is empathy at a very obvious level, blind and uncritical. To the best of my knowledge it was Brecht who first drew attention to the danger of that method of acting which aims to provoke the state of empathy in an audience at the expense of judgement. It was to counter this promiscuous tendency on the part of the modern audience to identify that he formulated his 'distance-theory' of acting, a method calculated to inspire a more active and critical kind of participation. Unfortunately, Brecht's theory has had no impact whatsoever on popular entertainment. The zombies remain; the spectacle grows more spectacular. To adapt an epigram of a friend of mine: *Si nous ne voulons pas assister au spectacle de la fin du monde, il nous faut travailler à la fin du monde du spectacle.*[3]

Such art as had claim to be called serious touches popular culture today only by way of the fashion industry and advertising, and for many years it has been infected by the triviality attaching to those enterprises. For the rest, literature and art exist side by side with mechanised popular culture and except in an occasional film here and there have little effect upon it. Only in jazz, which retains the spontaneity and vitality deriving from its proximity to its beginnings, can we see an art which springs naturally out of a creative ambience. But already more adulterated forms tend to be confused with the authentic. In England, for example, we are confronted by the absurd craze for 'trad'; a rehash of what went on in New Orleans in the early Twenties, simple, obvious, repetitious, overshadows almost completely the vital tradition of the post-Charlie Parker era.

For a long time now the best artists and fine minds everywhere have deplored the gulf that has come to exist between art and life. The same people have usually been in revolt during their youth and have been rendered harmless by 'success' somewhere around middle age. The individual is powerless. It is inevitable. And the artist has a profound sense of his own impotence. He is frustrated, even confounded. As in the writings of Kafka, this fearful sense of alienation pervades his work. Certainly the most uncompromising attack on conventional culture was launched by Dada at the end of the First World War. But the usual defence mechanisms were soon operating: the turds of 'anti-art' were solemnly framed and hung alongside 'the School of Athens'; Dada thereby underwent the castration by card-index and was soon safely entombed in the histories as just another school of art. The fact is that while Tristan Tzara *et alii* could point deftly to the chancre on the body politic, could turn the spotlight of satire on the hypocrisies that had to be swept away, they produced no creative alternative to the existing social order. What were we to do after we had painted a moustache on the *Mona Lisa?* Did we really wish Genghis Khan to stable his horses in the Louvre? And then?

In a recent essay[4] Arnold Wesker, concerned precisely with this gulf between art and popular culture and with the possibility of reintegration, refers to the threatened strike of 1919 and to a speech of Lloyd George when the strike could have brought down the government. The Prime Minister said:

> . . . you will defeat us. But if you do so have you weighed the consequences? The strike will be in defiance of the government of the country and by its very success will precipitate a constitutional crisis of the first importance. For, if a force arises in the state which is stronger than the state itself, then it must be ready to take on the functions of the state. Gentlemen, have you considered, and if you have, are you ready?

The strikers, as we know, were not ready. Mr Wesker comments:

> The crust has shifted a bit, a number of people have made fortunes out of the protest and somewhere a host of Lloyd Georges are grinning contentedly at the situation . . . All protest is allowed and smiled upon because it is known that the force – economically and culturally – lies in the same dark and secure quarters, and this secret knowledge is the real despair of both the artist and intellectual. We are paralysed by this knowledge, we protest every so often but really the whole cultural scene – particularly on the left – 'is one of awe and ineffectuality'. I am certain that this was the secret knowledge that largely accounted for the decline of the cultural activities in the Thirties – no one really knows what to do with the philistines. They were omnipotent, friendly, and seductive. The germ was carried and passed on by the most unsuspected; and this same germ will cause, is beginning to cause, the decline of our new cultural upsurge unless . . . unless a new system is conceived whereby we who are concerned can take away, one by one, the secret reins.

Although I found Mr Wesker's essay in the end disappointing, it did confirm for me that in England as elsewhere there are groups of people who are actively concerned with the problem. As we have seen, the political-economic structure of western society is such that the gears of creative intelligence mesh with gears of power in such a way that, not only is the former prohibited from ever initiating anything, it can only come into play at the behest of forces (vested interests) that are often in principle antipathetic towards it. Mr Wesker's 'Centre 42' is a practical attempt to alter this relationship.

I should like to say at once that I have no fundamental quarrel with Mr Wesker. My main criticism of his project (and I admit my knowledge of it is very hazy indeed) is that it is limited and national[5] in character and that this is reflected in his analysis of the historical background. He takes the 1956 production of Osborne's *Look Back in Anger*, for example, to be the first landmark in 'our new cultural upsurge'. A serious lack of historical perspective, the insularity of his view . . . these features are, I am afraid, indicative of a kind of church-bazaar philosophy which seems to underlie the whole project. Like handicrafts, art should not be expected to pay. Mr Wesker calls for a tradition 'that will not have to rely on financial success in order to continue'. And so he was led to seek the patronage of trade unions and has begun to organise a series of cultural festivals under their auspices. While I have nothing against such festivals, the urgency of Mr Wesker's original diagnosis led me to expect recommendations for action at a far more fundamental level. Certainly, such a programme will not carry us very far towards seizing what he so happily refers to as 'the secret reins'. I do not think I am being overcautious in asserting that something far less pedestrian than an appeal to the public-spiritedness of this or that group will be the imperative of the vast change we have in mind.

Nevertheless, at one point in what remains an interesting essay, Mr Wesker quotes Mr Raymond Williams. Who Mr Williams is and from what work the quotation is taken I am unfortunately ignorant. I only wonder how Mr Wesker can quote the following and then go out and look for patronage.

> The question is not who will patronise the arts, but what forms are possible in which artists will have control of their own means of expression, in such ways that they will have relation to a community rather than to a market or a patron.

Of course it would be dangerous to pretend to understand Mr Williams on the basis of such a brief statement. I shall say simply that for myself and for my associates in Europe and America the key phrase in the above sentence is: *'artists will have control of their own means of expression'*. When they achieve that control, their 'relation to a community' will become a meaningful problem, that is, a problem amenable to formulation and solution at a creative and intelligent level. Thus we must concern ourselves forthwith with the question of how to seize and within the social fabric exercise that control. Our first move must be *to eliminate the brokers*.

At the beginning of these reflections I said that our methods will vary with the empirical facts pertaining here and now, there and then. I was referring to the tentative, essentially tactical nature of our every act in relation to the given situation, and also to the international constitution of what we might call the new underground. Obviously, all our operations must be adapted to the society in which they take place. Methods used effectively in London might be suicidal or simply impracticable in Moscow or Peking. Always, the tactics are for here and now; never are they in the narrow sense political. Again, these reflections themselves must be regarded as an act of the new underground, a prescriptive document which, in so far as it refers for the most part to what is yet to happen, awaits baptism by fire.

How to begin? At a chosen moment in a vacant country house (mill, abbey, church or castle) not too far from the City of London, we shall foment a kind of cultural 'jam session': out of this will evolve the prototype of our *spontaneous university*.

The original building will stand deep within its own grounds, preferably on a riverbank. It should be large enough for a pilot-group (astronauts of inner space) to situate itself, orgasm and genius, and their tools and dream-machines and amazing apparatus and appurtenances; with outhouses for 'workshops' large as could accommodate light industry; the entire site to allow for spontaneous architecture and eventual <u>town-planning</u>. I underline the last because we cannot place too much emphasis on the fact that '*l'art integral ne pouvait se réaliser qu'au niveau de l'urbanisme*'.[6] In the 1920s, Diaghilev, Picasso, Stravinsky and Nijinsky acted in concert to produce a ballet; surely it does not strain our credulity to imagine a far larger group of our contemporaries acting in concert to create a town. We envisage the whole as a vital laboratory for the creation (and evaluation) of conscious situations; it goes without saying that it is not only the environment which is in question, plastic, subject to change, but men also.

It must be said at once that this quick sketch of our action-university is not the product of vague speculation. Not only are there numerous historical parallels, past situations, fortuitous or controlled, some of whose features are manifestly adaptable to our own project; during the past decade in many countries we have already conducted sufficient experiments of a preparatory nature: we are ready to act.

It used to be said that the British Empire was won on the playing fields of Eton. During the eighteenth and nineteenth centuries the British ruling class was formed exclusively in such institutions; the deportment they conferred on a man was vitally relevant to the growth of England at that time. Unfortunately, the situation at Eton and similar establishments did not continue to inspire its own improvement. Inertia set in. Forms that were once successful hardened until they were devoid of contemporary relevance. In the age of relativity we envisage the spontaneous university as filling the vital formative function of our times.

The Jewish settlements in Israel turned a desert into a garden and astounded all the world. In a flowering garden already wholly sustained by automation, a fraction of such purposiveness applied to the cultivation of men would bring what results?

Then, there was the experimental college at Black Mountain, North Carolina. This is of immediate interest to us for two reasons. In the first place, the whole concept is almost identical to our own in its educational aspect; in the second, some individual members of the staff of Black Mountain, certain key members of wide experience, are actually associated with us in the present venture. Their collaboration is invaluable.

Black Mountain College was widely known throughout the United States. In spite of the fact that no degrees were awarded, graduates and non-graduates from all over America thought it worthwhile to take up residence. As it turns out, an amazing number of the best artists and writers of America seem to have been there at one time or another, to teach and learn, and their cumulative influence on American art in the last fifteen years, has been immense. One has only to mention Franz Kline in reference to painting and Robert Creeley in reference to poetry to give an idea of Black Mountain's significance. They are key figures in the American vanguard, their influence everywhere. Black Mountain could be described as an 'action university' in the sense in which the term is applied to the paintings of Kline *et alii*. There was no learning from ulterior motives. Students and teachers participated informally in the creative arts; every teacher was himself a practitioner – poetry, music, painting, sculpture, dance, pure mathematics, pure physics, etc., – of a very high order. In short, it was a situation constructed to inspire the free play of creativity in the individual and the group.

Unfortunately, it no longer exists. It closed in the early Fifties for economic reasons. It was a corporation (actually owned by the staff) which depended entirely on fees and charitable donations. In the highly competitive background of the United States of America such a gratuitous and flagrantly non-utilitarian institution was only kept alive for so long as it was by the sustained effort of the staff. In the end it proved too ill-adapted to its habitat to survive.

In considering ways and means to establish our pilot project we have never lost sight of the fact that in a capitalist society any successful organisation must be able to sustain itself in capitalist terms. The venture must pay. Thus we have conceived the idea of setting up a general agency to handle, as far as possible, all the work of the individuals associated with the university. Art, the products of all the expressive media of civilisation, its applications in industrial and commercial design, all this is fantastically profitable (consider the Musical Corporation of America). But, as in the world of science, it is not the creators themselves who reap most of the benefit. An agency founded by the creators themselves and operated by highly-paid professionals would be in an impregnable position. Such an agency, guided by the critical acumen of the artists themselves, could profitably harvest new cultural talent long before the purely professional agencies were aware it existed. Our own experience in the recognition of contemporary talent during the past fifteen years has provided us with evidence that is decisive. The first years would be the hardest. In time, granting that the agency functioned efficiently from the point of view of the individual artists represented by it, it would have first option on all new talent. This would happen not only because it would be likely to recognise that talent before its competitors, but because of the fact and fame of the university. It would be as though some ordinary agency were to spend one hundred per cent of its profits on advertising itself. Other things being equal, why should a young writer, for example, not prefer to be handled by an agency controlled by his (better-known) peers, an agency which will apply whatever profit it makes out of him as an associate towards the extension of his influence and audience, an agency, finally, which at once offers him membership in the experimental university (which governs it) and all that that implies? And, before elaborating further on the economics of our project, it is perhaps time to describe briefly just what that membership does imply.

We envisage an international organisation with branch universities near the capital cities of every country in the world. It will be autonomous, unpolitical, economically independent. Membership of one branch (as teacher or student) will entitle one to membership of all branches, and travel to and residence in foreign branches will be energetically encouraged. It will be the object of each branch university to participate in and 'supercharge' the cultural life of the respective capital city at the same time as it promotes cultural exchange internationally and functions in itself as a non-specialised experimental school and creative workshop. Resident professors will be themselves creators. The staff at each university will be purposively international; as far as practicable, the students also. Each branch of the spontaneous university will be the nucleus of an experimental town to which all kinds of people will be attracted for shorter or longer periods and from which, if we are successful, they will derive a renewed and infectious sense of life. We envisage an organisation whose structure and mechanisms are infinitely elastic; we see it as the gradual crystallisation of a regenerative cultural force, a perpetual brainwave, creative intelligence everywhere recognising and affirming its own involvement.

It is impossible in the present context to describe in precise detail the day-to-day functioning of the university. In the first place, it is not possible for one individual writing a brief introductory essay. The pilot project does not exist in the physical sense, and from the very beginning, like the Israeli kibbutzes, it must be a communal affair, tactics decided *in situ*, depending upon just what is available when. My associates and I during the past decade have been amazed at possibilities arising out of the spontaneous interplay of ideas within a group in constructed situations. It is on the basis of such experiences that we have imagined an international experiment. Secondly, and consequently, any detailed preconceptions of my own would be so much excess baggage in the spontaneous generation of the group situation.

Nevertheless, it is possible to make a tentative outline of the economic structure.

We envisage a limited liability company (International Cultural Enterprises Ltd) whose profits are invested in expansion and research. Its income will derive from:

1. Commissions earned by the Agency on sales of all original work of the associates.
2. Money earned from 'patents' or by subsidiaries exploiting applications (industrial and commercial) evolving out of 'pure studies'. Anyone who has spent time in an art workshop will know what I mean. The field is unlimited, ranging from publishing to interior decorating.
3. Retail income. The university will house a 'living museum', perhaps a fine restaurant. A showroom will be rented in the city for retail and as an advertisement.
4. Such income as derives from 'shows', cinematic, theatrical, or *situationist*.
5. Fees.
6. Subsidies, gifts, etc., which in no way threaten the autonomy of the project.

The cultural possibilities of this movement are immense and the time is ripe for it. The world is awfully near the brink of disaster. Scientists, artists, teachers, creative men of goodwill everywhere are in suspense. Waiting. Remembering that it is our kind even now who operate, if they don't control, the grids of expression, we should have no difficulty in recognising the spontaneous university as the possible detonator of the invisible insurrection.

BOMB CULTURE

Jeff Nuttall

. . . Letters were pouring in from all over the world. My mind was everywhere. Lovers were my other selves. Coloured electric tremors seemed to be passing through humanity, flashing liquid across my perceptions. Nightmares walked my house – familiars. All things coming under my senses quivered with a crazy potential.

I spent a lot of time with Keith Musgrove. We went to Writers' Forum meetings. We planned and performed happenings in North London. We did a book together. We sat and talked. We roared and raved and were expelled from a number of pubs and restaurants. Mostly we just drank. I remember a party at Nick Watkins' studio. Travelling there, the shop signs flashing across the car windows strung themselves together into messages. Thoughts rattled across my brain like disconnected bursts of machine-gun fire and the snide bastard in me that watches me for kicks capered about in eldritch delight, had me hurl Keith into a hedge, had my life thronging through the world and the world rattling through my senses like a motor-driven rosary.

I woke up one morning at this time, early summer 1964, to find a loosely packed parcel thrown on my bed, thrown by my wife with a certain amount of resignation. It contained two typescripts from Alexander Trocchi – *The Invisible Insurrection of a Million Minds* and *Sigma, a Tactical Blueprint*.

I read through them quickly . . .

The web was connecting up its separate strands. Between Criton, me, Burroughs in Tangiers, Trocchi, Weissner, Pélieu, something was clearly happening.

I answered Trocchi by return, saying simply, 'What do you want me to do?'

. . .

Sigma, however, was Alex Trocchi's name for the cultural tendency to progressive alienation and for his own ideas. It was a term he applied to both praxis and process of the whole movement. It was also a bid to convert a stage in social evolution into an international spiderweb with himself at the centre. Since then it has become evident that the movement is linear rather than concentric, that there are no power figures, and that there is no centre for such a figure to occupy.

Trocchi arrived in Britain in 1963 from the United States, accompanied by his wife and child. At Edinburgh he was joined by Burroughs for the International Writers' Conference organised by John Calder. At the conference Burroughs gave the first public demonstration of his cutup technique. Together he and Trocchi moved down to London.

In London they became the pivot round which a number of people revolved – Charles Hatcher, Tom Telfer, McGrath, Philip Green, myself …

Trocchi launched sigma; Better Books, owned then by Tony Godwin, opened its paperback shop with a wild mod décor and a succession of influential managers, Bill Butler, Miles, Bob Cobbing; Jim Haynes launched his Edinburgh bookshop and his theatre, the Traverse; Dave Cunliffe started his *Poetmeat* magazine from Blackburn, and deliriously, within about twelve months, everything started to grow together. Jimmy Johns' Peanuts Club, all that was worth saving of CND, with the brilliant Mike Osborne Quartet and hellroaring left-wing poets like Dick Wilcocks and Del Foley, was a favourite meeting place.

The first Edinburgh Writers' Conference was followed by a series of conferences and carve-ups at which different groups converged. The unofficial Edinburgh poetry conference, the utterly chaotic Cardiff poetry conference (called the Commonwealth Poetry Conference and attended by a chorus of bewildered Commonwealth delegates), the Better Books Writers' Nights, Strip Readings at the ICA organised by Eric Mottram and Bill Butler – the potsmoke eddied and the wine flowed free. The high point of these activities was Allen Ginsberg's visit to London during his grand tour of 1965 which drew a line of contact from India, through Greece, Yugoslavia, Czechoslovakia, Poland, to London, back to 'Frisco, and gave London a direct taste of something new, disturbing and intoxicating. At the huge Albert Hall reading organised and presented in six hectic days by John Esam and Dan Richter, not only were Trocchi, Corso, Ferlinghetti, Horovitz, Brown, Hawkins, Richter, McGrath, Lacey, Esam, MacBeth, Logue, Hollo, Jandl and Fainlight (the real star of the show), performing together but all our separate audiences had come to one place at the same time, to witness an atmosphere of pot, impromptu solo acid dances, of incredible barbaric colour, of face and body painting, of flowers and flowers and flowers, of a common dreaminess in which all was permissive and benign. It was also an occasion when two important poems were read which laid the ghost of our previous sickness. Ginsberg's 'The Change' and Fainlight's 'Spider' meet the projected spectres of torment face-to-face – 'Shit! Intestines boiling in sand fire/burned yellow brain cold sweat/earth unbalanced vomit thru/tears, snot ganglia buzzing/the Electric Snake rising hypnotic/shuffling metal eyed coils/whirling rings within wheels/from asshole up the spine/Acid in the throat the chest/a knot trembling Swallow back/the black furry ball of the great Fear'[1] – 'I WANT TO VOMIT UP A SPIDER'[2] – and disarm them with sheer love – 'I am that man trembling to die/in vomit and trance . . . Come sweetly/now back to my Self as I was'[3] – 'Flowers where I still lie amidst my slime . . . The lovely shame of knowing myself deep in my heart an adorable young female spider. (It is the point where you start thinking of the hair as fur that it no longer seems so sinister).'[4]

There was a frisson for us all to savour as there had been at the first Aldermaston, and the Underground was suddenly there on the surface, in open ground with a following of thousands.

It seems fastidious to pretend that the overriding agent which produced this new bizarrity, the new relaxation and colourful contrast to previous earnest tight-lipped attitudes, was not Lysergic Acid.

After the Albert Hall I wrote to Klaus Lea crying: 'London is in flames. The spirit of William Blake walks on the water of Thames. sigma has exploded into a giant rose. Come and drink the dew.'

Trocchi lived in the hotel where I'd met Burroughs. We talked. A place, a week-end conference, even. Duplicating.

Coffee around the corner on the Queensway in a brash, crowded mod restaurant. He bought me ten Players. I didn't know whether to be charmed, touched or suspicious. Was he really hip enough to pamper the anxious child? Was that the part I wanted to play?

The next time I had the new copies of *Invisible Insurrection* duplicated for him. Bob and Jennifer Cobbing were with me. Lyn Trocchi came in while we talked. She had the child, Mark, with her. She leaned against the wall by the door in her black leather and looked like a young Susan Hayward.

The third time Alex and I sat in a pub near Marble Arch. He drank rum and coke and I drank beer. 'Let's get this clear,' he said. 'What this is all about is the complete rejection of *everything* outside that door.' The letter of his meaning indicated that society was to be rejected, fine, but it flashed through my mind then that the door represented the seven holes in Alexander's skull and therefore all but self was to be rejected, perhaps the only way that such a self could live.

Later, in his room, I said, testing something that was worrying me – 'I want to work for sigma as an artist. Let's have *that* quite clear.'

'After a while it wouldn't make any difference.'

'Well' I said, 'let's get it launched and see.'

'D'accord,' purred Alex. He took a fix. Watching somebody fix is like watching them masturbate.

I was in a hurry. There were two organisations Alex knew of; a group of mad doctors at Millbrook centred around a man called Leary (who, after their expulsion from Mexico, had advertised in London papers as a group of schizophrenics who wished to set up shop in Britain) and a group of mad doctors in Finchley centred around a man called Laing. Alex wanted to contact them both. One thing uppermost in his mind was his safety. Doctors meant protection. 'I hate doing anything outside the law,' he said.

Mark Trocchi ran in. He'd run away from his mother in Queensway and come to Dad. Alex embraced him and looked worried. Lyn came in. 'Oh so he's here,' she said. She seemed curiously unconcerned.

I wrote to Brazier's Park in Oxfordshire. Would it be possible to run a weekend conference there? We made a date to see Ronnie Laing. Alex and Lyn went to dinner.

I went to a pub where a bunch of the lads were playing – Gas Griffiths, Johnny Fry, Ken Kennedy. I sat in, blew some crude showy horn. Feeling on top of the world I showed up on Ronnie Laing's doorstep with a bruised lip. I talked to Lyn and Mrs Laing. Beautiful women again. Mrs Laing was a husky, ironic redhead. Alex fixed somewhere. Ronnie prepared the front room. Shortly Beba Lavarin (late of Centre 42 – background of left-wing fund-raising and bad art), David Cooper, Aaron Esterson, Sally Gooch and her poet husband arrived.

Everybody but the wives went upstairs to talk in Ronnie's office. We filed in and sat in a ring, most of us on the floor. The old conflicting divisions – ban-the-bomb politics and eastern metaphysics. Some wanted to talk mind. Beba, a little militant, wanted to talk money. Ultimately Mrs Laing, proclaiming that we all had the manners of pigs, summoned us downstairs. Another familiar hangup – business or pleasure, yes there is a difference, always a difference.

Downstairs a new start. Alex moaned. Mrs Laing took him aside. Alex stopped moaning. Ronnie played a Billie Holliday record to cool our minds. Beba fidgeted and Mrs Laing, bless her, took the piss out of Beba's Hungarian accent.

Ronnie introduced the Philadelphia Foundation. Beba and I sat, a little amazed at his 'deep speech' bit. The Glasgow hardman's accent, wreathed face, his 'ah'm-fucken-taillin'ye' expression (remembered from God knows how many lance-jacks in the Royal Scots Greys) dressed in a Presbyterian resonance and a junkie's speed. He finished, bringing his hands up close to his face, as though holding the 'No Theng' (Noh thing? Refusal thing?) and said 'The only way – the only way we can define our aim is as this: to reveal the greater glory of God.'

Beba – bewilderment, after years of business-like, fast-moving committee work with Arnold Wesker and chums.

Alex – patiently absorbing the sinister monosyllable into his evil atheistic soul and smothering it.

I – suddenly interested.

Mrs Laing – loyally suppressing her giggles.

Alex did a little seductive purring and name-dropping – Bill Burroughs, Francis Bacon. Good old Alex.

Then a growing fragmentation, talk breaking into groups, half a dozen different conversations. I thought Esterson looked as though he had been in a concentration camp – a sort of lucid bestiality about him that put him, somehow, in that setting. I asked him if he'd ever been in a concentration camp. 'No,' he said. I told Cooper I felt that I should have been in one, that this would have been tantamount to suffering the century. 'To suffer society is enough,' said Cooper. 'Society is a concentration camp.' Christ what a nut.

I was still in a hurry. No sidetracks. I could perhaps kick this introspective shambles into a body that would take up where the Committee of 100 had failed. I was wrong. I needed a reputation for that. Professional rank was, finally, fairly rigid.

But time and the wailing clarinets of the whiskey indicated I should leave, and I'd promised Beba some concrete decision.

I willed down the alcohol. 'How would it be if I fixed a weekend conference in the country? Would you all come?'

'*Yes,*' said Ronnie loudly.

'I'll do it then,' I said. In fact, I already had.

Nevertheless I had to persuade the people at Brazier's Park to accept a series of afterthoughts and additions amongst the guests and act as a go-between for two grotesquely different groups.

The community at Brazier's Park, a little colony of quiet, self-sufficient middle-class intellectuals, totally square with heavy overtones of Quakerism and Fabianism, was anxious to extend every kindness and expected, in return, good manners and an observation of the minimal regulations they imposed.

The group I represented was turned into the examination of their own minds, partly driven there by their fear and hatred of anything outside their own minds, with an angry contempt for most ordinary conventions and all regulations, with no intention of playing guest to the Brazier's Park host, merely wanting to pay their way for a place where they could go a little madder than they already were. I put down twenty-one quid as a deposit, and on that sunny Friday, got off school early and made my way to Reading. At Reading I missed the bus so started out on the Oxford Road. An old man gave me a lift; courteous, kindly, at peace with himself; he seemed the embodiment of all that was good about the way of life we were out to destroy.

He put me down on a high road where cornfields lay around like sumptuous mothers, apple-green and gold, russet, bread-white, toasted brown, on all sides. The breeze stirred the wildflowers in the shallow hedges.

'Brazier's Park is down there,' said the driver, pointing to a lane. He drove off and I walked down the gentle side of the swell towards a family of trees, mossy, sooty-black and green, clustered in the hollow. I could see the little minarets of Brazier's Park above the trees. I felt exhilarated, moved by the shimmering cleanliness of the summer and the light.

Rounding the curve of Brazier's Park drive, I saw a group standing in the porch, recognised Esterson. I waved but nobody waved back. I laughed aloud for contempt and waved again.

'Hello,' I said. Esterson nodded his reply, introduced me to others in the group. 'Nice evening,' I said. It was such an understatement of my obvious exhilaration I must have sounded grotesque. It was a beautiful place and a beautiful summer and we were going to stop the squares scorching it to death (what, sixty miles from London? Outside the blast of one hundred megatons – just fires and roast flesh and heavy fallout).

Opposite the porch was a high elm sodden with light, luminous and liquid masses of foliage clotted sumptuously to a regal altitude. Esterson said, 'I wonder if you could guess the height of that tree.' I knew immediately that we were in for trouble. Their eyes were closed.

I was eager to begin, to meet, to talk. Was Alex here? Where was the clueless nit? Wandering round the Oxonian downs with a dropper up his nose? I talked to the hosts. They were anxious to give out with a formal welcome at dinner. Yes, we had all been asked to be there for dinner. But dinner came and went and still no formal announcement. That would have to wait till after dinner. Tom McGrath showed with wife and baby. Cooper and I went to meet Laing and look for Alex (visions of him put down facing in the wrong direction by a bus conductor and wandering off to the south). Cooper whipped along the lanes in his flash car. We met Ronnie. He was with Clancy Sigal and Joe. We chased around the lanes looking for a pub. In the pub I said to Sigal, 'I can't see you.' 'Oh sorry,' he said. He lifted his shades.

Joe rode back with Cooper and I. A Hungarian brain surgeon with huge maudlin eyes and a big Jewish yearning in him, Joe talked about the play he was writing. 'This is Kafka,' he said, indicating the bleeding landscape. I thought, 'For these cats everything is Kafka.' I said, 'You should have seen the sun earlier this evening – like a bloody great fried egg.' So Joe smiled and that looked a bit more promising.

Half the people had been in to dinner. There were two times suggested to meet after dinner. Alex arrived, nerve-wracked from Jim's driving, wanted to leave this evening informal until morning. Joe and Ronnie wanted to go on the piss. The hosts wanted to give their welcome and outline their regulations. I was beginning to stretch between appeasement of the hosts, excitement at the place, and a powerful unassuaged thirst of my own.

By ten-thirty we were assembled – wanderers back from the pub but Alex in his room. The Philadelphia representatives were a little sceptical about the whole project. What the hell was sigma anyway? I started to try to tell them. Tom sloped off to get Alex. Alex, irritable, came down. For all his inadequacy and megalomania there was something warming about him and his wife – there always is – a warming virile whiff of sheer jazz about them.

Confrontation between Bob Cobbing and Alex. Alex sitting crosslegged on the floor painting a piece of driftwood in Cryla colour.

Cobbing: 'Where is the money coming from?'

Trocchi: 'The money is *no problem*.'

Cobbing: 'Where is it then?'

Trocchi: 'I've *got* the fucking money.'

Cobbing: 'How much?'

Trocchi hurled his driftwood at Cobbing. Cobbing grinned.

Trocchi: 'Have I got to sit here all night looking at your fucking ugly face?'

Play this man right like an instrument, I thought, and you'll get a good song. Thinking vaguely that the Philadelphia Trust must be trusted with something, I said, 'It's okay Bob. There is money.'

At this point the host, Mrs Faithful, came in to deliver her official welcome. She had waited patiently since dinner four hours ago. 'I don't want to listen to any administrative details,' growled Alex.

Later we fixed a meeting for ten in the morning and broke up. Sigal, McGrath and I talked. 'You're awful hung up on art,' said Sigal.

John Latham had a pint of whisky. He shared it. Joe crooned Hungarian Yiddish lullabies to Beba Lavarin.

In the morning Alex overdosed. I began to get the pattern of his habit. It was, basically, a kind of worrying towards self-perfection. Thus he had lasted longer than most. He came down to the meeting late. By the time he came down Ronnie, Joe and Beba had gone off on the piss again. Another pattern. These people *dreaded* meeting one another. Deeply they *dreaded* it.

So through most of the morning session Tom McGrath and I talked about an art centre and nobody dug the idea too much.

We had lunch. Ronnie, Joe and Beba were back, picnicking with wine and garlic sausage on the terrace. 'My obligations do not go so far as to have to eat their fuck-awful food,' said Ronnie and hurled a stone out into the park.

The picnic got wilder and drunker. Wine got into people like the sun got into the butter. The picnic table became an image of the whole meeting. Discordant, messy, runny, sticky and finally abandoned.

I began, doggedly, to make mere meeting times my business. That final abandonment was not going to happen if I could help it. Graham Howe had already left in disgust.

In the afternoon Ronnie sat in a centre chair, magnificently slewed with a litre of wine at his foot. 'I want everyone in this room who is not prepared to be a fucken' *general* in this campaign to walk out of that door now.'

The discussion started circling. Joe asked, '*What* is this sickness in society you refer to?'

Everybody sounded off abstractedly. Joe kept asking. I said 'Ronnie, will you for Christ's sake give Joe some definition of the social sickness so that we can move on?'

Sigal said, 'Jeff, you're beginning to bug me.'

That was it. I crumpled into a chair with the wine and held back angry tears. There is a movie somewhere of my beergut rising and falling on that occasion, tumultuous with suppressed wrath and frustration.

'Why put down Jeff and not Joe?' said Tom.

'Because Joe seems to have a little more behind his asking,' said Sigal.

Laing pointed at McGrath. '*You* are an innocent man,' he accused. John Latham burned a Skoob Tower.

In the evening there was a hurtling drive to Oxford. Beba Lavarin's teenage son, who suffered with a violent nervous twitch, sat in the front of the car. As we crashed the traffic lights or hurtled towards slowing vehicles Jim, driving, threw his left arm across the boy's chest. And a hell of a lot of good that would have done had it come to the crunch.

At dinner I sat by Joe and the boy. Joe, well-plastered by now, talked to the boy about his twitch, then screamed 'For Christ's sake stop it!' The boy froze. Joe turned to me with an expression of dreamy benignity: 'I'm winning,' he said.

The bill for dinner came to a hundred pounds. Somehow Ronnie paid it.

One of Cooper's patients drove me back to the Park. I had to get petrol for him on the way – conned a passing motorist into driving me to a garage and back with the can. A mile from the Park we ran dry again. Joan, Sid, the driver and I piled out and pushed the car home.

In the house everybody was stoned. Alex and Ronnie squatted cross-legged on the floor, forehead to forehead, eyes closed. Sigal had some jazz records. I listened for a while – Joe Turner – then turned in.

A smell woke me up. On the stairs it was stronger, a cheap scented chemical kind of smell. I expected chaos in the lounge and vaguely intended clearing it up. That at least I could do for the Faithfuls (who, I later discovered, had sat up all that Saturday night with a gun). I opened the lounge door. John Latham met me with a steady staring eye. There's something about Latham at such moments that is mad beyond madness. A staring immovable shocked and shocking inner violence. Latham had taken a book (an irreplaceable book belonging to a pleasant little

Chinese friend of Alex's), stuck it to the wall with Polyfilla, and shot black Aerosol all over book and wall in a big explosion of night. That was the smell. Otherwise the room was tidy.

Until breakfast-time John reassured me that the Faithfuls had given him permission to do a mural. Later it caused serious mental distress to aged community members. That Sunday morning it stood, overlooking the talk, a stark, beautiful, violent emblem to pure action, the most graphic condemnation possible of our evasive ineffectual waffle.

So that Sunday morning Cooper and Laing spoke well. Calm after the party, relaxed, knowing us now and we knowing him, Laing enacted a catatonic ceremonial, summarily describing its magical function. 'It's a question,' he said, 'of coming down from the surface of things, from the surface of yourself, down to the core of all things, to the central sphere of being of which all things are emanations.'

At midday we fled from one another with colossal relief . . .

'I'm glad we had it,' said Ronnie over the phone.

Through that summer of 1964 we turned our possibilities over between us like enigmatic stones. Alex and Lyn moved back together. Lyn had kicked her habit successfully. Their flat was a three-room place near Westbourne Grove. The discarded cars rusted away in the street.

I spent long sunny afternoons sitting on the balcony playing with little Mark, sitting in the pub talking to Lyn. Our intentions and schedules submerged into a warm ambience, compounded of Lyn's gentle slatternly beauty, the soft purr of Alex's voice, an ambience of tenderness, intelligence, total licence and crackling undercurrents of a kind of sad cruelty.

Alex rigged up his study like an office. People passing through London dropped in, Jack Michelin, Gregory Corso, Bob Creeley, Ian Sommerville. Posters went up on the walls, statements of policy, plans of action. I drew up a plan for a sigma poster magazine and found a cheap printer at Hertford who'd print it like a wrestling poster. Alex didn't like it. He drew up his own mock-up and passed it on to Sankey at Villiers Press.

I duplicated the sigma portfolio and Alex and I went up to the unofficial poetry conference at the Traverse with something to sell. Jim Haynes' vast Edinburgh flat was like a Bedouin encampment. Actors, poets, folksingers, dancers came in, dossed down and passed on. A man from Millbrook showed up – actual tangible proof of the psychedelic movement.

The dream was strengthening. My best things I said to myself — auto-responses to passing remarks and half-memories. A little man called Jack Moore held my hand in the Traverse Bar. I caught my nose in the door of a telephone kiosk on the Royal Mile and a fat man called Adrian Henri released me. Chinese lunch with Alan and his bird. Ferocious embrace from Roddy Carmichael. George Lawson like a wren. George MacBeth like a predatory spider. Martin Seymour-Smith and I and the two vacant American girls. The Corries late night at the Traverse reminding me of Dennis Winnie and Dennis Winnie dying. Looking for Bill McArthur and selling the Festival Special Mag. Sunday morning sunshine waking the beatniks dossed out in rows in the castle gardens.

Phil Cohen found the Kingsley Hall. What was the Kingsley Hall? A beautiful hall, says Cohen, what you might call Bypass Ecclesiastical. Who's running it? Oh some trust, some collection of social workers, working more or less under David Sheppard (who was, at that time, unsullied by *Last Exit to Brooklyn*). — Gandhi slept there — Social centre in the East End. What are they doing with it. Absolutely fuck all.

The exhibition. Yes, the exhibition. I went to see the Kingsley Hall. Latham has his Skoob Box, a strange dark environment, in the basement. Cohen was dossing in the organ room. The Philadelphia Trust wanted it for their community. Cohen wanted it for a youth recreation centre. I wanted it for Criton and me, to house our exhibition. I contacted Criton and called a meeting. John Latham, Bruce Lacey, Islwyn Watkins, Criton, Dave Trace, Phil Cohen, Keith and Heather Musgrove, came.

Meanwhile I learned something more of Alex and the price of his self-perfection — how each step towards his own apotheosis cost him dearer in terms of need — a veritable Faustian progress with the Devil upping the price all the time, so that each project that his aspiring sensibility conducted him towards, each ideal, each aim, each plan too huge and too audacious for unstimulated minds, carried with it its sad reverse of negatives. Each gesture of self-realisation carried an aspect of snide self-gratification. The funds poured in. But the funds also poured out. In September Tonk sent me ten bob from Liverpool with the note, 'Is this any good for sigma?' I sent it back by return . . .

The sTigma closed at the end of March 1965. Ginsberg arrived in May. Unannounced he wandered into Better Books one day and introduced himself. He offered to read anywhere for no fee. His first reading at Better Books was the first healing wind on a very parched collective mind. The sourness, the negativity in the air before his coming was almost tangible. Was certainly poisonous.

We sat, packed tight, rather self-conscious. Bob Cobbing looked triumphant. I was drunk and insane and in love. Bill Morris was sick in the metal wastebasket noisily.

Ginsberg read and it registered that what had seemed over-messianic, grotesquely self-exposing and self-lacerating in print, was, in fact, a gay thing, the violent images delivered with a mischievous twinkle, an incredibly milky gentleness flowing out from this one man into the minds and bodies of the audience. After the reading he sauntered down into the audience – cigarette, hands in pockets, not a prophet, not a great poet any more, just a friendly Yank, said: 'Well, where's the party?'

Two women with flowers on their faces whisked him away. Days later, in Marcus Field's room one floor down from Alex's, a crowd of us sat in a circle. Field, a young and capable Australian, had been doing my job for sigma since we began work on the exhibition, doing it far more efficiently than I. Allen was tired. Was I Nuttall? Did I know that Burroughs was against the flesh? I was surprised that he knew. Did the young people read Blake? Rather in the same way that American reporters thought the Beatles were queer because of their haircuts, so Allen seemed to think that any long-haired British youth was steeped in Proust. The misunderstanding reached a hilarious peak when, stark naked, he encountered Lennon and McCartney (at that time very sharp little mods) at a party and demanded their embraces. It seems to indicate an insight beyond error, that now two years later both the Beatles and their fans would enjoy Proust very much indeed.

It was a new and elevating summer, a long warm time of colours merging, changing, in a slow exploding orgasm of events.

At the Albert Hall reading John Latham and I were to have a battle. We dressed in blue paint and huge Aztec costumes of books which we were to tear off one another. Trocchi forgot to signal our entrance. As we waited in the wings John passed out. There was a fight with one of the British Legion attendants who tried to prevent Cohen and I from using a door as a stretcher to carry John to Sir Malcolm Sargent's dressing-room. It was the same attendant, pulverized by the goodly Anglo-Saxon pouring forth from Jewish lips down in the auditorium, who burst into Sir Malcolm's bathroom, found John and I giggling and washing one another, assumed the worst and staggered away in an advanced state of shock.

The summer was out of control. I behaved, I am told, intolerably at one of John Calder's parties. Most people, I am told, behaved intolerably everywhere. Sigma office was crowded with people wearing flowers. Gregory Corso, a pretty girl and I sold newspapers in the Portobello Road. I wrote real poetry at last. In September Allen went home and we all went to Cardiff. At Cardiff Jean-Jacques Lebel, Tom Hudson and I put on a happening. Cardiff School of Art was full of beautiful young people. The Park Hotel was full of local queers affecting disgust at visiting poets. Henri, Patten and McGough floated on a sea of black sullen faces. Patten took the shoes put out for the bootboy and threw them down the lift-shaft . . .

PROJECT SIGMA: CULTURAL ENGINEERING:

Manifesto Situationiste, 1960, sigma edition

Alex Trocchi and Philip Green

The *coup-du-monde* must be in the broad sense cultural. With his thousand technicians, Trotsky seized the viaducts and the bridges and the telephone exchanges and the power stations. The police, victims of convention, contributed to his brilliant enterprise by guarding the old men in the Kremlin. The latter hadn't the elasticity of mind to grasp that their own presence there at the traditional seat of 'government' was irrelevant. History outflanked them. Trotsky had the railway stations and the powerhouses, and the 'government' was effectively locked out of history by its own guards.

So the cultural revolt must seize the grids of expression and the powerhouses of the mind. Intelligence must become self-conscious, realise its own power, and, on a global scale, transcending functions that are no longer appropriate, dare to exercise it. History will not overthrow national governments: it will outflank them. The cultural revolt is the necessary underpinning, the passionate substructure of a new-order of things. – *The Invisible Insurrection*

(*Editorial Note*: For many years now we have been to some extent involved in the theoretical evolution of that dialectic which goes under the name '*situationiste*': the manifesto which follows is based on the *Manifesto Situationiste* of 1960. But as all situationist documents have been at all times provisional in the sense that they are to be understood as tactical manoeuvres or 'happenings', we have taken the liberty now (at the end of 1964) of making certain changes. Thus, although the original was faithfully translated by our collaborator, Philip Green, we have proceeded to develop some of the original theses, always, nevertheless, in accordance with the natural evolution of the situationist point of view. The fact that we are able to do this without perverting the original, bears out our contention that the invisible insurrection is happening in many places simultaneously . . . NOW.)

Contrary to the absurd prejudice of certain evolutionists who regard evolution as having, with present-day man, come to an end, a new (or perhaps very old, 500,000 years old, for all we know) force is active in human becoming, a force so subtle that existing 'cadres' will be incompetent to contain and stifle it. *It does not exist except for those who are with it.* Our contemporary police systems are thus outflanked by the very nature of their 'adversary': the institutional nature of the world is in the process of being turned upside down. The evolution of this force is rendered daily more certain with the irresistible development of technology whose more than logical outcome is automation (and compulsory leisure), and is stimulated by the growing dissatisfaction of individuals all over the world with the . . . [missing line] . . . was for our GRANDFATHERS WHOSE CORRELATIVE institutions moulder on and constrict us: those capitalised letters are in question) to exploit the vast potential of that technology to render the world safe for human beings to live in.

Neither alienation nor oppression, no matter what form they take, can in the long run be rationalized to provide a permanent solution to the problem of the individual in society; such states must be discarded or, better, *transcended*, along with society itself. Finally, there is no way out of our infinitely complex age of crises except one which is fundamentally revolutionary (cf. *The Invisible Insurrection*, etc.).

What new perspectives are available to a society which will authentically reorganise production on bases compatible with the free and equal association of its constituent individuals? Automation and a general 'socialisation' of vital goods will gradually and ineluctably dispense with most of the necessity for 'work': eventually, as near as dammit, the complete liberty of the individual in relation to production will be attained. Thus freed of all economic responsibility, man will have at his disposal a new *plus-value*, incalculable in monetary terms, a *plus-value* not computable according to the accounting of salaried work. *PLAY-VALUE*. What is becoming is *homo ludens* in a life liberally constructed. There is no solution within the conventional economic framework. Trade unions fear automation because under present conditions men fear to be 'out of work'. Evidently these conditions will have to be changed to fit a future we cannot (and should be foolish to want to) evade. If we are not to become so many ants on an ant-heap (or be annihilated in a nuclear holocaust), we should do well to explore the creative possibilities of the leisure situation now and adapt our findings to the education of future generations. Such practice in '*ludic creativity*' is the guarantee of the freedom of each and every one of us. Forced labour, passive leisure: such notions, being in direct conflict with our contemporary revolt, must be consciously transcended. The liberalising influence of a ludic situation functioning imaginatively is startling and wonderful to see.

In another age the Church burned sorcerers to suppress the primitive ludic tendencies conserved in popular festivities. In present-day society, massively technological, and 'rich' in pseudo-games in which the individual does not participate . . . in an atmosphere of such spiritual desolation, all authentic artistic activity tends to be . . . [Missing line] . . . invoked against the *Living Theatre*, Beck and Malina, against loft-living in Manhattan, against 'poetry-readings' in the Village . . . discussed in *The Floating Bear*, *The Village Voice*, etc.; and in England, the recent seizure of *Cain's Book* as an 'obscene' work, etc.) are a small part of this universal tendency. Art has become semi-clandestine and appears as often as not in the form of scandal.

What do we mean by the word 'situation'? Within an experimentally constructed context, due attention paid to what we call 'psycho-geographic' factors, the situation is the gradual and spontaneous realisation (articulation: happening) of a superior game in which each participating individual is vitally involved. At the same time, it is the conscious provocation of the game inspired by the posture of the individuals involved. Revolutionary players of all countries must evolve the technique of acting together to raise the whole tenor of daily living beyond the level of stock response: we must break out of these stifling conventional doldrums which future historians will undoubtedly regard as evidence that present-day man is sunk in what they (the future historians) will regard as a kind of 'pre-history', a period of human history during which man is still without techniques to control his own destiny.

Bearing all this in mind, we propose immediate action on an international scale, a self-governing (non-)organisation of producers of the *new culture* beyond, and independent of, all political organisations and trade and professional syndicates which presently exist; for there is not one of those which does not have the fogs and vapours of ataxia in its own basement. They can, that is to say, initiate nothing at a sigmatic level which would not finally imply their own obsolescence. The exception (which proveth the rule) is one organisation which, relatively speaking, is in its infancy: U.N.E.S.C.O.

The worldwide bureaucratisation of art and culture is an entirely new phenomenon and at the same time it expresses the common ancestry of all the social systems of the world, and a common ancestor who is precisely as Burroughs sees him: 'an old and evil man from an old and evil cave'.

Principles underlying those systems: what we might call 'the principle of eclectic conservation' and, broadly speaking: that of the reproduction of the past. The response of revolutionary artists to these conditions has to be a new kind of action, one which cannot provoke conventional forms of reaction (destructive reaction). The kind of reaction we must provoke is that of 'potlatch'[1], and at the same time the point-counterpoint is the game of tennis. The very existence of such a concentration of directorial cultural power, 'situated' in a single building, favours '*une mainmise par voie de putsch*'.[2] But this 'putsch', like the insurrection in general, must be 'invisible' to be effective. Now as this institution is presently quite evidently destitute of all possibility of sigmatic exploitation, as it is, from our 'subversive' perspective, quite obviously *beyond the pale*, it is up to us quietly to infiltrate and seize it (cf. *The Invisible Insurrection*). And we shall have it.

Even if, for the sake of argument, such a 'seizure' proved to be temporary, we are resolved to attempt it, because we feel we would be in a position to do works which would remain (inspirational) long after our

TOP: Trocchi and Richard Seaver, Paris. Photograph: H. Riemens, courtesy of Jane Lougee.
BOTTOM LEFT: Patrick Bowles, George Plimpton, Jane Lougee and Christopher Logue, Paris, 1953. Photograph: Otto Van Noppen, courtesy of Jane Lougee.
BOTTOM RIGHT: Trocchi and Jane Lougee at Cap d'Ail, South of France, 1953. Photograph courtesy of Jane Lougee.

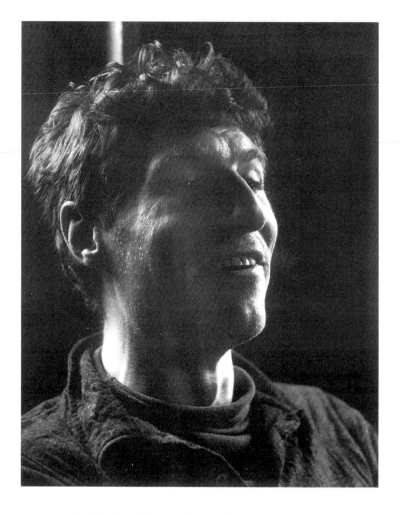

ABOVE: Trocchi, New York. Photograph by Jane Lougee.

rocchi on the scow, New York. Photograph by Jane Lougee.

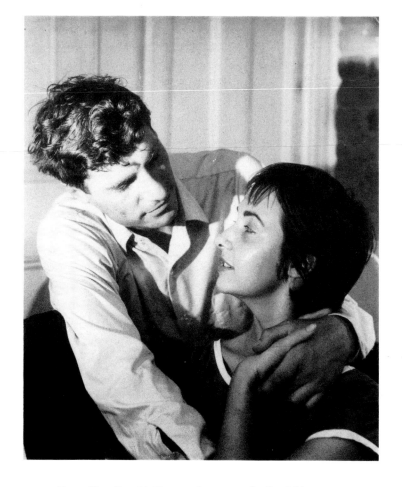

ABOVE: Alex and Lyn Trocchi. Photograph courtesy of Sally Child.

ABOVE: Trocchi. Photograph courtesy of Sally Child.
BELOW: Lyn and Mark Trocchi, New York. Photograph by
Jane Lougee.

ABOVE: Lyn, Mark and Alex Trocchi in London. Photograph courtesy of Sally Child.
BELOW: Alex and Lyn Trocchi. Photograph courtesy of Sally Child.

ABOVE: Trocchi and Sally Child. Photograph courtesy of Sally Child.
BELOW LEFT: Mark and Nick Trocchi. Photograph courtesy of Sally Child.
BELOW RIGHT: Trocchi at the Chelsea Arts Club Ball. Photograph courtesy of Sally Child.

ABOVE: Alex Trocchi. Photograph courtesy of Sally Child.

evacuation. We are confident it would not be like the Jacobite campaign, for example. Our '1715' would, we feel certain, be followed by a successful '45'.

Then, what would be the principal characteristics of the new culture, particularly compared with the old? In the place of spectacle, a true situationist culture would introduce participation (in the game).[3]

We would replace the excessive accent on the conservation of art with a strong accent on the artistic organisation of every lived moment. The present is, finally, all we have. But it is enough, as some mystics have always known. To be truly in the present is to be already in eternity. Here lies whatever immortality is ours.

Against compartmented art, situationist culture would encourage a kind of universal practice which would include and transcend every employable element. Without in the least threatening the individual, it will tend naturally to collective production, and anonymous production certainly in the sense that individual works by individual artists will not be stocked as merchandise, in the sense that the situationist culture in general will not be dominated by the hysterical need to 'leave traces'.

A whole revolution in comportment is implied, along with a dynamic and globally orchestrated town-planning, 'infinitely' complex in its immediately sensible correlations. Alongside the art of the individual, sigmatic culture would inspire the art of the dialogue, the art of interaction. Individual artists . . . cultural elements in general . . . have come to be cut off from the normal process of society, just as, by (at least partly) conscious choice, they are cut off from one another. But, even before the present historical impasse was reached, art was essentially 'unilateral', and only unconsciously part of a dialectic: from time immemorial, it has been in this sense *'sans réponse'*.

It seems, therefore, as though an era is in the process of being transcended.

Nous nous attendons au tournant, qui est l'inévitable liquidation du monde de la privation, nous qui nous occupons avec la construction de notre propre vie, la privation sous toutes ses formes. Tels sont nos buts, et ils deviennent les buts futurs de l'humanité.

Philip Green
Alex Trocchi

THE LONG BOOK
Alex Trocchi

In his fortieth year, according to the most exact sigmatic informations, Joseph Necchi, alias the sexistential – one of the last men – inherited the earth. At least, it seemed to him he had done so, or was doing so, and would be doing so, momently, thereafter. He discovered the decision in himself there and then, wherever and whenever it was, and felt it and himself from then on renewed, at each bright moment of confirmation. 'It is here and now,' he wrote to another of his shadow kind in another land. 'It is happening. The future is our inheritance.'

The Long Book (shades will recognise the noumenal foetus of the sigmatic toilet roll) was constructed of and on behalf of what has come to be known as the 'invisible insurrection'. – 'God-speed all cosmonauts of inner space!' cried Necchi in the falseteeth of some manufacturers of moral rearmaments, and would there and then have mounted the naked lady in the McEwan Hall, like the rampant ram he was, had not the lion in him been tempered by his foxy Roman ancestry. Old fox of Rome that he was! And inventor of numberless identities. . . . When asked by a critic, to whom was he referring when he spoke of 'they'? – he replied: 'When they come into my room and find me with my eyes closed, for them I am asleep: they are the enemies of contemplation, dull motor-ataxiane cut off from the himalayan horizons of the third eye . . .'

The idea was finally committed to writing in this period following the roman's return from the United States, the deed done in the living in that part of his permanent temporary quarters given over to the holy-of-holies, deftly done and tentatively, amongst substances, instruments, and engines of experiment. Aaram had gone into the futique-shop caper in sheer desperation, having tried during devious wanderings amongst natives of divers contemporaneous civilisations in sondrie laundes, high and low, far and wide, north and south, east and west, tried, even laboured under effort, to live his life freely, without absolute commitment to one and all of the patent relativities teeming about him. These he would have liked to stuff into the paper bag in which he kept his spike and his condom, a piece of agate, a small dungcoloured nob of the finest hashish, and two thighs in rut for his fleshwriting. But it rained and the bag burst, and another bag after that, and indeed he could never find the right container. Moreover, there was always some joe gander or plooknecked customs' artificer to interrogate him along thirty feet of tressle tables through his flyman's telescope, and, alas! he had found himself pressured persistently in all places, in cities and in prisons and in villages and in hospitals, to define himself clearly in terms familiar to the rudest of those about him, and to act accordingly, on pain of death or harsh confinement. And there was ever the problem of the unorthodox container. If it didn't burst, it farted!

Inevitably, wherever he paused to acquaint himself with the local situation did he encounter men who had got themselves into groups to govern as did kings and parliaments according to tradition. This group and its appointed vicars, in whatever land, were the guardians of that land's conventions. And the scene around our Soris was, by all extent conventional standards, unusual, and while a Martian might have considered it less outlandish than, for example, the works and worship of the congregation of the first presbyterian tabernacle in little frankenstein, arkansas and in terms of raw process altogether more logical (as ripe pregnancy after lust), vicars of all established denominations smelled the winds of change and tightened hempen guyropes.

General Apathy K.B.E. would have no truck with Martians, whom he regarded as outsiders by definition (can we really tolerate green pricks in our white runts?) and the general was quoted by the society columnist of the botulist bugle of hysteria pogromshire as saying of joseph necchi. 'This man is a notorious sexistential, and unrepentant pervert, and a self-confessed dope-fiend, one million of the d. . . breed which, secretly and with malice aforethought, has been landing during the past few decades on this unsuspecting planet . . . '

'Like blowflies on shit,' Coriolanus said to a visiting dean.

For more than two decades, indeed, the uncategorical imperative had been flaring like a (black) beacon across continents.

Now, Daedalus had noticed that every such group without exception assumed the power of life and death over individuals who chanced to be or go within its jurisdiction. Wherever he went, therefore, Eros did his utmost, within the limits of sigmatic expedience, to initiate the processes of operation outcry. Sometimes, and more frequently with the passing of the years, it was his good fortune gradually to discover such processes, begun before his arrival. Then he felt himself invaded by a kind of brainwave . . .

> How many zealots could we have? At present we had nearly
> fifty thousand: sufficient for the day. It seemed the assets in this
> element of war were ours. If we realised our raw materials and
> were apt with them, then climate, railway, desert and technical
> weapons could also be attached to our interests. The Turks were
> stupid; the Germans behind them dogmatical. They would
> believe that rebellion was absolute like war, and deal with it on
> the analogy of war. Analogy in human things was fudge,
> anyhow: and war upon rebellion was messy and slow, like eating
> soup with a knife. − *T. E. Lawrence*

One hundred and twenty planes bomb N. Vietnam from Ratten Tot
(Lushington, March 31). Today has seen the greatest air activity of the
Quietcon War. While over 120 United Brutes and South Vietnamese
planes were bombing six separate targets in the North, seventy other
planes were dropping tons of napalm bombs and barrels of fuel oil in an
attempt to burn out Tryiton guerrillas from a nest near New York . . .

Hon. Agatha Hardon's blue eyes moved gently on to her cornflakes.
No news, of course. Just the usual good morning scream implying a
woman had far more to defend these days than the garters to whose protection Victoria Regina had dedicated her widowhood. Blonde Bunny
will hitchhike to Mars. Male must be Martian. The ghost of the late em-
press lingered on however, and many women of her granddaughters'
generation still emulated her. Murder, panic, and corruption reported in
the *News of the Church*. Permeability amongst the miles and miles of news-
print. But, in fact, few minds were capable of absorbing and being affected by the flesh and blood behind the print. People were stunned by
too much of it. Click! they turned off: in self-defence. (Turn an cooler!)[1]
It was true what the sexistential had said to her the previous night: that
we were condemned by our own institutions, about history's being 'amok'.
Visit one's M.P. for reassurance? He'll sell us a policy? So, most women
returned to defending their garters, as excitingly and as profitably as
possible. And some committed suicide. Most of the men of her acquaintance never seriously considered the problem. And if they were carried to
that point in a conversation, they remembered that polite-conversation-
is-never-serious or they lapsed into the God-gave-us-courage-and-hope

routine, bishops' banalities. And women performed polite bird-motions to sustain their men. So that it seemed jack the raper would be top of the pops eternally. At least it had seemed so until the evening her roommate, Ophelia D'Arce, forgot an appointment and Agatha twanged like a supple English longbow at the touch of the sexistential's flat front.

Hon. Agatha Hardon remembered that occasion most vividly as she lifted the cornflakes off a yard away across the table and poked her spoon into fresh grapefruit. Ophelia D'Arce was her lifelong friend and sometime lover. 'A really super girl'.

'Miss Agatha Hardon,' said the sexistential sweetly to her there in that long room.

'Then I too shall come to the point,' said she, darkly.

When their smouldering passions had inhabited one body and were (warmly) subsided, she told him what Ophelia had said to her an hour earlier as she collected herself and dashed out of the flat:

'Of God, I forgot!'[2] said Ophelia all of a sudden, raising her slender hand from her soft sweet amazonian heats where the thick slabs of her powerful thighs came together at the wild fulcrum of her lower abdomen sticky and stenching after wenching on a bed of burgundy grapes. Agatha's body remembered the other body soft and haired as silken gooseberries against the netherlip. 'How could I forget! I was to be astride rat-Levy's blue mug with no drawers on and dripping, my dear, at eight o'clock sharp! It is after nine, in case my darling failed to notice, and here I am wallowing like a pig in your damn grapebath and died redder than any wife of MacBeth! Five hundred pounds is at stake!'

'Cash?'

'Cash. You could have ordered white grapes, Ag, you luscious slut!'

'And forfeit the blood?'

'Bugger the bloody blood!'

'Five hundred pounds?'

'Five hundred pounds.'

'It's not enough,' Agatha said, turning on her belly amongst broken, bruised grapes. 'The man can't wait to get his moustache between your legs. You said so yourself. His lapels are stiffened with one hundred dollar bills, remember?'

'He's not a rat, my darling, because he likes to be prepared for pogroms, nor indeed because he likes to prise my marble pillars apart with that blue chin of his; he's a rat because he's furtive when he bucks. He always turns off all the lights before he begins. I never know which direction he'll come from. And then, there he is, just a shadowy hulk, quivering like a rat beside me. Rat-Levy, yr Ophelia D'Arce is on her way!' And the big pretty pink girl stepped under the shower.

'*I Am a Prostitute*, by the Hon. Agatha Hardon S.V.P.,' said Agatha, selecting a large unbroken purple grape from her fruity bedding, and plopping it unbroken through lovely lips into her mouth. The bow of the lips, the set of the face, the painted eyes, were Egyptian.

With the steam rising from the shower came the immaculate voice of Ophelia D'Arce, singing the latest pop hit:

I lie here wondering
about it all, how
it wasn't like that at all.
How you bucked me thru
the slit in my overall . . .

And then: 'Do you know, Ag, what that louse Fink said about my apparent addiction to Jewish men? he said it was racial prejudice! My subconscious, I suppose, is a kind of Auschwitz . . .'

'How do you feel, darling, when you've sold yr body, or a short lease anyway?' said Agatha at the bundling steam.

Huskily, 'Rather depends on what one's had for dinner, doesn't it?' Ophelia replied.

'I miss Phee,' Agatha said now across the breakfast table to Ferdinand.

'Men turn away from the implications of their thoughts like commercial travellers from their bastards,' he replied. 'Phee? Ophelia D'Arce? Yes. Why don't you invite her to come to Tangiers?'

'Do you think she would come?'

'She might. And, not to shirk the implication of my own thoughts on the subject: I can't imagine anything nicer than to be the filling of a sandwich with Phee and yrself as the bread.'

'Sam Sandwich spread, soon him dead,' said Agatha demurely. 'Him dead, him washed.'

'Such waste as can has already taken place,' retorted the sexistential. 'Let us send at once for Ophelia D'Arce!'

'God,' said Godfrey, 'is always in the first person, like a man at crap.'

He had been telling Agatha about a book he was writing; the act he was perpetrating: *The Long Book* (or *The Addict in the White House*). 'It is of the future of continents conceived in the urinals of my pure heart,' he has said. They were lying on the low round bed, twelve feet in diameter, which stood at the end of the studio. They had gone there after a swim after breakfast. Beside them, set into the nearest wall was the red plastic face of the radio, nine inches high, three feet long. 'Sick, sack, suck a bum's abuck!' said the announcer. 'Superior thin vaseline: Axel's Axlegrease: makes buggering easy as peasebrose!'

'What station's that?' Agatha said.

'Mars,' he replied. It occurred to Hamlet as he lay beside Agatha, that thinking, silent or out loud, was ineffectual, the way writing was. Baked, fried, or steelblue and gleaming from the hook, the mackerel was dead however it was presented, nor even was 'mackerel' outside 'my' thinking. *I* am in more senses than one an 'idealer'. I am a kind of funeral director of what is essentially wordless. Each thought is a coffin for what previously lived. Black coffins, white coffins, coffins with brass handles . . . what's the difference? I bury things even when I praise them. Jean-Paul Sartre out of Mark Anthony. How did I ever think I could get nearer to things if I thought out loud, nearer, that is, than if I were to write my thoughts down? No matter how spontaneous my utterance, each word is a nail in the coffin of the corpse I wished to touch undead, unsymbolised. I deal in ideal or not at all. Nevertheless, I often thought . . . no, I often felt . . . If I thought out loud and spontaneously I'd get nearer to something, by a process of overspill, evade the censor, catching myself out. Catching whom out? The same sordid half-existence who sat down early this morning and took a fix? *Que suis-je?* A pseude-entity[3] out of inertia with a thirst to be. A microscopic speck of consciousness on the dark tide of unbeing, with athlete's foot? A swift fix makes nonsense of whatever definition, rings an epistemological bell. Still, that is the kind of question that interests me, the illegitimate question, the 'meaningless' one, the one in which is involved a host of ambiguities, a morass of symbols, a swarm of bees, word chasing sense, sense chasing words, and out of which, suddenly, as a ship out of fog . . . an image, a crisis, a sound . . .

On. Again. Along a road, there is still a road, the same road, blank and categorical like a state highway in the desert, and friends as old as lizards with their stone grimaces . . . how swiftly they scuttle when surprised! That isn't what I meant to say, not at the beginning when I sat myself down. It's the same road, different, bars of particulars, unfolding itself towards the red suppuration of sun at the long blue horizon, which might be volcanic, or a burning man. At the road's edge, a few scrub oaks, stones of many colours, quartz, feldspar, fluorite, garnet, gold. In the desert emotions take on a nakedness that could be offensive in the salon. There was, as I remember, dust clinging to the woman's thighs which had been wet and weren't any longer, and it clung there as wet sand clings, forming ridges against her white flesh, a glinting leafedge against the soft northern city-protected loins of a city woman who kept on her nylons and her garterbelt for ye oulde prospector who sprinkled her fine melon-belly with the golddust of his strike . . . Goldenballs Gannon of I-o-way, dogone died a year later in Las Vegas, Nev., in the stroke of his passion . . . Jesus Christ the oulde fart's croaked! At the beginning, her first thought for insects that crawled . . . before she was persuaded, because she remembered the day just off the highway between Nogales and Guaymas, and the exhilaration at having escaped at last across the border into what might have been another century, and the climb down over the embankment at the side of the road to the small bridge under which we lay with our naked legs entwined, when suddenly she felt the red ants and saw them move like a minute river of blood over her skin. There is nothing that is not in some way or other ambiguous, dialectical, in time. It was along the road these moments at which I was out of time, at which the world was like a perfection at my senses, whether it was a woman or a stone, it was those moments which provided me with a hieroglyphics out of which I was able to construct it again; and it is so even now again as I go on.

Igor chose the desert to begin with, not because anything began or came to an end there, but because of its relative emptiness, because, especially in remembering, he didn't wish to be at once overcome with a profusion of things, much as he supposed Descartes had chosen his *cogito*: to have an apodeictic posture from which to be going on. He said, 'There's a specific character in all the acts in the life of a man, an awful sameness in all his various situations. Even his accidents are affinitive. And every man is alone in a night world in which the beacons of responsibility have gone out.'

'In Las Vegas,' Ophelia had said, 'there's nothing like gold for correct friction.'

This is the long book. I should say: this will be (or, this is becoming) the long book. For what form this book will take enters my conscious mind gradually as it is written. I have the feel of it, and, in that sense, could be said to know what it is about, but whether it will lie, a bible in a brothel, a textbook in a factory for human engineering, or hang, a toilet roll in the lavatories of the enlightened . . . certain historical facts and factories seem to be beyond my immediate control, Dr Kildare . . . where was Noah without the flood?

'When can you let us have your next novel?' Jeremiah's publisher had asked him.

'Call it a spade, not a shovel,' Kubla Khan replied. 'If you'd really dug where I was at in the last, you wouldn't keep asking that question.'

'I do wish you would be serious, Bla. I'm running a business.'

'It's called *Notes Towards the Tactical Revaluation of the Human Process*,' Necchi replied. 'And it should be printed on toilet rolls and hung like an air-freshener in the lavatories of all lands.'

'Poof!' said Pottle the publisher. 'That's old hat! Didn't someone do something like that before somewhere . . . I'm sure I heard . . . now who was it . . .? I . . .'

'Sir Izal Germicide,' Necchi said, 'and *imperm'eable,* as I remember.'

'Lionel, it wouldn't sell!' Pottle insisted, 'and anyway, the bookshops wouldn't stock it. You know how they treated *Cain's Book* . . .'

'Pottle, it is precisely because they have damned and insulted and labelled as obscene and caused to be burned by the public executioner the fealthy dorty wordes of yr humble's . . . I demand the privacy of a lavatory where I can tickle yr balls for you when you're alone with yr wig off and yr bum down, if you take my meaning?'

'Mmmm,' Pottle pondered, placing one small pink crocus-like hand at his round chin and smiling in his blue eyes, remembering the naked lady he had caused to be transported in flagrant sin and trembling, history of literary supplement. Again he saw the outraged headlines. 'Who would print it, Mathieu? I doubt if it could be done . . .'

'Thy will be done, Pottle,' Mark said. 'Don't you see the relevance, how fitting the toilet roll? Nasty man banished to lavatory. Shine a

bright light in the crazy corridors of those toilet-trained consciences?
Just a wee bit? Like a new hymn:

> Jock lost his sporran
> is dangling free
> God cares for he . . .

A toilet roll now would be a bestseller, Puttis. Evil Epigrams Encapsu-
lated, Publishers. Build a fire under the turkey-necked bastards!'

'It's all very well for you,' Pottle now protested. 'You can simply take
off for Tangiers if things get out of hand. I can't. I'd look very silly
pushing a barrowload of toilet rolls!'

For the sexistential the long book was an act, a making, an outbreak, a
measured scream. He might have said: this book is written to kill, or, less
melodramatically: I keep a log. He might have called it *The Case of the
Proscribed Informations*, the long book, this further gambit in the boardless
chase-game wherein it was his misfortune to discover himself already at
play and with no knowledge of the relevant dimensions. But Pottle had
required a title at once, and Joe, after all, had Ag to think of. She required
her scents and her greasepaints. And her golden nipple-cups he found
charming, as well as her delicately wrought bellybutton-stud. The long
book it was therefore, or would be.

'Now it is a game I am going to play,' Necchi might have quoted, if he
had known the rules . . . but I should have been lying, perhaps smiling
one of my finer false faces. Was it in fact or fiction that I creased her
massive centrale, moving my carcassone down through her pziroknees[4]
into her softs' pain? The distinction has grown confused over a quarter
of a century. The problem of truth and falsity I bequeath to those who
come after me along with my second sharpest hypodermic needle. Meanwhile, I should like a man to be alone when he reads this document: he
should imagine an oval of glazed, cream-coloured enamel chipped black
at one edge by unknown vandals, its surface anastomosed by cracks and
written on in the usual urinal brown, a little plaque screwed to the door
in front of him where he sits in the cubicle of a public toilet where he has
no one to turn to nor caper for. Then he will not use me as a foil, at least
until he has read what I have written (the which he could be grateful for,
having no other reading matter), or what he thinks I have written, or
what he thinks he thinks I have written, or . . . but in my universe

where no road leads to Rome, where every avenue becomes a road becomes a path becomes a track and eventually undisturbed sand, such regressions once implied may be taken for granted, although nothing else can.

(When they appeared it was as Romana[5] in the streets.) The man then, should be alone; each member of a jury can avoid my gaze and, at the subsequent conclave, evade the real encounter and insolently condemn me. As for my judge, let him come down from where he picks his nose behind his magisterial bench and expose his short hairs. All that symbolic paraphernalia of conventional power, lumber out of the past, is anachronism, stage scenery for old arguments. The cripple can't walk until he dispenses with his crutches. The man at crap is at my level, squatting more or less comfortably on his naked haunches, at serious purpose with himself and beyond equivocation in his need to rid himself of the accumulated poisons of the living process.

> The slack white body
> of yr dead Aunt Peg
> had a pink confection
> for a face, the day
> they buried her.
> — Gone in her prime,
> like yr gin and lime!
> Candy kisses . . .
> Meet a dark stranger!

As for those dicte of koanst[6] any immodesty is in the reverberations of the mind which contemplates them. What kind of hocus-pocus ever led men to think otherwise? Ponder these things before you speak of improper suggestions and complain to the attendant of a flagrant obscenity in Cubicle Zed.

'When you speak of the "cannabis problem",' Peter went on, placing the wee green-black turd of some of the finest hashish of Asia Minor on the delicate curve of Ag's creamsweet abdomen, 'I take it you mean that of assuring the supply of fine-quality goods, of improving the yield and quality of the hemp plant in both hemispheres, of evolving efficient grading methods, and so on? Did I tell you that this piece came all the way from the secret cellar of Ghengis Khan?' And his forehead fell forward and down until it pressed against the nut of hashish and the lozenge of his lips closed like a cockle to the cream.

'Eat me!' said the Hon. Ag with a laughing husky groan, and she raised one sleek thigh like the neck of a white mare in the gold of the late morning sunlight. Her hand stroked his tangled hair.

From a narrow slit in the masonry at the other side of tile court the lens of a powerful telescope protruded. In the high heat of the midday sun Finck, German agent of the yellow peril (alias Dr Yu No Fok), was still at work. His employer was not interested in the prevailing meteorological conditions in northwest Africa. If the sexistential had been at the north pole, Finck would have been expected to be there, 'tapping' him . . . follow that iceberg!

For it had long been suspected by the repressive elements of various governments in the world that the man who was known as the sexistential was engaged in activities which amounted to sedition on a global scale, but most deviously and with great subtlety, since up till now, and in spite of the energies of divers public prosecutors, he had been seen to commit no actual felony, not once in all his travels which, in themselves, were highly suspicious in the opinion of upright men; for they served no obvious purpose. Had Finck not already produced as evidence a certain scrap of paper retrieved from Necchi's wastepaper basket on which the following had been noted? – 'New York, 1960. The hero as junkie, confounder of conformities, sinker of moral ducks, alone with his twilight detergent, in his original posture, in his every shuddering act, he resists his times. With the bad fiction of international politics he wipes his pile-encrusted arse. Can't buy vaseline these days without a prescription. (Was that true?). Where would the Empire City be without its pariahs, the blue geek with his sliding walk, slobbering the poetry of his liver-loose lips at the sanitation squad sent to dispose of him?

'Where he lay on a stoop, a hoarfrost of his peculiar perspiration, snailglint, and five cigarette stubs left over from a previous work of fiction – lying extinguished in their own long ash. It got dark a short while ago a long while ago and the fog and the night wrapped themselves up in each other until suddenly under the pale yellow cone of light from the lamp post, transparent parvenu amongst my sensations, is myself.'

* * *

The man (and here Finck placed a questionmark in parenthesis) was elated all the time. It was unnatural. You would call him a failure . . . a man who idled away his time, more often than not under the influence of some drug or other, many of them obtained, Finck was ready to swear, from some underworld acquaintance, a certain West Indian most probably, yes, the man sat or sprawled all day, fiddling with a tape-recorder and composing articles which were often obscene and perhaps subversive. How, with his life based on such foul delights, did the fellow contrive to appear elated all the time? The man, too, showed no regard whatsoever for money, was up to his neck in debt, and unemployed so long as to be unemployable. And yet this Uranus seemed to prosper. . . something was wrong somewhere, that was to say, not right . . . and Finck hinted at some dark purpose as yet unrevealed. It was his (Finck's) business to penetrate that purpose and to expose it in such a way that the more liberal elements would be forced to side in this matter with the ultra-conservatives, whose secret agent the yellow peril was. And so the telepscope[7] tilted downwards now to take in the yard into which an Arab was now leading a camel. '*Gott in Himmel!*' breathed the intrepid agent as the telescope came to focus on the face of the man who walked there below in the yard. 'It is Dahou himself!' Finck dashed down the stone stairs three at a time to the cellar where his secret radio transmitter was cunningly installed.

'It is over ten years now since Midhou left me in Athens,' Sir Victor said to the Hon. Ag. The lovely lady was in the process of affixing the ruby stud to the whorl of flesh at her navel.

'Must you dress, Darling?' said the sexistential when he noticed. He noticed too that her posture was most alluring and simultaneously felt his centre of gravity shift downwards like an invisible sea towards his crotch. The smoky blue runt was a strange flower in the white grotto of her groin.

Joseph Necchi had begun to experiment with visual objects in a serious way in the middle Fifties, first in Paris and then later when he was living in California near the Mojave Desert. Of course, he had always been concerned with visual experience, though, until now, his reputation had rested mainly on the excellence of his prose. And even during his editorship of *Mainliner* (the Anglo-American literary quarterly published in Paris in the early Fifties), he was already constructing his habitat about him.

He had owned a tiny cubelike room in Montparnesse, two minutes away from the Dome where latterly he had come to make most of his mysterious 'connections': a studio, monk's cell, and buckpad, where at any hour he might quiet the ferocious wild beast in his loins, a holy place in short, the bed-centrepiece of which was an altar. 'I'm a real holy bucker already,' he said once in the Bronx. His bookcases were a multi-coloured structure of variable planes built to allow him to read efficiently when horizontal (a frequent posture for an inveterate smoker of hashish and opium). An important prop this, it resembled in some respects the portable pulpit with which Necchi sometimes confounded the Enemy on the night streets of Manhattan. Mounted on it, with paints, brushes, and various masterly 'futiques' in front of him, he considered himself, and usually was, improbable enough to offset and outflank all the facts of New York City. Of course it could only be a temporary measure, and in the end he had fled out of that land, wisely, and in the nick of time. The facts, he knew, were breathing down his neck.

He had returned via Montreal, the Newfoundland icebanks, round the northern tip of Scotland one early translucent dawn, to the ancient granite city of Aberdeen, and thence by way of Glasgow (city of his 'birth') to London, a thin grey figure, lamppost or ghost, the idea of the coup-de-monde close under eyelids, an electronic load, an unwritten book, a plan in four dimensions, a shadow one, taking as given that complex of informations called London 196– as raw material for his engraver's tool, and calling at list, finally, for poet's rule.

'Weenie, weedy, weakie,' said William the Conqueror as he stepped ashore at Aberdeen. He had half-expected an escort on arrival . . . a small black car perhaps (in contrast to the bleaming[8] white spaceships of Las Vegas), with two tall fellows in plain clothes.

'Niatzschie?' one of them would say.

Discovered!

'Nothing concealed abt yr parson? In a hollow tooth? Behind yr foreskin? Up the old bungho?'

Smelling the seat of a bully's body, the sexistential decided to turn off, and, availing himself of the martian technique of elision, he dematerialised and regrouped his faculties alone in a context with no men and only his own deceit to confront, in his own bottle, airy or earthy, as it happened.

*   *   *

The book Xerxes was flipping through was in French . . . a book which around 1948 had made a lasting impression upon him. Translating as he went: 'You're a coward,' I said. 'You're a motherbucker. The fuzz is still too good to you. One of these days you'll really be licking their boots. Maybe they'll go visit you where you're baged and shove their pricks up yr arse.' Said to Stiletana or Michaelis? Anyway, 'all old and evil presence from an old and evil cave,' as his friend, the dean put it. And that led, naturally, to his thinking abt the dean. And he remembered saying to him: 'Cut up or boil down, it doesn't seem to matter what technique so long as it doesn't become an institution.' The dean agreed with him. Wherever he went Yehudi found individuals whose posture was, at times anyway, metacetegarical[9] as his own. There was the ground of his tentative optimism. He was not the only man who knew he was alone.

The barbecue was executed at noon precisely on that day in a secret chamber somewhere in the bowels of the Institute. It was supervised by Dr Hare Q. Kildare, prominent medical telecaster who headed the disciplinary board at the Institute and who, at a recent general meeting of the A.M.A. was highly commended for a speech entitled: 'The Health of the Citizen under Free Enterprise', in which he stressed the importance in a democratic society of a man's paying his own medical bills, issued a warning against foreign bodies of all kinds, at the same time calling for a strict international ban on narcotics as a muse for civilisation as we know it. In their various official and unofficial capacities, the following lords, ladies, and gentlemen were present: the Reverend Filing Delinquent of Lisreggub,[10] Prof. Horat Nesel,[11] Obersturmfuhrer Doktor Mengele of Auschwitz Sanitorium, Lord Jeremy Stoppit, Mrs Remember Gomorrha, and the elegant Countess Dracula, sophisticated spouse of the Enemanian Ambassador, which lady herself is recognised as a noted student of moral science, and who studied under the late Commissioner Manslayer.

The jolt or brainbouncer was what is considered average in this kind of case, Rev. Filing Delinquent informed his colleagues, slightly more than is ordinarily employed in current European practice, considerably less than that recommended in Ambassador Dracula's country.

'Enough,' concluded our distinguished cleric, 'to dissolve neutral tissue without causing body-odour.'

At the third jolt the patient's body was seen to shudder like a tall jelly within the leather harness, and a wisp of blue smoke issued from red nostrils, a reaction generally regarded as a symptom of what, in techni-cal nomenclature, is called 'reintegration'. The patient reintegrated slowly, the shuddering subsided gradually over a period of two and a half hours, after which he was returned to the deep freeze as a precaution against pong.

It was the practice, Dr Kildare pointed out to those present, to wait three days before attempting to estimate the results of the operation, since further changes not unlike those of terrestrial subsidence (earthquakes, volcanic eruptions, etc.) were often met with during a period of up to forty-eight hours after the barbecue. The patient's eyeballs, which had been driven out of their sockets by the electric brainbouncer, had a vaguely cooked look which, explained the eminent telecaster, could have sinister implications, and this naturally made him reluctant to predict success or failure at the present time.

Mrs Remember Gomorrha spoke afterwards, calling for the stimula-tion of public interest in the various modes of electrocution. 'This poor fellow,' she declared, referring to the electrocuted catatonic, 'is now no longer a menace to himself or to others.' She concluded her remarks by insisting upon the urgent need for the immediate segregation of that por-tion of the population which was infected. In this she was eagerly sec-onded by Obersturmfuhrer Doktor Mengele who offered to place his sanatorium at the disposal of the committee. His engineers, he averred, were already studying the possibility of chain treatment.

Dr Hare (Bunny to his friends) Q. Kildare returned to his study with the other members of the committee, and when they were all provided with some fine dry sherry which he kept for such occasions, he began 'Trouble was, though I'm reluctant to say it, the man failed to distinguish between two kinds of perspiration, the physical kind and the mental kind. Science shows that in the glands of the mature male and the glands of the mature female perspiration caused by anxiety emits an offensive odour. For two thousand years man has sought to avert this embarrassment. Poor Cleopatra had to spend twelve hours a day in milk baths and having ex-pensive oils and elixirs rubbed into her skin, particularly during political crises, and all to avoid what nowadays we call . . . I am sure the ladies present will excuse me! . . . bee-oh! Yes, body odour; like the poor, it has always been with us . . . ha! Nevertheless (the forefinger of Kildare's right hand pointed triumphantly up), with our modern techniques, in this instance, electric-shock therapy, we have devised a way to abolish all thought, and thus, Ladies and Gentlemen, all anxiety and the resultant offensive odours ...'

Polite exclamations, applause and a smattering of handclapping, interrupted all of a sudden by the ringing telephone.

Reluctantly, our eminent physician surrendered his captive and, with a gesture of impatience, lifted the pastel-pink receiver.

'Yu No Fok here!' a voice came urgently from the other end of the line. 'For Kildare the yellow peril immediately here speaks now, please!'

'This is Kildare, Dr Fok. Is there some trouble, Sir?' he cupped his hand over the receiver and flashed a glance at his guests. 'Fok,' he said quietly to the unvoiced question on their various faces, 'Central Security ...'

His guests turned away discreetly to converse amongst themselves. Mengele addressed the Rev. Filing Delinquent: 'As I was saying earlier, Delinquent, fortunately I was able to expose that fool who accused me in short order. "Lies," I said. "All lies! You say we National Socialists made soap from murdered Jews. That is a patent falsehood. Fat is required to make soap and concentration camp victims were too thin for that!" Ha! You should have seen his face! I thought the lying swine was going to have a coronary!'

'Ha!' said the pigs, and 'Ho,' and 'Ha, ha! Hee, hee, hee! ...'

'Trouble?' said the voice on the telephone, 'Yourself be judge, my friend. I haf reported to me by one of my best agents of a certain Mohammed Dahou. Thees man is arriving an hour ago in Tangiers ... on one camel!'

'Good God!' Kildare exclaimed, and then, recovering his composure under the startled glances of his guests, he said in a firm voice: 'If this information is correct, we must inform General Apathy!'

The reunion of Mohammed Dahou and Zorro (alias Joseph Necchi alias the sexistential) took place towards the beginning of the end of the beginning (so to speak) in the Tangiers residence of the Honourable Agatha Hardon, runaway heiress, step-daughter of Mrs Remember Gomorrha, and niece of General Paralysis, esteemed colleague of Apathy K.B.E., of whom, each and every one of them, we shall hear more anon.

JOHN CALDER

In publishing terms Trocchi's estate seems more chaotic than most. Why is that?

Trocchi always lived very much from day to day. He lived in Paris, to a certain extent, by writing pornographic books for Olympia Press and became very friendly with Maurice Girodias, who ran Olympia. They were rather similar personalities, both free living, free spending, great womanisers, liked good food, good drink and so on, they'd have lunch together all the time. Trocchi was very fast. He could turn out a two-hundred-page novel over a weekend and hand it over and be given money for it, but there was never any contract. Girodias had no idea that a book would last beyond one or two editions, and Trocchi wasn't thinking that way either, you know, he would just write another book and get more money and Girodias would just hand him whatever he happened to have in his pockets when Trocchi needed money, providing, of course, you know, that sales were going reasonably well. Now, all of these came out later on in pirated editions from which Trocchi received no benefit whatsoever. There are only two of his novels really that are in normal copyright.

English language publishing is much messier than publishing in other languages and other countries. First of all, America in particular has a great many small publishers who start off one day, last for a few months, and then disappear. They will pick up a book that they have found some-where else, or buy a manuscript, usually not even pay the advance, never pay any royalties, and if things go badly, well they simply disappear from sight and start up again under another name. Trocchi was a victim of all that. Nobody knows how many hundreds of thousands of books were sold in unauthorised editions. Besides, in the States it was assumed that anything pornographic you could get away with, you would never have to deal with the author.

He was always very hopeful that films were going to be made of some of his books, that the big deal was going to happen. Film producers, some of them very fly-by-night, would come and see him all the time with big, big promises – it never did happen. Everything disappeared. *Young Adam* is being filmed this year.[1] It's the first time that anything of Trocchi's has actually been filmed.

How much are you able to say about the pirating of Young Adam?

Young Adam came out in two versions. He wrote it as a serious novel, he was looking for a publisher for it, then Olympia Press asked if they could do it but they would like him to add a little bit more sex and spice, which he did.

Young Adam has been pirated many times and Trocchi lost a great deal of money. Nobody knows how much. I would say at a guess probably three, four hundred thousand copies of *Young Adam* and also of some of his other books have been turned out by small presses in America, paying no royalties and without contract and it's a great pity but the cost of trying to establish copyright and trying to claim for companies that very often don't exist anymore, would be too astronomical for anything to be done. Unfortunately, you know, Trocchi's life work yielded him very little money and is not going to yield, in my opinion, very much to his heirs.

Then *Young Adam* was published first of all by Heinemann in Britain, had various not terribly successful editions, until we finally added it to our list. It is a good book because it's a book that anticipates the French new novel. It's a book that is outside conventional fictional morality in that the hero is also the villain who gets away with it, but you are never quite sure to what extent things are happening in the mind and to what extent things are happening in reality. It's a book he believed in himself and I think it's a better example of what would have become of the writer had he been able to continue. *Cain's Book* is a much more famous book and was a bestseller, but it's a book put together much more by accident. It is a straightforward account of his experiences on a barge on the Hudson River in New York where he was simply a caretaker for the barge, you know, stopping it being stolen. Which gave him the time to write, the time to read, the time to think, always very much under the influence of heroin. Ultimately, probably *Young Adam* is going to be the book that will last longest, although *Cain's Book* has much more sensational material in it and also was the centre of a trial in Sheffield in 1964, which brought something new into British Law – that the description of drug-taking can constitute obscenity under the Obscene Publications Act.[2] It's a very dangerous precedent and has been used in other cases since.

When he wrote pornography, you know, he wrote it very well. He wrote with style, he created real people, he created backgrounds. His best writing about Glasgow, in fact, comes in books like *Helen and Desire*, where he describes the old Thirties scene when the Gorbals was ruled by razor kings and life was dangerous but very exciting. Now Trocchi, growing up in Hillhead, would not have had any personal experience of what was going on in the Gorbals, but of course it was part of the folklore of the day and certainly would have been appearing in the newspapers the whole time.[3] He was able to make use of that and he documented second hand a great deal of the old pre-war Glasgow life and that, I think, has a sociological as well as a literary value.

So if that sums up Trocchi's career as a writer, if that was behind him at the time of the Edinburgh Conference, how did he occupy himself thereafter?
Trocchi had a great deal of genius in him, you know, he was very quick, very talented and he had a very much all-round talent. He wasn't wrong when he thought he could do anything he wanted to do, until the heroin took over. But aside from that he was very much a rogue and when you got to know him you realised that he could never really be trusted. He was so incredibly convincing, you know, so sincere the whole time that everybody naturally believed him, but he was a conman, a complex character who underneath it all really believed that he was there to help save the world.

One of the ways in which he was going to save the world was through an organisation that was never defined, called sigma. Sigma was simply going to be a general movement of goodwill and peace that was going to move through all nations, that all people who were of goodwill would get together. Sigma was, in my opinion, simply a way of wasting time and making himself interesting. He loved to be surrounded by admirers. He would collect around himself people who were ambitious to get in to the literary life one way or another, students. His last serious book was *Cain's Book*. After that he never really was able to do anything that required a sustained effort.

He had an idea for a book which was never defined, to be called *The Long Book*. I don't think it was a joke, *The Long Book*. It might have been. We signed a contract for it. He signed contracts with many other publishers in London, without us knowing about each other, simply to be able to get the advances. He would do odd jobs like translations. He did many for us. We had to pay him by the page because after he'd been paid he would never sit down and do anything. *The Long Book*, I'm sure, never got beyond one or two paragraphs, or even went that far. I think he intended to write it; at the funeral of his wife he said, now that Lyn is dead I really must get on with *The Long Book*, I promise you it will be finished within six months, but by the next day of course it was out of his mind again. There is simply a lost writer there, lost because of heroin. I've known many drug addicts, I've known nobody who was able to cope with it as well as Trocchi, but it killed his talent. He's the biggest example I know for not getting in any way involved with drugs.

What claims would you make for Trocchi as a writer?

As a writer he had a good background knowledge of literature generally. He studied English literature, philosophy, he had an international knowledge of literature. He knew the difference between different styles, he could imitate almost anybody's style. He perhaps came closest to his own style in *Cain's Book* where he was really writing a kind of diary. In a way he was a man of many masks who never really discovered who the real Alexander Trocchi was, you know, who was the man behind all these different facades, all these different ambitions. It's a great pity that talent was never realised because it was a major one and I think almost everybody who knew and who met him realised there was a great promise there. The promise unfortunately was never fulfilled.

How did you feel about The Long Book?

I never worried very much about how much money one was making or losing with Trocchi. My relationship with him was a friendly one. I knew he was a rogue, I knew he was not to be trusted. I signed a contract for *The Long Book*, I paid him a first advance of £250, he would have had more on delivery and more on publication, but I had no great expectation I would ever see it. I knew the depths of his heroin addiction, I knew the difficulty of actually sitting down to write anything. There was a hope that something might develop. He could be convincing, he could even convince me at times that something was really happening, that he was working on it, but that money was of course lost and I was in no way particularly surprised. I had never had any great expectation of Alex that anything would ever really develop, other than what I'd published. His poetry I'd published, but I had to go and almost break in to his flat and go through his drawers and find all the poems that he'd promised me and edit them myself and put them into order and then publish them. He was quite happy when I did it but could never actually find the time to get them out because he just couldn't be bothered looking through them again and editing them and improving them and so on. I did that for him.

I was able to get things out of him by always taking the necessary precautions, especially on the translations that he did for me where I only paid him, you know, after delivery. I helped him in as many ways as I could. I even gave him a character reference when he was involved in a possible burglary at the Savoy Hotel on one occasion. I gave him a testimonial that he could not possibly have been involved in this, he was a distinguished writer and so on, but who knows? Trocchi was capable of almost anything that he felt he would get away with that would make him some money. And he would do things just for the sheer devilry of it, you know, for the excitement of being an outsider, of being on the fringes of criminality. He certainly knew a great many very dubious characters and he could get excited by any kind of new experience. I would not have put too much past him. In spite of which, I liked him, I enjoyed his company, we were always good friends when we were together. Strange, complex, dubious, talented man, died too young. But to have lived into his sixties after nearly forty years as a junkie was still not too bad.

One shouldn't concentrate too much on the black side of his character. I mean he was, when he could be, generous. Very helpful to other people, particularly if they were people who were around him. He wanted to be the big man. He wanted to be helpful and he genuinely was helpful, could be very imaginative in helping other people. Some of the people he helped might not really have deserved it but, you know, that's incidental. Underneath it all he had a certain personal morality that I think was genuine. He was not a bad person. He took advantage of people who really could afford to be taken advantage of and who, from his point of view, rather invited it . . .

£ S D

(love, sex, death

pounds, shillings, pence

lysergic acid)

Alex Trocchi

Iron leaves glint,
where wind broke in,
red rot in rain:
my death is lead,
cloven by slow,
radium-sharp shark-fin.

In my soft tree-bole
bleeds pearl,
spreads spoor
of wee, unhungering,
ceaseless vole.

An end to blue and green
and tune;
no more delight
in the black cave
of yr feminine night:

the poor silt of my years
is thin to spread . . .
after I am dead, 'Margarine,'
it will be said,
'he mistook it for butter.'

An end to the sun,
moon, sky,
no young girl now will lie
in hot halter of a pregnancy.

... young witches,
old bitches,
silvered resilience
of stagelit thighs,
hot, husky cries,
mascaraed eyes,
all manner of highs,
excruciatingly artificial.

Few virtues,
threadbare ascription ...
clues: blues
  cruise
  unpaid dues;
... dropped Plato
like a hot potato;
wouldn't work:
hashish of the Turk ...

There was a door between
him and himself.
Out, like the biff-ball
from the bat,
the limit taut,
feet sunk in cement,
tripped over himself,
a closing hinge:
himself something
upon which he couldn't impinge.

LETTER TO MAURICE

Alex Trocchi

Dear Maurice,

I wonder if you *can* imagine how it has taken me so long to get round to writing this letter to you? From one point of view, and in some contexts, you would undoubtedly insist that anyway it was up to my agent to concern himself with these matters . . . 'I would much rather deal with an agent!' Indeedy, indeedy, amen. No doubt you would prefer me to be represented by a custodian. But, eventually, unless the agent really understands what he's about, the situation would become absurd. In all my life, I feel I have never been so ineffectually represented. Like, before we allow ourselves to become involved in some new agreement, what about the one we signed a while ago? You [your associate] published *Helen and Desire* nearly a year ago now. While, a few months ago, you could fall back on the legalities bit about not actually being bound to pay anything 'yet', royalty returns for the first period in respect of *Helen and Desire* became due on the 30th of June. And, man, that was straining it to the point of unfriendliness. However, I have sufficient imagination to understand how you got yourself into that situation. From your point of view, you felt justified in being annoyed with me. But this is past. And we can't afford to be concerned with it. Now, the situation is this: on the one hand you appear to expect me, loyally and industriously, to go ahead and write more work on your assurance that you will treat me favourably and even generously. On the other hand, you appear to have reduced my agent to a state of floundering and bewildering incompetence so that he seems to have resigned from contesting anything and is beginning to be, figuratively speaking, as a elusive Pimpernel Girodias.[1] I have to remind young Victor that it is not my purpose to be a victim perpetually. Meanwhile, he is presently and most exasperatingly 'trapped' somewhere out in suburbia by the present railway strike. I might tell you how I am presently to go under the scalpel as I am now under a dangerously leaky roof and subsisting on a dangerously insubstantial overdraft, but really, that is all quite irrelevant and I am sick and tired of feeling constrained all the time to stoop to such tactics. Surely to God you are sensitive enough to understand how awkward it is for me [to] accept as fact something which

I, myself, together with two separate witnesses, know to be not quite so. . . . I am referring to what those of us heard as '65,000' and to what you insist was, on the contrary, 'sixty-five per cent'. As you know, on that point, I did not insist. I accepted the [considerably lower] estimate, and got nothing in return for my compromise. I hate to say, what I accepted as sixty-five per cent – not even that was paid. It could legally be shelved, and was so shelved until the six month royalty statement was due. But, *tempus fugit*, and here we are again. And by the crab-like scuttling of the aforesaid agent whenever, over the past four months, I have reminded him of the monies which should have become available with the June royalty returns, I am regretfully led to the familiar nasty suspicion that I am about to be witness to more side-stepping.

MICHAEL X

Alex Trocchi in conversation with
Allen Ginsberg and Peter Orlovsky

ALEXANDER TROCCHI: Do you remember Michael X?[1]

ALLEN GINSBERG: Yes.

AT: He's dead. You know that?

AG: I know. I was involved in trying to stop it out of New York but god, it didn't work out, so what was behind that?

AT: Oh well, I think I know. One of the things that was brought up in Michael's trial was this International Communist Conspiracy called sigma!

AG: Oh really!

AT: Yes.

AG: That's interesting.

AT: A conspiracy of drugs! To put drugs everywhere! But not only that. Did you know that Michael, when he went to Trinidad, his main point was to establish a university there. Ronnie Laing, Feliks Topolski, a whole load of us were going to go out there – John Lennon was in it too, you know, there was money – we were going to Trinidad and create an island where we could register ships, you know, whatever . . . but we wanted an international university which would be based in Trinidad . . . we had all the pop stars who were going to come too, you know, with the money and the kudos and that kind of thing . . . and Michael was the forerunner, he went out there, and he obviously became too big for his boots before the power got behind him, you know . . . Look, I don't know what happened. Michael wrote me letters.

I would have liked to save him. Do you know why he got into trouble the last time? My fault! Do you know a little boy called LeRoi? A member of the Living Theatre?

AG: Er, yeah. A black fellow?

AT: Yeah.

AG: Went to India later.

AT: Well all right. Now, LeRoi was living with me in London and he needed some bread and he did some cleaning, cleaning houses et cetera, through an agency, and the agency didn't pay him properly, or something like that, and he gave them his watch for an advance or something, right? And, well, the day that LeRoi comes back crying to me about this, about what had happened, Michael turns up. Now Michael's a bit of a motherfucker in his own way you know.

AG: Because he had a reputation for having worked for some housing man?

AT: Oh, but that was a long time back. . . . He used to come along when I was in trouble or something like that, and he'd put his fucking cheque book down and his gun, and he'd say, which do you need? — as though I need a fuckin' gun! But Michael was that way, you know. He was like . . . hot-headed. I didn't approve particularly, but whenever Michael was with me I was able to shut him up. Anyway, he came to me and I said to him, look, poor old LeRoi, they won't give him his pay, because he didn't want to work anymore, they won't give him the pay, and he had a whole bloody week's pay to come. So, of course, that's a wrong thing to say to Michael. Black boy is being bullied by white boys in this country. He walked down and he kidnapped the boss of that fucking firm! He took him down to the Black House — remember the Black House in London? — he put chains round his fuckin' neck, chains round his fuckin' wrists and he danced round him. The man was scared out of his fuckin' life, you know. I said, oh Michael, for Christ sake, you know this is ridiculous! But he says what do you want me to do? That's what they did to my fathers and my mothers. You know, I couldn't say, no, not true. On the other hand, Jesus, Michael really lit it for himself because this cat went to lawyers and Michael was immediately arrested and was to come up in court for kidnapping . . .

AG: Did he let the guy go?

AT: Yes of course he did. He was just trying to scare the pants off him.

AG: Did he collect the money?

AT: He didn't as a matter of fact.

AG: So, well, that's the reason not to do such things! You just get done on kidnapping charges and you don't get the money!

AT: Well, put it this way, I don't know whether he did or not in the end but at the office he didn't. And that's why he took the man, you understand?

AG: Yeah.

AT: He's a literary man, Michael. I mean, it wasn't serious. He wasn't going to kill the fucker, you understand?

AG: Yeah, but the guy didn't know that.

AT: The guy didn't know it. He might have had a heart attack. I mean I'm with it and I'm against it. But you know it was I who pointed out what was wrong with LeRoi when he arrived that day with three of his boys and I feel responsible.

But let me go back just a moment . . . Michael was a friend of John Michell's, a good friend, close friends, well, I said to Michael, Michael, I need money for sigma. He says, how much do you need? I said, a million pounds. He didn't have a million pounds. He said, you can have a hundred. I said okay, when? He said, I'll give you fifty pounds now, and fifty pounds next week. Nah, I mean it was sweet. John Michell, of course, could have afforded it, if he'd cared to write a cheque, but it was Michael who said it.

AG: Michael was getting . . . what year was that? '67?

AT: Oh Christ I can't quite remember . . .

AG: Because he was getting money from Panna O'Grady.

AT: Was he? Well he was getting money from a lot of people. Anyway, I took the fifty pounds and I bought two dozen red roses for the wife of a publisher here in London. Michael found out about it the next day and he said, what have you done with the money? And I said, well, I bought two dozen red roses for so and so. Now, I bought her two dozen red roses because I knew that, two dozen red roses for this lady, it would be a gesture – and I was working for sigma . . . He flipped his fuckin' lid! I gave all my hard-earned money and you spend it on two dozen fuckin' red roses for this bourgeois something something. But I wouldn't back down an inch. Because I knew what I was doing, you know. And eventually, he agreed, he understood what I was doing, saw it was worth it. As a matter of fact, I think I got a couple of thousand quid out of that! Oh dear, I wasn't trying to con anyone, or anything like that, but you know, like, you have to communicate with whom you can communicate, in order to bring the money into sigma, that's what it was. Okay, well, that is the kind of thing that Michael could understand, you see. This was something I always found with Michael. If I explained it to him, he could understand, you see. And, dammit, if I had been in Trinidad at that time, that other motherfucker would never have bullied him into whatever . . . I can't tell the whole story just now, you know, because it's too long . . .

AG: I don't understand what happened there though.

AT: I don't understand.

AG: The bodies were found on the lawn and he was blamed but he wasn't around or something like that and there were . . .

AT: It seems his cousin was . . . I'm not even sure that Michael was innocent but . . .

PO: Did you know Michael as well?

AT: Intimately, intimately. As a matter of fact, one year when I came back from Spain and Lyn was really pissed off with me, she left me . . . and I had taken her to live with Michael – because we had no money and I had nowhere else to go – and Michael had said, Alex, you and Lyn have nowhere to go? You come to me. But Lyn just flipped and left, so I stayed with Michael for three months . . . so I know his kids, you know, I know the man like I know a brother.

I know him so well, so intimately, and you know, I'm not an inconsiderable fellow. Michael never did anything that I told him not to – ever. That meant he was an intelligent guy, you know. I'm no idiot and I wouldn't let the man do things that would be stupid and get him into trouble.

PO: But why did he carry a gun with him?

AT: Well, Michael could afford to. He had to do it to persuade the other boys that he was one of them. Why did he not have Black Power to defend him? . . . Because he had too many white friends.

AG: Well, no, now wait a minute, it's a very complicated matter.

AT: Okay.

AG: The Black Nationalists, separatist movement, you understand, that says, don't work with whites, that was, secretly, the party line of the FBI.

AT: Well maybe it was.

AG: And I have the documents here to show you.

AT: All right, okay.

AG: It's very interesting.

AT: I'm sure it is.

AG: LeRoi Jones was also pushing that line from '65 on, and LeRoi later found out his tutor in that, his guru in that particular thing, was being supplied with money by the FBI, precisely for that purpose, to split black and white.

AT: I was absolutely horrified in the last period that I was in New York, I had four or five real good close spade friends, they loved me, you know, and I loved them, and I was close to them and I could really talk to them, but came a day, one day, when I went to talk to them, and there were two real stony-faced cats from Chicago or somewhere.

AG: Likely FBI agents in disguise bringing the new party line.

AT: And these cats said that you don't want to trust whitey, you know – and so you're called 'whitey' by your old friends! But the point is, that Michael never fell for that bullshit, and Michael never had any of the black activists to go on his side, he didn't have a halfpenny worth of help from them when he met his doom, the only people who were going to help him were his white friends.

AG: Look at this. These are FBI files under the Official Secrets Act or . . . two from Detroit . . . Counter-Intelligence Program . . . Black Panther Party . . . SDS . . . this is 1969.

AT: Jesus Christ . . . where did you get this?

AG: I have a lot of stuff like that.

AT: Where? Where did it come from?

AG: Under an American law called the Freedom of Information Act, you can get your own files, as much as they'll give you, and, short of murder, they're giving most of them out now, and this was from Jane Fonda's file, because she got a copy of a letter that was . . . no this was LeRoi Jones' file . . . let me see . . .

AT: Doesn't matter.

AG: Oh, Ann Arbor.

AT: Allen, you're convinced that this is valid? Solid?

AG: Oh sure . . . I have my own files here . . . it's real . . . a Xerox of . . .

AT: You know, I'm sorry, but I've got to be a little bit . . . you know, if I read something like this, it's shocking, isn't it?

AG: Read that and I'll tell you the context.

AT: Oh Christ . . . well . . . Leary had a whole bit, you know, with them in Algeria.

AG: And the FBI was responsible . . . but you read this and then I'll get on to the others.

AT: Jesus Christ, it's so down-to-earth, so cool.

AG: Do you remember John Sinclair, the White Panther Party?

AT: Sounds familiar, but I can't remember.

AG: Sinclair founded the White Panther Party in sympathy with the Black Panthers, because Sinclair was a poet, friend of Charles Olson . . .

AT: God it reads like Bill Burroughs doesn't it!

SALLY CHILD

When you met . . .

. . . I was there for a week's trial. I was introduced to Alex by Penny, who'd married Robert Creeley. Alex needed an au pair because his au pair had gone back to Italy. I had just arrived in England and didn't have any work. When I met Robert and Penny they said, Alex is the salt of the earth, a writer and a really wonderful person and he needs someone to help. We met in a pub and we agreed that I'd come on a week's trial on both sides to see how things worked out. So, it was three days into that, that Mark died and so I stayed.

What was Mark's diagnosis?

I'm not entirely sure, but he died of, I think it was probably leukaemia or cancer of the bone marrow. He was very, very thin when he died. He went through this horrible treatment and was in incredible pain. The whole thing was gruesome beyond belief.

Did Trocchi ever speak to you about why he was unwilling to write?

The only thing I can remember him specifically saying about not writing was that after the death of Mark, what was there to say?[1] And, that's all he said, basically. But I think the death of his son was too much. I think that because for Alex writing was so personal that ultimately to go back inside himself and deal with the death of Mark was just not fair. And I think it frightened – I don't know if frightened is the right word – it was like, when these things happen, what's the point of saying anything? That was the impression I got. He did want to write about Julius Caesar, something historical, interestingly enough. He read a lot of books constantly around the subject and wrote various things. But I don't think he ever wanted to write about the present ever again, because of the death of Mark. He was very close to Mark; they had a very close relationship at the end. Mark was eighteen when he died. They used to talk a lot about literature and history and writing. They had a lot in common. He never felt he understood Nick, which was very sad, but Nick was very young when all that happened. Mark took about four years to die and the last eighteen months Alex was basically his nurse and was really caring for him and they got incredibly close. There are some extremely moving notes that Alex has written about Mark and things that Mark said, that are in the notebooks. What do you say about the death of a child?

This seems to demonstrate a completely different side to Trocchi . . .

Alex was extremely loving and caring. He was extremely good at looking after people, I mean really looking after them. Mark was at home with Alex right up until the week that I actually met Alex, when I actually moved in, and he had to be taken to hospital. It's very sad that, because I was there Alex had not gone to the hospital one particular visiting hour, and that was the time he died. I can still remember Alex just howling like a wounded animal, absolutely beside himself with grief.

How did Trocchi change after that, after he'd met you?

Alex literally sat in front of the television and drank advocaat. Although he never got drunk. He was either watching television or reading a book. He was just very gentle. He was a recluse basically. He didn't really say anything much to me and then gradually, I suppose, because of circumstances, because of Nick . . . We went away on a book-buying trip to Scotland and the car broke down and we got stranded. The only hotel we could find had only one double bed, and we had to put Nick in the middle. I mean, I hardly knew Alex at this point, it was all very strange. I suppose, gradually . . . it was my fault; I fell in love with him, it was all my doing. It wasn't his idea at all, to start with.

Trocchi as an antiquarian bookseller is a curious thought.

That's what he was, basically, when I met him. Most people that he had dealings with were other antiquarian booksellers. They didn't know who he was, they certainly didn't know he was a heroin addict. He loved books, he loved going to auctions. He hated having to sell them. That's what he did. Which is also why he didn't write; he had a couple of businesses to run.[2]

I think Alex was quite proud of the fact that he used to be employed by a Harley Street doctor to take blood from patients that nobody else could get blood from – of course, he was an expert with a needle. He used to look at my arms and say what lovely veins you've got. The other way he used to make money was to rewrite his manuscripts in longhand and sell them as the original to various buyers who collected such things . . .

Typical Alex lived in the moment. I mean when he had money he spent it. He didn't save it, he didn't, sort of, think ahead. He lived well when he could. He really liked nice food and cheeses and things like that. Typical Alex was all just a bit chaotic. It was just not very organised, hard to explain really.

He was perfectly capable of being extremely irritated with things, not so much people but things, and you could often hear the voice yelling bastard, bastard, and you'd come running round and find that there was some bit of equipment that wasn't working. Particularly a dictaphone that he'd bought. He thought he was going to give up actually writing by hand and he would just speak into this machine and then the slaves would transcribe it, but he couldn't get it to work. I found that he just had the volume turned down and he thought I was a genius. But then he used to complain about this wretched woman he lived with who wouldn't even run him a bath, and when she did she scalded him. And that was me of course.

Did he ever speak about his background?
He spoke about his mother. He loved his mother, that's probably why he loved women so much, and he used to stroke her hair when he was a little boy and he used to stroke my hair, which was one of the things he used to try and persuade Nick to do as well but Nick was having none of it.

Some men love women and they're quite unique. I don't think there's that many of them and Alex was definitely one of them and whether that came from his relationship with his mother I don't know, but he definitely was one of those men that loved women.

His father, I think he always felt a bit guilty about the way he betrayed his father in *Cain's Book*. I think he thought it was perhaps just a little harder than it needed to be. I think he thought maybe he'd hurt his father.

How did he feel he'd betrayed his father in Cain's Book?

I don't think he thought he'd betrayed him but I think when things go on record they're not the whole truth. I think when he was looking back I think he felt perhaps more sympathy for his father than perhaps you would expect from reading *Cain's Book*.

Can you give us an idea of how the usual day with Trocchi would have been?

Daily life with Alex? Well it started with him leaping into his Mini and dashing off to the chemist to pick up his prescription and at the same time he'd pick up fish for the cats. We used to cook for both the cats – well, Alex used to cook it because I couldn't. And so the whole place used to stink of fish and then he would have a fix, basically, and then he would get on with his life which was either going down to the bookstall, sorting things out, or going to the pub, or going to buy books or whatever.

He took a lot of heroin. He took five times as much as normal people would need and he had special methadone made up to get him through the night. He couldn't even last a night without methadone. But it was a bit like living with a diabetic, I mean it didn't really affect him other than, you know, he needed to take it regularly.

Did Trocchi ever talk to you about why he took drugs?

I don't think he really wanted to take them as much as he did. He would have liked to have the option but he didn't have the option. Because if he came off being a registered addict, then he was sunk.

There was no way he would ever give up taking heroin completely but at times it was inconvenient to take it. He would have quite happily... he would have preferred to smoke a pipe of opium, basically. He told me once, because I was curious, that he took drugs, particularly heroin, because they made him feel inviolable. He was a very sensitive person and I think, you know, he needed some sort of protection. But Alex on heroin was, I mean, most people didn't know he was on heroin. Most people who came in contact with him just thought he was a book dealer and they had no idea. I think he drank too much. I think if there was a drug problem it was alcohol and certainly not the heroin – but it also had become, I suppose, part of his being.

He was curious. He wanted to experience everything. I mean drugs, whatever, anything. He didn't see any limits.

What happened to the writing?

He was terrified of writing. We rearranged the house so that he could have a study, but it meant that he just had more space to make more chaos really. He said that after the death of Mark, what was there to say. Terrifying.

When you embarked on your relationship Trocchi gave you a copy of Thongs. *How did you react?*

When I met Alex I didn't . . . I'd never read any of his work. I met him just as a person and he gave me *Thongs* to read and I was completely horrified because I'd been making love to this man who'd written this book and I can remember saying to him, you know, my God, Alex, where did this stuff come from and he said oh, just off the top of my head. I kept thinking my God, if that's at the top, what's at the bottom, but he just treated it very lightly. It wasn't serious to him. It was just fun, experimenting.

There are some people who think Alex was evil. There are people who have even said to *me* that they thought he was evil, which I find just totally incomprehensible. I can only suspect that they had bad intentions towards him. He was wicked in certain ways. He was very cheeky in certain ways but I only ever knew incredible kindness and humanity. I just can't see the rest. But I met him at a particular time in his life and I don't doubt that there were times when he was less than perfect, in terms of perhaps . . . I don't know. Everybody that I knew who met him, I mean all my family and friends were completely charmed by him and just had incredibly warm feelings towards him and even when he was in hospital, I mean, the nurses all adored him and all just thought he was charming.

What about Lyn's prostitution? How did you feel when you heard about that?

I think the thing about Alex which you have to remember is that he . . . he didn't have one law for himself and another for other people. I'm sure if he could have got money by prostituting his body he would have done it, but obviously it was probably more convenient the other way round. I think the story is a bit sensational. I think when you're really up against it – and they were really up against it – those things are just necessary. They're neither particularly good or bad, they're just what you have to do in the circumstances and I don't think Alex thought that sex was that important in that way, you know, that there was a deeper loyalty and love that wasn't really touched by those sort of activities. I know that's true in our relationship and I'm sure it was probably true with Lyn.

Did Trocchi ever seem bitter about things?

He did sort of see himself as a mixture of Julius Caesar and Jesus Christ. Maybe that was his way of dealing with the fact that things hadn't really gone as well for him as for some other people who perhaps weren't as talented and who perhaps didn't really deserve it as much as I think he did. But then I think it was a choice he made and perhaps he couldn't make any other. I mean that was the sort of person he was. He wasn't manipulative in the sense of furthering his career. You know, he was more interested in . . . sort of other investigations, other experiences.

There's a couple of Alexes. I mean, Alex was obviously a very complicated person. There was a side of him which knew he was a good writer. There was no question about that; if not a great writer, if not the greatest writer. There's also a side of him which found the whole thing extremely difficult and he had lots and lots of doubts. I think on the whole, I think he knew his own talent. I don't think . . . He used to jump up and down and say that I didn't know who he was. That I should have more respect.

I think he felt cheated, not because he was particularly not known but because he hadn't been paid what was due to him. He was very bitter about that, extremely bitter – and probably getting more bitter in his old age about that sort of injustice and, I think, rightly so. He used to say that because people regarded him as a junkie they didn't feel that they had to pay him. They just thought, well just don't bother paying, he'll be dead in a month or so. He battled with this his entire life, I think. It was extremely unfair the way he was treated. He was bitter about it, no question.

You see Trocchi as a man who was willing to help others . . .

Alex's attitude to people who had problems . . . he had an expression of poor wee people, which wasn't patronising at all. It was just quite matter of fact. He often thought they were . . . they just needed help. Alex always felt that he could help them and quite often he was right. A lot of quite confused, lost people ended up at our door and Alex would do his best to talk to them and encourage them to be creative and give them confidence and people would always say things like they felt better after being with Alex, they felt more hopeful, you just felt better after being with him and I can't really . . . understand quite why except you've got an extremely generous and intelligent man giving you attention, and giving you serious attention, and perhaps some of these people had never been given serious attention before and it was. . . sometimes I think it was his way of distracting himself. I think the idea that these people needed help was an excuse for him not to get down to other things like writing but, I mean, he just wouldn't turn someone down.

He was always trying to help people. Even when people sort of turned round and kicked him in the teeth. There's a very good example of a man who worked for him and was totally dishonest and had ordered books under Alex's name and hadn't paid for them and Alex had got in to all sorts of problems with bookdealers and Alex just kept helping him out. To the extent that, you know, when he stopped giving him money, he was giving him cheese sandwiches.

I COULD HAVE TOLD IT MUCH BETTER I'M SURE

Alex Trocchi in conversation with Allen Ginsberg and Peter Orlovsky

8TH NOVEMBER 1979, LONDON

ALEXANDER TROCCHI: Oh God Allen, if you knew, if you only knew, like the hang-ups, the hang-ups I have when I come to write . . .

ALLEN GINSBERG: Yeah, well, I don't know, maybe you take it too seriously.

AT: Well, yes, but I don't really, you know. On one level, I do. On another level, I don't take it seriously at all. I mean, I know it's all for the birds.

AG: Now will you just start telling me that whole story that you told me before, all over again please, this time into the tape recorder.

AT: Oh my God.

AG: Okay, tell me another story?

AT: Well, I don't know whether this is a good one or not, really, I really don't.

AG: It's not supposed to be either good or bad.

AT: Okay, it's neither good nor bad. Well, about last March, I had a sudden phone call from Paris and it was a Jane Lougee . . . have you heard of Jane Lougee?

AG: Years ago there was a girl . . .

AT: Jane Lougee was a girl with whom I lived with in Paris for a number of years.

AG: Yes, she was involved in the old *Paris Review* or *Merlin*.

AT: She was actually the publisher of *Merlin*. She was the editrix of *Merlin*, the magazine of which I was the editor from 1952 to 1955.

AG: I don't think I ever met her.

AT: I don't think you ever did, Allen. Anyway, she rang me up and wanted me to drive down with her, suddenly, this past summer, to Mallorca where a lady called Joanne Lasch had left her – not let her – had left her – a nice cottage, a rather large one, next to Robert Graves', down there in Deià – flattering but, needless to say, living with Sally [Child], I had to say, well really Jane, for God's sake . . .

AG: I'm an old married man . . .

AT: I'm an old married man now and its many, many years ago since we were together – but, no, she insists, you must do it, here I am contacting you and after twenty years, there's nothing sexual about it, nothing like that, I just want to meet you and drive down . . .

And man, it struck me as rather nice, you know, that she should get in touch with me after all this time. So I talked it over with Sally and we, I decided I would go down with her and . . .

Actually, my last night in New York I'd been with Jane. That night I told you about? When I was going to pick up those bottles of Demerol in one of the chemists and lost my nerve? I said I'll have that doll over there, that big doll! So, once I'd bought the doll, I asked for the bottle of Demerol, got back to Jane, met with Jane and Baird Bryant – they'd got married you know – that's who Jane Lougee is by the way.

AG: I didn't know Baird married her.

AT: Yes, Baird married her. In Paris, while Jane and I were living together, she hated Baird Bryant's guts, wouldn't touch him, wouldn't look at him, but, just as soon as I got married to Lyn, she married Baird. Anyway, the night before I left, that's the last time I saw her, hadn't been in communication with her for all that time, until suddenly, last March, there she is on the telephone.

So I say, okay, Jane, but get back to me in a couple of weeks. I check it with Sally.

Now, unfortunately, at the beginning of July, I run into a real tragedy with my book business. I bought a load of books, on the advice of, well, a false friend, books that were supposed to be worth £1500 – and I didn't know whether they were or not frankly – there's areas in the business which I know nothing about. Turns out he was getting his own back on me for something and I find out that I've considerably overpaid, and, you know, for me to take off with my car and go to Spain, drive to Spain, that was going to cost some money. My business isn't that good – that I can just take off anytime, and, anyway, as you know, I have the drug problems, I've got to make all kinds of arrangements up front.

I decided, halfway through July, that I could make it for the week but not for the fortnight that Jane wanted me to, so I decided, well, I'll meet her in Paris, we'll spend a little time in Paris, look up the old scenes and then, if she wants to go down to Spain she can go, but I'll just stay, come back to England.

So here I am arriving at my lovely old Paris just at the beginning of August, last August . . . Now, when I had seen Jane last she had been a beautiful black-haired young lady who looked like – who was the existentialist singer?

AG: Juliette Greco.

AT: Juliette Greco. She used to be mistaken all the time for Juliette Greco in Paris. Well the lady I met had grey hair hanging down her shoulders! Dear Jane, I thought, dear Jane, so what are you trying to prove? But nonetheless, don't get me wrong, she still looked lovely. We went out and had a meal and set out for Spain the next morning.

AG: By train?

AT: By car. Listen, this lady was, as far as I knew, a millionairess but, you know, when she goes with her old friends, perhaps it's not like that. I don't believe she's strictly a millionairess, she's got stuff in land, her father is her benefactor but her father died and her brother is looking after her money, that kind of thing so, no doubt she doesn't have a lot of extra cash, but, well, anyway, she discovers, much to her surprise, that an American Express card will get you a car, so we booked a car and we started off – and the first day was beautiful. We drove, there was sunlight, and it was absolutely beautiful.

I'm not telling this very well, I don't think.

Anyway, every bloody place we stopped, we got terribly expensive hotels, terribly expensive meals . . . and they were lousy! We hit all the wrong places! It got worse and worse and worse as we went down through France . . . and you must remember that I am personally driving away from my drug supplies. I couldn't arrange on such short notice to have my drug supply provided for more than a week.

So we stopped at this place and at that place and we tried to get the very best, you know, real good meals, but, every single time, it turned out to be silly. We spent too much money on nothing, we were not satisfied, and, by the time we were very near the Spanish border, we were really, quite frankly, a bit on each other's nerves. I was wondering to myself, Jesus, why the fuck did you come here, Trocchi, in the first place, when she said to me, well, next year, if you don't know, it is the twenty-fifth anniversary of *Merlin* and I was thinking of having a reunion in Paris of all the writers of *Merlin* and I wanted to get together with you to do it.

And I thought, what a nice, pretty idea, you know, I'll go along with it. Understand we weren't sleeping together or anything like that, Jane and I – I was fond of her, you know, but, sexually speaking, there was nothing between us by this time. She looked like the Witch of Endor or something! She'd been looking after her farm, she has dogs et cetera, she won't put on any make-up, and she's the same age as I am, fifty-four, you know I love her, you know, I love her, but, on the other hand, I'm not attracted to her, I can't get romantic about her in any kind of way. I do love her though and, like, I put my arm around her and hold her, that kind of thing . . . but she really begins to get on my goat as we travel along.

So, eventually, she decides to allow me to drive.

Well I'm driving on the right-hand side of the road instead of the left as we drive in England, and at one point she says, it's that-a-way, so I turn that-a-way, and then at the last moment she says it's that-a-way! and crash! . . . So I take a mudguard off another car you know, and I'm a good driver, I've been driving for – what – about forty-five years without an accident . . . not forty-five, I'm exaggerating, forty, right. But anyway, so I take this mudguard off this other car. And of course we argued.

I'm trying to tell you a story but I'm not doing it as well as I wanted to, you understand?

AG: The universe is already empty.

AT: And anyway it doesn't matter.

AG: It doesn't matter, and we're not gonna get anything out of it. We're all gonna die. We're not gonna get out of here alive!

AT: Now, I had decided to bring a little good hashish with me. And having seen that film, *Midnight . . .* something?

AG: *Midnight Express? Midnight Special?*

AT: . . . The one in Turkey where the man got caught with hashish and was put away, yes, *Midnight Express*, I didn't particularly want to be arrested for any hashish crossing a border of any stupid country.

Now Jane actually, shortly after we met in Paris she says, Did you bring any pot with you? and I said, Well, as a matter of fact I did but . . . you know . . . best be a bit cool about it, you know, like here it is, in my pocket. Well, when we arrive at the Spanish border we are really angry at one another and Jane, she's brought her dog along with her. She didn't want to leave her dog – I almost dug that, and approved of it, you know – that she didn't want to leave it, her dog is her best friend, this is the person she's been living with – and it's a nice wee dog but when we get to the border she dashes out the car with her dog and dances around like a sixteen-year-old little girl! I don't know but I'm sitting there with, in my pocket, the hashish that I'd bought. Oh boy, I was really . . .

Oh Allen, I haven't led up to this very well. If I ever come to write it I will build it up a little more strongly.

But anyway I was flabbergasted and, oh man, they weren't nice to me at all when she dashed off like that! They said, now what's all this about? They ask me what is she doing? They opened the trunk. They took our bloody cases, they put them down, they went through them like nothing on earth. Oh my God, you know, she's gone crazy, she's dancing around with her dog.

She took my freedom in her hands and played with it.

AG: Did she know she was doing this?

AT: I suspect she did. I suspect she did, Allen. You know, like, oh man, I was horrified. I wanted to go past the Spanish border so quietly, so yes-mister-very-'umble-Mr-Copperfield-like, sail by it, you know, but here I am, they make me get out, they ask me, what is this woman doing over there? I say, well, you know, her dog wants to pee. And they don't speak English! And I don't really speak Spanish! I can speak in French but they're not interested in any foreign language.

AG: Did you make efforts to distract them?

AT: I probably did but it didn't help very much. They were still annoyed an American woman was coming on like this, and here was I in the car and they had my case open and my clothes out . . . I'd never been searched at a border like that before in my life – never! So, anyway, she finally comes back – and fortunately they didn't actually search my jeans pocket and get, you know, a hold of the hash. I was still a free man, but I was a free man who wasn't very interested in speaking to Jane anymore, I really didn't want to go to Deià anymore, you know, because it was costing more than I felt I could afford and . . . when we left Paris she had said to me, Alex, if you don't mind, with your £500 (which was what I had kind of set as the maximum I could spend, you know), you spend that and I'll give it back to you when we get to Deià. Understand? So I had lost all my bloody cash! All my bloody cash was gone by the time we got to the Spanish border! All to try and bring back old times. Now look, our old times were never like that you understand – we didn't have that kind of money in those days. So anyway, when we crossed that border, well, basically, I wasn't speaking to her at that point.

AG: You'd explained to her why you were offended?

AT: Yes.

AG: And what did she say?

AT: Don't be stupid, you're paranoid. I said, maybe – but you know who I am and you know the possibility of my being arrested is like . . . very likely. If I were nabbed – I mean – Jesus Christ! It's all right for her if she gets arrested, but if I get arrested, oh boy, I go to perhaps a foreign prison and I don't have any of my drugs, so I'm dead, or I'm screaming, or something. So you know . . .

AG: What did she say to that?

AT: Oh just paranoiac again, you know. Well, by the time we got to Barcelona, we weren't speaking to each other at all, so she dropped me off at the first hotel we found and we said good bye.

And I must say at this point I had forgotten that I had paid all the expenses on the way down. I wasn't thinking of money at the time. So I went into this bloody hotel and of course I discover that I'm paying twenty-two pounds a night. In this fucking hotel you know. Spain? Twenty-two quid a night! I had a bathroom, you see. By God! I needed a bath that night. So I took this damn room . . . Okay that was Saturday night, I was sad, you know, that she had gone off like that because, dammit, we'd been close. I really felt sad about it and I hoped that she'd be feeling sorry too and would soon get in touch.

All day Sunday I wandered around there, thinking back about my earlier days in Barcelona (because I'd spent some very happy days in Barcelona, earlier on), couldn't see the car, couldn't see her. Sunday night, about ten o'clock, I came back, a bit sadly, to my hotel. I had just gone up to my room when I get a telephone call from the front desk. There's a lady here to see you. Yeah, that was so nice. I dashed downstairs – they wouldn't let her up, ten o'clock at night in Spain, she wasn't my wife, so they wouldn't let her go up to my room, I had to go down and talk to her in the hall. So what had happened to her was . . .

AG: She got robbed?

AT: She lost her fuckin' car keys! You know she was flipped a bit too. She'd lost her bloody car keys. She'd gone into another hotel, not far away, but she couldn't open the bloody car – and it was a Hertz, so we had to phone up Madrid, and they told us that they'd have the keys, the second set of keys, sent in from Madrid – they would be ready for us first thing Monday morning. So I went to bed actually quite happy that night – grateful – she hadn't run off at least. On the other hand, happy only to some extent . . .

AG: Then what happened? Go on.

AT: Monday morning I go and meet her at Hertz Rent-A-Car, where the keys are going to come. So she says, well, are you coming to Deià? We'll fly. I suppose that meant she would pay for the tickets and all the rest of it but already I was beginning to worry about being back in Paris for the right time to get back to get my drugs, you know.

AG: But you didn't explain that to her?

AT: Oh I explained that to her. She knew everything. So when it came to the bit where she says, well are you coming? I said, no, I'm exhausted. I think I'll just make my way back quietly to Paris. I'll see you later. You know it all went wrong. And I should have gone. I think I should have gone. To tell you the truth the reason that I didn't go was because I said, well Jane, I'm pretty broke, so I'll have to cash a cheque, and we went to a bank where she cashed some traveller's cheques and I cashed my cheque, and well, honestly, I felt that she really shouldn't have made me cash that cheque, since I'd already spent like, you know, probably 350, 400 quid already, on the way down. There was no need for me to cash a cheque at that moment. This was a cheque that I didn't intend to cash and so, when she allowed me to go through with cashing it, I felt . . . Alex, time you went back home, you know.

So I went back to the hotel and said you must book me a seat in an *avión* you know . . . they finally got me a ticket on the Thursday, they got me a ticket to go off at 2.30 . . . so I'm on the plane for Paris, but Jesus! That was the most expensive holiday I ever had. I had a miserable time, a fuckin' miserable time you know . . . everything went wrong you know . . .

I could have told it much better I'm sure . . .

WE DRIVE EACH OTHER UP THE WALL

Alex Trocchi in conversation with Kit Lambert and Rt Hon. George Rodney

17TH MARCH 1981

KIT LAMBERT: . . . It's like toilet training this, with a dummy potty.

ALEXANDER TROCCHI: On the other hand, sometimes even in this potty training I can be brilliant . . . All right we're talking. I will tell you, there's nothing happening on that tape until we put it there, so don't worry about the tape. Just let it be sung . . . No, it's for the typist. Let us bore the typist.

KL: It should stay in your possession and be typed up. We're looking for a woman, presumably with a very good pair of tits, I imagine, and a nice ankle.

AT: If a woman does not have good breasts, I am not in the least interested. Oh, yes. I don't quite know what we're going to try to do.

AT: Do you know you can go from London to Glasgow for nine pounds in a bus and see two films like *Jaws* and everything else on the way? For nine pounds! You get there in about seven hours. This bus thing is absolutely marvellous. Jules has told his dad, don't go by train, it costs too much, go by bus and you can watch some films. So Jules paid nine pounds, Edinburgh to London. Now, that's a third of what you pay on the train. He saw two films on the way down and had lunch at a nice hotel on the way . . . in a coach, sitting back on a nice chair, watching films all the way down. And they charge you twenty-seven pounds on the fucking train! They bring you coffee . . .

RT HON. GEORGE RODNEY: Can you do it the other way? Can you go to Glasgow?

AT: Yes, I have actually got the address. We'll go straight up there, man! We'll watch a couple of films on the way up. We'll take Kit with us, show him how to buy books. I'll show you both Glasgow. (*Tape stops and restarts*) I had two nights in Kelvin Park when I was young, one of them was a man, one of them was a woman. Fortunately, the time that I was caught by the police, it was a woman. They came with their torch and pricked me out of the dark . . . and there I was, fucking this married woman. Didn't blame me at all, I was just young.

KL: My fancy at the moment is Aberdeen. There aren't any good book shops up there, are there?

AT: Ah, shit! Where? In Aberdeen? Ah, yes, indeed. I'll show you the granite city of Aberdeen. On the other hand, it's very expensive these days. There's a lot of oil in Aberdeen. We'll have to take your pop groups up there.

KL: That's how I got up there. I had a showdown fight with a theatre owner. I said, take your coat off!

AT: The minute we cross the border of Scotland, I can look after our tourists!

KL: Oh, my God! Ha! Ha!

AT: You people, you have to look after England and you're not doing a very good job at the moment, I must say.

AT: . . . Now, you tell me that this man around the corner is a CIA agent? Well, we ought to phone him tonight!

KL: No! No! No!

AT: Why? Stop it, man, stop it. We can get this man, bring him down.

KL: You were asking why I thought he was CIA . . . the word was around.

AT: No, the word was not around. I just turned round, during the conversation and said, frankly, old man, you're from the CIA.

KL: Yes, you did all that.

GR: I heard that he could have been from the CIA.

AT: I said that as a joke. Kit went along with me . . . and the guy could be from the CIA, actually.

KL: By the same token, he represents no kind of threat to Alex whatsoever. I'm not being paranoid, I've only met two people from the CIA and he resembles . . .

AT: . . . He is your typical Chicago Jew, you know, the man with the thick spectacles, brilliant and liberal and all the rest of it. Now, how many of them are really in the CIA?

KL: You must understand, Alex, we're not talking about guns in railway carriages.

AT: I know we're not!

KL: We're talking about intelligence collectors, about the mood of a country; they are observers. An observer in Venice is required, an observer in London is required. I think you flatter yourself.

AT: This is my specialty, old man.

KL: He reports on intelligentsia; a minor sleeper, that's the category I'd put him in. He is not licensed to carry a gun, he's never been on special operations.

AT: This is just your trouble, man! You are absolutely caught up in this CIA image now. You're going to put it over George and me. Whether he was CIA or not, it doesn't make a fucking halfpenny worth of difference. You're getting caught up with this in a way that makes you a mad man!

KL: You're challenging me and alleging paranoia on my part. By agent, I mean a stringer, somebody on a retainer.

AT: I know about all these terms, old man. So what are we going to do with him? I'd like to take him to bed, frankly.

KL: It doesn't matter a fart!

AT: I'll give him my wife, I'll give him my son, I'll give him my friends. What are we going to do with him?

KL: It doesn't matter, they're not after us, they're just observing a scene. Your views and George's views are interesting . . . One is the King and country debate, that this house will not fight for King and country.

AT: This house will always fight for King and country! (*Sings*) I will fight for King and country! God save our gracious Queen, long live our noble Queen! Now look, you, you're making a fool of yourself at the moment. You're making a fool of yourself on tape. Just sit . . . He is not the CIA's person and although he is feeling absolutely pissed off tonight and out of it, he can't walk round. He will come very shortly and talk to us all.

KL: The people I have met from the CIA have been selected for . . .

GR: Their brilliance, their absolute brilliance.

AT: But, my dear, I am their employer, so I know who . . . I don't mean that, Kit, but honest to God, I mean, I've met them all. This man here is not the CIA person, on the contrary, he is a Jewish liberal over here, trying to . . . Yes, I know there are Jewish liberals in the CIA.

KL: They don't choose fools. For crying out loud!

AT: Damn it! It was I who said he was in the CIA, not you. You supported me as a joke to begin with and then you got caught up with it.

KL: I want to cocksucking prove that I'm not paranoid *vis à vis* the CIA! What on earth would they want with me?

AT: They wouldn't want anything with you.

KL: So where is the source of my paranoia?

AT: Fuck it, man, I was joking in the first place. You take everything so fucking seriously, you know.

KL: I certainly do, in such a matter. It is a matter of caution.

AT: No, it's not, man, that's the whole point. You're an Englishman, you should know, you can take something with a sense of humour. I don't know if the man's a fucking CIA agent or not. I don't give a fucking hell whether he's a CIA agent because I'll pee on him from a great height!

KL: That's what I'm worried about.

AT: All right, you'll have to manage me, yeah? My flat here is about to be raided by the police because you're talking so loudly. This is what I call insanity . . . But on the other hand, like, I know about insanity myself, you know?

KL: How nice.

AT: I wouldn't be otherwise. But on the other hand, I don't want to be arrested.

KL: You couldn't get arrested! Ha! Ha!

AT: Ha! Ha! They gave me six months. I had to fight like hell. I'm not going to get arrested again. Probably, I will be. Anybody who arrests me, will have to apologise later on, because I'm not staying in, wherever they take me. What they said to me was six months and I was waiting for 'suspended'. And they didn't say 'suspended'. Imagine how I felt, standing in that fucking little dock. My lawyer had promised me before that even if they did put me in, that he would get me out on appeal. And so he immediately walked forward and appealed and they said they'd allow the appeal. What if they'd said they wouldn't allow the appeal?

GR: You'd have gone down.

AT: George, help me. What was the book that was written, you know, the man who wrote the book about the eighteenth century chamber maid who fucked everybody?

KL: *Tom Jones.*

AT: *Fanny Hill* . . . Well, I'll tell you what happened to me. When I was up in court for, you know, et cetera, et cetera . . . Well, *Fanny Hill* got all the publicity. I didn't get any fuckin' publicity; I got three lines.[1]

GR: *Fanny Hill?* That ages you a bit. When was that?

AT: It was exactly the same time as *Cain's Book* got banned and burned in Sheffield . . . and *Fanny Hill* got all the things, the whole . . . I got nothing.

KL: Poor old Troc!

AT: Poor old Troc, yes! Now, don't give me that bullshit because publicity is fine so long as they spell your name correctly.

AT (*directly into tape recorder*): You see, we'll turn it off, shall we? Because they're all gone now, into the kitchen for the moment . . . When they come back in we'll turn it on again but, eh, we've got to get hold of ourselves, all three of us, to work together because – honest to God – we drive each other up the wall.

AT: I can tell you the story about Peggy Guggenheim and myself.[2] I went in to Peggy . . .

KL: Now, wait . . .

AT: I went in to Peggy to make love to her because she put me in the bedroom next to her. I was Sinbad, her son's, friend.

KL: Sinbad . . .

AT: You what? Sinbad, you know about Sinbad?[3] Okay. Listen . . . I'm not competing with you in this story.

KL: Sinbad . . .

AT: Shut your fuckin' mouth!

KL: . . . had a motorbike.

AT: He's a little, spoiled, stupid prick, not with a halfpennyworth of his mother's intelligence, right? Okay. Okay. Never mind Sinbad, I'm talking about Peggy. So, I'm put in this bloody bedroom next to hers with the door open. In Venice, yes. Under the Calder silver sculpture and the bed . . .

GR: What era is this, Alex?

AT: Between 1953 and 1955. There it was, my bed was there . . . There was a Picasso on that wall and there was a ... I'll tell you his name later, but he's a ...

KL: We want it now!

AT: I don't have it now. I cannot remember.

KL: It was Ernst.

AT: It wasn't Ernst. He was ...

KL: Surrealist?

AT: No.

KL: Cubist?

AT: No.

KL: Leger?

AT: No, no, man!

KL: American?

AT: You see what he does?

KL: I want to know what the other painting was on the wall.

AT: Oh, yes, you want to know that fact, so you'll stop me telling all the other brilliant ...

(*Here tape fades, then overdubbed voice of AT can clearly be heard:* The man's name was Hans Hartung.)[4]

AT: I don't know that I want you to be my manager. I am sitting, I am lying under a beautiful Alexander Calder sculpture. Do you know what it was like? It was made of silver and it was over my beautiful double bed ... and Peggy's door is open like that, allowing some light to come through. I think, well damn it to hell Peggy Guggenheim, if your door is open you want me to come through! So I went through.

KL: Hi!

AT: Hi! Yes, I went through. I don't even think I ought to tell you this fuckin' story! I go there and there is Peggy. She's lying there as though she is the Queen of Sheba, you know?

KL: Well, isn't she?

AT: She isn't as a matter of fact.

KL: Fair enough. Proceed.

AT: And I go over to her and I say, Peggy, I suppose you wanted me to come in?

KL: You coarse old cunt!

AT: I wasn't a coarse old cunt. I was about twenty-seven years of age. And, eh, she laughed and I laughed and, eh, I put my hand on her belly, you know?

KL: Yeah?

AT: And she said, don't bother, Alex. I said to her, Peggy, it's a pleasure.

KL: Big of you.

AT: No, it was a pleasure. Do you want the story or not? She had a big old nose and hair. She had her nose operated on a number of times, unsuccessfully.

KL: She wasn't in cold cream or curlers?

AT: Yes, she was . . . She wasn't actually at that point.

KL: She must have been fifty . . .

AT: . . . More than that. I was already about thirty. She was about fifty-seven. She wasn't bad-looking, but she wasn't good-looking. Damn it, she had that nose operated on in a terrible way.

KL: She had never been considered a beauty.

AT: No, she had never been. Well, we had our arms round one another and we talked and we laughed and she said, listen, Alex, Sinbad . . . I know he's your friend but I really worry about him. I said, well, don't worry about him, Peggy. He's a good friend of mine and we're doing fuckin' well in Paris, you know? And, eh . . .

KL: Explain that. What was your relation to Sinbad? Were you working together on *Merlin*?

AT: No, he edited a magazine called *Points*. Well, the first time I met Peggy, to tell the truth, was the night I went to have dinner with Peggy, Sinbad, his poetry editor and myself.

KL: Did Peggy back *Merlin* or help towards it in any way?

AT: No, not at all. She was backing *Points*.

AT (*alone, directly into the tape recorder*): Never mind the bottom, I'll show you the fucking top. Or, never mind the top, I'll show you the fucking bottom, whichever you like.

AT (*alone, watching television documentary on David Hockney*): . . . The ghost of Sickert . . . The ghost of Sickert . . . That is sickening, absolutely sickening. The ghost of Sickert got this little, this little bitty boy Hockney '. . . But he did think it was very important and here he is saying that he was painting Divine . . . '

'. . . Put in the dark blue and I didn't just want it dark blue. I suddenly took these little, this kind of treatment and put it all over the back of Divine . . . '

'. . . And bore me, which I don't want to do . . . '

AT: Is that what you want to do? You don't mind boring us but you don't want to bore yourself. Is that right, David Hockney?

AT: Listen, there's a great deal to be told. Listen, I was very angry with you when Peggy died and I didn't see her before she died.

KL: She was so long in dying, right?

AT: Yes, I know, but . . . Damn it, she should have been with me. She should have seen me before she died, she fucking should. I was closer to that lady, I think, than practically anyone, for the short time I was with her, like, that was every summer for a little while.

KL: I'm afraid, Master Trocchi, that when the process of death begins and you take to your bed, you have to be visited and you don't go zapping around the world.

AT: Je m'accuse, je m'accuse, je m'accuse. On the other hand, you have no idea the things that got between Peggy and me.

AT: Hey, what's happened to Ursula tonight? Where did she go?

GR: She's at home.

AT: Oh, what about you now? So where are you sleeping tonight?

GR: Can I crash out here?

AT: Perfectly all right, George. (*To Kit Lambert*) Where are you crashing out? Are you crashing out here too?

KL: I've got money, I can . . .

AT: Hold on, what we can do is . . . Now, listen! If you two boys promise me not to touch one another, you can pull open the bed and you can both sleep here.

KL: No, I think that . . . I want to chase up . . .

AT: You can do exactly what you want to do . . .

KL: Basically, I want to go into book publishing . . .

AT: You swine! You little swine! Don't you realise that I am probably the greatest book publisher of the twentieth century already? Already! Everything good that Girodias ever did, I did. Girodias didn't do it. He was a stupid Belgian or a stupid something. No, he wasn't. As a matter of fact, he was a brilliant fellow. Kahane was his father, he did the Obelisk Press . . . Brilliant, brilliant and I have a first edition of *Black Spring*, Henry Miller, who was published, not under the Olympia Press but, eh, the Obelisk Press. Now, I myself think that Girodias is marvellous. He is . . . well, I wouldn't say that he worked for his writers.

KL: Well, that's where I would score.

AT: That's where you would score? Right . . . Listen, I'm going to tell you the whole bloody story. You've no idea how much I know, like, eh, I know more probably than any fucking man alive about, eh, the history of, eh, good literature in the Western world from nineteen, well, nineteen hundred and forty to nineteen hundred and ninety.

KL: I think you should do a travel series . . .

AT: All right, we'll do the travel series, but meanwhile, if you have any questions, I don't mind answering them.

KL: Well, we aren't really going to have a serious taping session.

AT: We've already shouted, shouted, shouted, we don't want to do that, we just want to sit down cool and talk because, honestly, we all have a lot to talk about . . . it's games, man, we play together, we sit on our arse and play together . . .

KL: I don't think that you're so unequipped with ideas . . .

AT: Of course I'm not. I have seventeen ideas to give to your sixteen, Okay? Now, let's get on with it.

KL: I prefigure, if you allow me to say this, a sort of another *Merlin*. I've read *Merlin* from cover to cover.

AT: You have?

KL: I take particular note of writers and dates.

AT: I'm very glad to hear it.

KL: I deeply appreciate the innovatory and revolutionary status . . . I mean, startling in the way that Cubism or Surrealism was startling . . .

AT: I know exactly what you're saying.

KL: . . . The editorial flair which you have is something which is rather akin to myself as an editorial chap putting a record company together. However, the status of *Merlin*, now defunct but not disgraced, is something which can be revived, which is one segment of the huge pie. Segment two . . .

AT: I'd like to talk to you about two before we go on with the whole story. Store it and get on. (*Into microphone*) Is it on again?

KL: I'm stating my ambitions. Segment two is for myself; I know that I can be a book publisher . . . I don't know if I can make a great deal of money.

AT: I think, actually, it will fall on you like a gold charm.

KL: Very likely, very likely.

AT: Never mind talking about yourself again, get on with the story.

KL: In the rare book field, capital injection is probably something we can stage. In conjunction with rare books we can do what the French do, which is deluxe editions, both records and books.

AT: Could I interrupt you for just a minute? Would you allow me, as an older man . . . and I'm exhausted . . . and I just want to tell you one little piece of story. Now, what would you say if you had published *Watt*? You're a rare books dealer, you understand . . . and you had published *Watt*.

KL: I don't know.

AT: Well, let us talk about *Watt* by Samuel Beckett.

KL: Oh, I see . . . *Watt*.

AT: And we publish, eh, a thousand copies plus twenty-six copies, ABCDE up until the end of the alphabet and a few others, you know, because we print a few more. They sell now for about a thousand pounds apiece, these twenty-six copies and, eh, the extras. I had eighteen of them but they were stolen and later sold for, I think, for about two pounds each by Gaït Frogé in the English Bookshop [Paris] when I was in America. These things happen, they happen. Fortunately they didn't find his manuscript, which I had. But I had to sell that, you see? In the 1960s I had to sell that for, well, £400 . . . I have so many things to say about the past, about the literary scene, here and there, Paris, New York, California.

AT: Have we got a tape that is not going to click? Well, I am not going to start and talk if this is going to start and click in two minutes.

KL: Cut! Cut!

KL: . . . The question is, why do you think you have lost your entitlement? Is it a mess of potage on *Cain's Book*?

AT: No! No! No! It's nothing to do with *Cain's Book*. It wasn't on *Cain's Book* that I made my money.

KL: Baby, what rights did you sign away and to whom, and how, and is it legal and possible? Everyone will pay you royalties when you ask. When did you last ask? I want to see the correspondence on the royalties. It strikes me that it's a lot of guilt-ridden claptrap, the whole thing. I don't think it's possible for you to be signed out of your rights. I saw Lionel Bart's case.[5] If you took a substantial advance, which has not yet been paid back and they fiddle their accounts subsequently, then you are making sense. In other words, if your American publishers gave you a sum of money, then until that money is recouped, then indeed you are not entitled if a series of negative, but decreasing statements . . . *viz.*: Trocchi, advance $1,000; copies sold 300, royalty rate . . . balance . . . minus . . .

AT: It wasn't like that at all.

KL: That apart, I do see how a writer . . .

AT: Isn't it beautiful how things can happen that I can't be done out of my royalties? My contract wasn't verbal even. It's a little more difficult than you imagine. It's so beautiful, I can tell you every fuckin' little movement. So long as you have enough tapes, I am going to tell you everything . . .

KL: You're so long-winded about it.

AT: I am not long-winded, but you knock me, you go on, stand up there like a little fucking Hitler. And it was like this, it couldn't be like this! And that kind of thing. Bullshit!

KL: Fine.

AT: Well, I'll tell you what happened. I was writing . . . Shut up! I don't want to hear your fucking voice for the next ten minutes, right? I was in Paris and wrote a number of, eh, very good books, far-out obscene books for Girodias . . . What were you doing, George? Were you saying hooray, George, because he threw something on the ground?

KL: . . . Paranoid.

AT: I'm telling you, man, that I have no interest, unless you are interested, in telling you any story at all.

KL: I want to find out whether it's worth making a gesture for you which would perhaps make an income. I want to find out why, in an area in which I have vast experience, I am told . . .

AT: This delights me, absolutely delights me, old man. I will introduce you to my present literary agent, if you like.

KL: Who is that? What's his name?

AT: I don't remember the name of my literary agent, honest to God.

KL: It's me.

AT: No, it's not you, old man . . . and before him, I had another one.

KL: He's so fuckin' shifty.

AT: Oh, my God. Friends, friends, please have a little more confidence in me. They thought I was going to die.

KL: That I can understand.

AT: I was always going to die, next year, you know? Because I was a heroin addict. They wrote me off and they wrote me off again and again. The point is, if only I didn't happen to have slipped my disc at that point I would have had dinner and that big fat lady who couldn't walk up the stairs – I would have walked downstairs and had dinner and I would have got my royalties.[6]

KL: How did you sign them away?

AT: I didn't sign them at all!

KL: They can't put out your work and not pay you.

AT: Listen, man, you're a fucking young man. America did not even join the international . . . thing.

KL: You are trying to tell me that your writing was bootlegged in America?

AT: Oh, I'm bootlegged in America, old man. It's absolutely ridiculous, the way you're talking. Of course I was! Do you think I'm an idiot?

KL: No, Alex, I'm trying to find out why you are not getting royalty statements.

AT: I wouldn't get royalty statements, man. They've taken it. What I have to do is fight them in court. My little man who had, eh, what is it? What's the bloody thing you get when you're young?

KL: Polio.

AT: Polio, that's it. This polio man says, Alex, don't bother, don't even bother. This is down at Grosvenor House. Don't even bother trying to sue us because my brother-in-law is a judge. Don't waste your money . . . He gave me a thousand dollars.

KL: You received one thousand dollars US. What did you sign?

AT: I didn't sign anything! I just had the text because that was all I had.

KL: I find it very hard to believe that you didn't sign some kind of waiver.

AT: I'll tell you exactly what happened . . . No, fuck it, I can't remember. You're making it hard.

KL: Exactly, you can't remember.

AT: No, I mean I can't remember it this minute, I can remember it in two minutes. In two minutes, I'll give you the whole fucking thing. Now, stop it. Shut your fucking mouth and I'll tell you the whole fucking story.

KL: Alex, not tonight.

AT: Exactly. That's why I've been, eh, kind of, a little difficult to get together with. I'll tell you the whole fucking story, man. I had the best agents in America at the time but I can't even remember the fucking name!

KL: This won't do, Alex.

AT: What do you mean, it won't do, Alex? Don't worry, I've got it all upstairs in my, eh . . . You want these things, I've got every piece of information that we need . . . so, we'll go up.

KL: Believe you me, boy, I have to believe you. I do think that maybe I can investigate, check out . . .

AT: . . . It would waste my fuckin' time. I'm going to write such wonderful things in future that I don't want even to waste the blood of my heart on this whole thing.

KL: I think we need something more like Random House than Brandon House this time.

AT: Listen, I have Random House. Now, Brandon House, I think I have them too. If only . . .

KL: The Who and I, who have audited American Decca seventeen times . . .

AT: What is it? Do we want a little whisky? Do we want a little smoke? I have some other stuff . . .

KL: There are other companies in the States.

AT: Of course there are. Listen, man . . . Let's give it to Richard Seaver.

KL: Listen, I'm a novice. I don't yet know which . . .

AT: What are you talking about?

KL: I'm a novice in a new area.

AT: In other words, you shut your fuckin' gob!

KL: Shut your fucking gob and you don't get any cheques.

AT: You shut your fucking gob and talk to me. If you, eh, in the quiet of our home overcome me, then okay, we'll go along with you and I'll be right behind you, but if you don't – then I'll tell you what to do. Fuck you! You fucking moron. You don't know what you're talking about.

KL: Very likely, but I'll find out tomorrow . . .

AT: Listen, man, I'll tell you. I think, actually, if only you were the man who had wanted to get me the royalties for my books when you were at the top of your, eh, thing, you might even have got it. I certainly would have got it myself if I could only have stood up on my two feet. I couldn't move. He thought I was dying of heroin.

KL: That I understand.

AT: Okay, right. What a fucking coincidence, you know? I couldn't move. I had a slipped disc.

KL: You were still adjudicated so as to be.

AT: What was so adjudicated so to be?

KL: You were dying of skag and you were . . .

AT: They always thought I was dying, man. When Katharine Whitehorn wrote a double page spread for me in the *Evening Standard*, it was taken out by the scientific editor who said I was going to be dead within a year and I didn't know what I was talking about. That was the day that *Cain's Book* was published in England and I had about fourteen of my beautiful sculptures on the grand piano in John Calder's place in Wimpole Street . . .

KL: . . . And?

AT: Katharine Whitehorn wrote a beautiful article for me, like, she said this man is an absolute genius. He is not only a great writer, he's a great sculptor, etc. Every one was round that piano. I had about twelve beautiful little miniatures, you know? Like these things there, but they were finished . . . These will be finished quite soon, so don't worry about that. They were standing on the piano and she had the whole bloody thing written up. The first edition came out and I wasn't there, second edition came out, wasn't there, third edition came out and I rang Katharine Whitehorn at the *Evening Standard*, she was there. She said, well, unfortunately, Alex, the scientific editor has said no, you mustn't publish it. She read it, she had . . . Sorry, I . . .

KL: No, I understand . . .

AT: No, hold on, hold on, I didn't tell you the story properly. Katharine Whitehorn phoned up and said, eh, Alex, I hope you'll be pleased. Here is the article I wrote about you and she read it over to me. It was absolutely superb. If that had appeared in the *Evening Standard* that night . . . that was it . . . Would you go and answer the door? If it's the police . . . Don't open the door if it's the police, okay? Hold on, we'll have to stop. (*Long pause, then whispering and laughing. Later, some indistinct comments from KL*)

KL: . . . She had it in her boob tube . . .

AT: Fuck you, off you go. I can't really have you working with me because, eh, you're going to crucify me.

KL: Yeah, yeah.

AT: No, I don't want you to crucify me, old man. Crucify me when I'm going to defend myself properly.

(*More whispering, then tape is switched off*)

DO YOU KNOW DE QUINCEY?

Greil Marcus

' . . . I remember long, wonderful psychogeographical walks in London with Guy,' Alexander Trocchi said in 1983, a year before his death. 'He took me to places in London I didn't know, that he didn't know, that he sensed, that I'd never have been to if I hadn't been with him. He was a man who could discover a city.' Guy Debord and Trocchi met in 1955 in Paris, where Trocchi was serving one god as a pornographer for Maurice Girodias' Olympia Press, another as the editor of *Merlin*, a sombre avant-garde quarterly. Joining Debord's group, the Lettrist International, Trocchi had to cut all ties, break with his friends and employers: 'I stopped speaking to them. I was to enter into a closed society, a clandestine group, which was to be my whole world.' He was near sixty when we met, and he looked forty; he was built strong, all power, his eyes set deep but piercing and clear. A huge, intimidating nose came out of his face like a claw. It was impossible to believe he had been a heroin addict for almost thirty years.

Though Trocchi left Paris in 1956 for the United States, when the Situationist International was formed, Debord counted him a founding, active situationist. In 1960 Trocchi published *Cain's Book*, an autobiographical novel in the form of a junkie's journal: '*Il vous faut construire les situations,*' he wrote in the last pages. He was speaking of the fix: 'systematic nihilism', but also 'a purposive spoon in the broth of experience'.

'For a long time I have suspected there is no way out. I can do nothing I am not. I have been living destructively towards the writer in me for some time, guiltily conscious of doing so all along, cf. the critical justification in terms of the objective death of an historical tradition: a decadent at a tremendous turning point in history, constitutionally incapable of turning with it as a writer, I am living my personal Dada. In all of this there is a terrible emotional smear. The steel of the logic has daily to be strengthened to contain the volcanic element within. It grows daily more hard to contain. I am a kind of bomb.'

This was the sort of person Debord wanted, but Trocchi never really returned. *Cain's Book* made him famous in bohemian circles in Britain, and in 1962, in London, he began project sigma, an attempt to unite every sort of dissident and experimental cultural tendency into an international corps of 'cosmonauts of inner space'. Debord published Trocchi's sigma manifesto in the review *Internationale Situationniste*, no. 8, January 1963, but there followed the ambiguous note that it was 'no longer as a member of the SI' that Trocchi pursued his 'technique du coup du monde', his 'invisible insurrection of a million minds' – to Debord, Trocchi's association with people like occultist Colin Wilson and Beat poet Allen Ginsberg, both of whom Debord had long since dismissed as 'mystical cretins', was a resignation *absent la lettre*.[1] To Trocchi, Debord's demurral was an exclusion, and he never got over it.

'Guy thought the whole world was going to collapse on its own, and we were going to take over,' Trocchi said in 1983. 'I wanted to do that – to take over the world. But you can't take over the world by excluding people from it! Guy wouldn't even mention the names of the people I was involved with – Timothy Leary, Ronnie Laing. I remember the last letter he sent me: 'Your name sticks in the minds of decent men.' He was like Lenin; he was an absolutist, constantly kicking people out – until he was the only one left. And exclusions were total. It meant ostracism, cutting people. Ultimately, it leads to shooting people – that's where it would have led, if Guy had ever 'taken over'. And I couldn't shoot anyone.'

'It wasn't a question of loyalty,' Trocchi said; he raised his hands. 'Guy has my loyalty. I loved the man.' Suddenly Trocchi turned away from me and shouted. '*Guy, Guy,*' he said, '*WHAT IS IT? I am talking to you now, even if you will never speak to me!*'

We were in a fifth-floor walkup in a seedy section of Kensington. Trocchi had plans for screenplays, movies, a memoir; he made his living dealing third-class rare books out of a tiny stall on Portobello Road. His apartment was littered with syringes and busted ampoules. The walls were hung with founding situationist Constant's diagrams of his own new city: 'In New Babylon, man has been freed from his burdens, builds life himself.' I copied the words into my notebook: this, I thought, was where the great situationist project of transforming the world had ended up.

Even in the moment, the irony failed to cut very deeply, perhaps because Trocchi had already circled away from the great project. He was speaking again of its smallest version, where the desire to take over the world was first the desire to be in the world, a desire driven by the conviction that one cannot truly be in the world until the alienation of each from all has been vanquished, until necessity has been banished, until the world has been changed. Trocchi was talking again about the dérive – there, he said, for as long as it lasted, you were in the world as if you were changing it, and there were intimations of Utopia everywhere you looked. 'The difficulties of the dérive are those of freedom,' Debord wrote in 1956 in 'Theory of the Dérive'. 'It all rests on the belief that the future will precipitate an irreversible change in the behaviour and the decor of present-day society. One day we will construct cities for drifting . . . but with light retouching, one can utilise certain zones which already exist. One can utilise certain persons who already exist.' Even if he had been used, that was what Trocchi remembered most sweetly, so he talked about getting drunk, chasing oblivion into the black hole, the way out, the Northwest Passage. 'There was a magical quality to Guy,' Trocchi said. He was almost smiling; the flux of emotion in the previous half-hour had confused both of us, but now he was happy. 'Distances didn't seem to matter to the man. Walking in London, in the daytime, at night, he'd bring me to a spot he'd found, and the place would begin to live. Some old, forgotten part of London. Then he'd reach back for a story, for a piece of history, as if he'd been born there. He'd quote from Marx, or *Treasure Island*, or De Quincey – do you know De Quincey?'

> I used often, after I had taken opium, to wander forth, without much regarding the direction or the distance, to all the markets, and other parts of London, to which the poor resort on a Saturday night, for laying out their wages . . . Some of these rambles led me to great distances: for an opium-eater is too happy to observe the motion of time. And sometimes in my attempts to steer homewards, upon nautical principles, by fixing my eye on the pole-star, and seeking ambitiously for a northwest passage, instead of circumnavigating all the capes and headlands I had doubled in my outward voyage, I came suddenly upon such knotty problems of alleys, such enigmatical entries, and such sphinx's riddles of streets without thoroughfares, as must, I conceive, baffle the audacity of porters, and confound the intellects of hackney-coachmen. I could almost

have believed, at times, that I must be the first discoverer of some of these *terrae incognitae*, and doubted whether they had yet been laid down in the modern charts of London. For all this, however, I paid a heavy price in distant years, when the human face tyrannised over my dreams, and the perplexities of my steps in London came back to haunt me . . .

AFTERWORDS

SEX AND DRUGS AND TROCCHI

James Campbell

Cain's Book, Alexander Trocchi's drug-related mastercrime, is a novel to give to minors, a book to corrupt young people. It has been banned, burned, prosecuted, refused by book distributors everywhere, condemned for its loving descriptions of heroin use and coarse sexual content. Trocchi died in London in 1984. Since completing *Cain's Book* a quarter of a century earlier, he had written hardly anything. It's not difficult to see why. *Cain's Book* is more than a novel: it is a way of life. The book is autobiography and fiction at once, the journal of a fiend, a stage-by-stage account of the junkie's odyssey in New York, an examination of the mind under the influence, a rude gesture in the face of sexual propriety, a commentary on literary processes and critical practices, a chart for the exploration of inner space.

Trocchi partnered Burroughs, Kerouac and others on the roads chartered in the 1950s; but he wrote with a sophistication shared by none of the other Beats. He was more keenly attuned to Literature, and therefore could refuse it and its terms more conscientiously. In Glasgow ten years later, we dipped into the mythology of the Beat Generation, borrowing what we needed and adapting it to suit our brand of Celtic Hip. Trocchi appeared to us a colossus, bestriding a narrow world, forging his own myths. And he was one of ours. Only a Scot could formulate an epigram so calculated to outrage the native temperament as, 'It is difficult to explain to the underprivileged that play is more serious than work.' Or, taking different aim, 'My friends will know what I mean when I say that I deplore our contemporary industrial writers. Let them dedicate a year to pinball and think again.'

Even before *Cain's Book* was published in Britain in 1963, Trocchi was shaping his terror tactics. At the 1962 Edinburgh International Writers' Conference, he listened to Hugh MacDiarmid promote his own work, denigrate everything English, dismiss *all* contemporary fiction out of hand, and proclaim Scotland's potential as an international force. When he had finished, Trocchi got to his feet and replied first by saying that the best modern prose had been written by novelists anyway, then dismissed the work of MacDiarmid and his clan as 'stale, cold porridge. Bible-clasping nonsense. Of what is interesting in Scottish writing in the past twenty years or so, I myself have written it all.'

As a stunt to publicise a writer still unknown in his home country, it was quite a success. Trocchi's neatly phrased hyperbole grabbed the front pages of the Scottish press, and he was invited on television as a 'self-confessed drug addict'. As the debate continued in the columns of the *New Statesman*, MacDiarmid denounced Trocchi as 'cosmopolitan scum' – which only enhanced his reputation further.

I don't doubt that Trocchi saw the humour in it all. He had written altogether nine books, but most of them were 'dirty books', which had appeared, under pseudonyms, in Maurice Girodias's Traveller's Companion series published by the Olympia Press in Paris in the 1950s. Nonetheless, there is a finger of truth in his words to the Edinburgh Conference, for Scottish prose-writing in the period 1942–62 has nothing to rival *Cain's Book*, which was published in Britain the following year (it had come out in the United States in 1960), for style, intelligence and formal originality.

Cain's Book provided a context. I first came across it in 1970, a nineteen-year-old literary minor living in the same streets where Trocchi had grown up some thirty years earlier. I refused to work, I was anti-university, I explored my 'inner space' with the help of hallucinogens. Play is more serious than work. All you have to do is say it, and – well, isn't it so?

Our view of ourselves was as outsiders, escapees from society's snares, gentle outlaws. But Trocchi really was an outlaw, being a determined drug-addict (there was also a rumour – true, I was to discover – that he had had to escape the U.S., and the electric chair, in disguise, being wanted on a charge of supplying narcotics to a minor). How far can a man go, he wondered, 'without being obliterated'? And he put himself forward coolly as the guinea pig for his own tests.

To adopt the identity of the junkie was to refuse society's own narcotics: work, marriage, civic responsibility, family duty; it was to make oneself avant garde, the anti-man; it was to escape the bounds of social consciousness, which deadened creativity, and take up residence in inner space. Trocchi went further. He implied that his was a moral position: 'to think that a man should be allowed a gun and not a drug'. Only by the way did he invoke the orthodox justifications for drug use, claiming he was 'experimenting', or seeking to unlock concealed compartments of the mind. Of Aldous Huxley – the pioneer of controlled experiments – he cheekily wrote in *Cain's Book:* 'He was a boyhood hero of mine, and I'm glad to see him on drugs at last.' Trocchi barely countenanced the notion that his addiction could debilitate him physically, or erode his talents. On the contrary, he made heroin sound positively beneficial:

> It's somehow undignified to speak of the past or to think about the future. I don't seriously occupy myself with the question in the 'here-and-now', lying on my bunk and, under the influence of heroin, inviolable. That is one of the virtues of the drug, that it empties such questions of all anguish, transports them to another region, a painless theoretical region, a play region, surprising, fertile, and unmoral. One is no longer grotesquely involved in the becoming. One simply is.

In addition to espousing original opinions on the drug laws (heroin should be placed 'on the counters of all chemists . . . and sold openly'), and taunting taboos in general, Trocchi was an authentic literary craftsman. This concerned us more than the drugs, which my friends and I would solemnly have described at the time as an objective correlative for alienation in the novel.

Trocchi's erudition was among his most attractive attributes. He had been properly educated (he didn't let on that he took full advantage of university before opposing it); he knew Latin, read Baudelaire in the original, quoted Unamuno; he breathed out phrases like 'the Aristotelian impulse to classify' as casually as blowing smoke-rings. Trocchi's Professor of Philosophy at Glasgow University described him as the best student he ever taught. The junkie and pornographer Trocchi was also a philosopher, one who plays the old logic trick by asking you to consider the contradiction in the statement 'This statement is not true'. For the ingenuity of *Cain's Book,* the tease that draws you into it again and again, is that it questions its own processes at every turn, consciously undermining its own validity as a 'novel', yet finally standing free as a work of art.

On my first copy, a picture of Trocchi's tough, hollow-cheeked face glowered from the cover like a Glasgow hardman advertising his prison memoirs. I set off on a year's travel through Europe and the Middle East, taking *Cain* with me, the alternative version, the lost Book. At every opportunity, I preached his gospel to believers in the false gods of plot and linear narrative.

In the pinball machine an absolute and peculiar order reigns. No scepticism is possible for the man who by a series of sharp and slight dunts tries to control the machine. It became for me a ritual act, symbolising a cosmic event. Man is serious at play. Tension, elation, frivolity, ecstasy, confirming the supralogical nature of the human situation. Apart from jazz – probably the most vigorous and yea-saying protest of *homo ludens* in the modern world – the pinball machine seemed to me to be America's greatest contribution to culture; it rang with contemporaneity. It symbolised the rigid structural 'soul' that threatened to crystallise in history, reducing man to historicity, the great mechanic monolith imposed by mass mind. The slick electric shiftings of the pinball machine, the electronic brain, the symbolical transposition of the modern Fact into the realm of play. (The distinction between the French and American attitude towards the 'tilt' ('teelt'); in America and England, I have been upbraided for trying to beat the mechanism by skilful tilting; in Paris, that is the whole point.)

The situation in the early 1950s in Paris – where Trocchi went after taking his finals at Glasgow University – was similar to that of the 1920s: a catastrophic war had recently ended, the city was cheap for foreigners, and artists were attracted by its reputation for freedom from social and sexual restraints. London in the 1950s was seeing the evolution of Angry Young Man, but in Paris there was Sartre, Camus, Cocteau, and Trocchi's mentor, Beckett . . . not to mention Richard Wright, James Baldwin, Chester Himes and others. Compared to this, Glasgow offered square sausage and the work ethic.

Basing himself in a cheap St Germain hotel, Trocchi founded the literary magazine *Merlin*, publishing Ionesco, Genet and others. *Collection Merlin*, an imprint of the Olympia Press, was the first publisher of Beckett's novel *Watt*, in 1953, and later issued the English version of *Molloy*.

When he quit the Left Bank scene and sailed to New York, it was ostensibly in pursuit of a woman, but the move had another significance. Greenwich Village, not St Germain-des-Prés, was the proper backdrop for his new drama. His leave-taking from literary society – and society at large – was fully planned. 'I reject the entire system,' he wrote in a letter of the time; 'I am outside your world and am no longer governed by your laws . . .' He found a job as a scow captain, shifting cargo on the Hudson and East Rivers; now he was living on the margin both while at work – his days were spent mostly alone, on the water – and at play. It was on the scow that he drew together the notes which had accumulated in Paris and elsewhere, and formed them into *Cain's Book*.

Trocchi writes of himself in the novel (as Joe Necchi) stepping between cities, luggage in hand, one suitcase packed with notes and scraps of text. Quotations are given in *Cain's Book* from 'Cain's Book', passages which do not appear in the main body of the novel. It took a long time to fall into place, but in 1959 it finally did so. On the last page, Trocchi writes as if discussing another book entirely:

> as soon as I have finished this last paragraph [I intend] to go into the next room and turn on. Later I shall phone those who have kindly intimated their willingness to publish the document and tell them it is ready now, or as ready as it will ever be . . .

I only wish that Trocchi's bold remarks to the Edinburgh Writers' Conference could be said to be pertinent still – 'Of what is interesting . . . I myself have written it all' – but he wrote nothing of moment before his death from pneumonia in April 1984. All play and no work? It makes a dull twenty-five years, and for a writer as talented as Trocchi – 'the most brilliant man I've met', Ginsberg called him – a pitiful waste.

What happened? There was the corroding effect of the drugs, of course. There was also the revolutionary movement, project sigma, to which Trocchi devoted a large part of the 1960s. The aim of sigma was 'the invisible insurrection', a takeover by the culturally enlightened of the 'grids of expression and the powerhouses of the mind'. Based by now in a West London flat, and with a body of support which included R. D. Laing, Michael McClure, John Arden and Robert Creeley, Trocchi plotted not the *coup d'état* of Lenin and Trotsky, but what he called a *coup du monde*, a gradual assumption of control by 'the creative ones everywhere'. In his manifesto, Trocchi set out sigma's aims:

> We have already rejected any idea of a frontal attack. Mind cannot

withstand matter (brute force) in open battle. It is rather a question of perceiving clearly and without prejudice what are the forces that are at work in the world and out of whose interaction tomorrow *must* come to be; and then, calmly, without indignation, by a kind of mental ju-jitsu that is ours by virtue of intelligence, of modifying, of correcting, polluting, deflecting, eroding, outflanking . . . inspiring what we might call *the invisible insurrection.* It will come on the mass of men, if it comes at all, not as something they have voted for, struck for, fought for, but like the changing seasons . . .

The Invisible Insurrection seems very much of its period, and very far-fetched now. Trocchi's prophecies – from the redundancy of the publisher ('we must eliminate the brokers') to the collapse of the nation-state – are mocked by history. The idea of a cultural terrorist seems foppish. But if the project appears blurred by the psychedelic patterning (Trocchi envisaged 'spontaneous universities' sprouting up like mushrooms across the globe), it also has a characteristic originality about it, and an intellectual and imaginative ambition which is endearing today, when underground movements mostly involve real terrorists with real guns.

Trocchi's admirers wondered why he was giving so much time to his manifestos and so little to literature. His London publisher, John Calder, (no doubt contemplating his forthcoming elimination) expressed annoyance at the failure to capitalise *(capitalise!* Trocchi would have shrieked) on *Cain's Book*'s success, and complained that no one really understood what sigma was all about anyway.

But the real question for the writer was: how to follow such a book?

Trocchi's art was confessional, and you cannot make the same confessions twice. And while the novel is structured on a number of clever devices, one of them is timed to detonate at the very second at which its creator attempts to sneak back to conventional narrative: at all its stations, *Cain's Book* announces: 'This novel is not a novel; such categories are hereby rendered defunct.'

In short, there is a negativity implicit in *Cain's Book,* to which Trocchi could do little but succumb. 'You write your future,' a friend of mine once said, and the writing in *Cain's Book* is much taken up with the then-fashionable topic, the death of the novel. The novel didn't die after all but, following *Cain*, Trocchi's part in it did.

Trocchi never lost the desire to shock. Nor the ability. 'If I'm not capable of satisfying my wife, for some reason, I've no objection to providing some young bull to pleasure her.' Those were among the first words he ever said to me. His wife Lyn, reading on the nearby sofa, looked up briefly from her magazine.

It was 1972 and I had lately become associated with a small magazine published from Glasgow University, called *Gum*. When the editor suggested I interview a writer for his series, I mentioned Trocchi. We got his telephone number from the publishers and on a wintry afternoon some two weeks later, Trocchi met me at the door of his Kensington flat. He was dressed in a shabby black t-shirt with short sleeves; I suspect now that he wore it on purpose, so that I could see for myself the ski-track scars running down both snowy-white arms where the veins had collapsed. He was very tall with an enormous nose and a grey complexion, and the girl who came with me said later that she could smell evil about his person. He made her think of another notorious figure associated with Scotland, Aleister Crowley, the occultist and black-magician who was known as the Great Beast. Trocchi would not have refused the compliment.

My first impressions were more mundane. I was dismayed to learn that the Trocchis lived a fairly orderly family life. Lyn, an American, made enquiries about old friends in Glasgow. She wore dark glasses even though dusk was pressing at the windows. Trocchi himself prepared café au lait and recommended a pastry – just hot from the oven, he chimed. There were two nice boys present, Marcus and Nicky. When their father told the younger one to lower the volume on the television, the instruction was quickly obeyed. Painters had recently redecorated the flat, so that the woodwork gleamed. Before leaving Glasgow, I had conferred with the editor over what to do if invited by Trocchi to shoot up with him. The editor said I must accept: 'It'll look great in the interview.' Fat chance. The gulf between the person I had read about and the person now before me was wide, and wrong-footed me: he was older, plumper, greyer, than I had expected, and while he still liked to tickle the toes of the moral majority from time to time, he had gone soft on hard drugs.

Trocchi was still an addict – it was one of his gimmicks to ask you to wait while he gave himself a fix – but he would advise any young person against getting started, he said. I read him a passage from an article by Cyril Connolly, which had appeared in a recent *Sunday Times*, presenting the addict in a familiar way:

> A striking observation is the anti-intellectual climate that prevails in the networks. All who have known someone addicted to drugs . . . will have remarked on the increasing indifference to reality, whether to the time of day . . . or reading, or any of the pleasures and passions, food, drink, love, sex, places of art or the acquisition of knowledge which makes life worth living.

Trocchi made a partial defence of his stance by referring to Coleridge and de Quincey: 'If nothing else, they were certainly intellectuals. But up to a point, it's true what he writes. What else can one say about it?'

I learned Trocchi's own version of his flight from America and the electric chair, in 1961. One year after the publication of the Grove Press edition of *Cain's Book*, Trocchi was arrested and charged with supplying narcotics to a minor, for which the penalty in New York State at the time was death. The evidence was strong – a prescription bearing his name had been found in the possession of a sixteen-year-old girl – and made a conviction look likely. Trocchi was bailed out of prison with the help of an old friend from Paris, but, once free, got immediately in trouble with the law again. This time it was for fixing up, with Lyn, on a station platform. Trocchi himself got away, but Lyn and their child were arrested and taken to prison. Supported by people on the Greenwich Village literary scene, Trocchi obtained a false passport, slipped over the border to Canada, to be met by Leonard Cohen, and made his way back to England, where Lyn and the boy Marcus eventually joined him.

He chose London not only because of his nationality but because it was a place where heroin was available to registered addicts legally, on the National Health. In this way, in the 1960s, Britain controlled its minor drug problem. There was no need to hustle on the street, to mug or to steal, except for the few who, for some reason, could not register for prescriptions.

However, to this we must partly attribute Trocchi's demise as a literary figure in the 1960s. While the easy availability of heroin comes as a relief to the junkie, it also cuts him off from his occupation – scoring –

which propels him from one day to the next. 'The identity of the junkie was consciously chosen,' Trocchi wrote in reference to his decision to go 'far out', to make himself an outlaw in a society of conformers. But who ever heard of a state-subsidised outlaw? Much of the energy of *Cain's Book* derives from the excitement of scoring, of settling on a safe pad, of heating the spoon . . . Legitimised, this act is deprived of its drama. Only a kind of pathetic, under-subscribed theatre remains. The junkie's determined 'outsider' stance turns out to be a bit of a fake.

With Trocchi, there remained a literary style, of course. In 1972 I was much inclined to look on the bright side, but I could draw scant information from him regarding current and future projects. *Cain's Book* was well over ten years old. 'You must be finding it difficult to do a follow-up,' I said, 'having written a book about the inability to write a book.' This drew from Trocchi the comment – which I carried back to Glasgow like a coconut – that I was 'quite perspicacious'. He was writing something called *The Long Book,* he said, and he read a portion aloud to me. I listened hard – I really wanted to hear it – for the old brilliance.

Trocchi relished the notoriety which first his drug-taking and then the book had brought him – more intoxicating than ordinary fame by far. A provisional title for *Cain's Book* was 'Notes towards the making of the monster', which, though charming in its way, reveals a certain deadly self-consciousness. Real monsters – like real outcasts – are not self-made. The necessary condition of the outcast is that he cannot step in. The black man (for example) in downtown New York in the 1940s and '50s, trying to find an apartment, trying to find a job, was an outcast in the way that a white, university-educated junkie can only imagine (I almost said 'long for').

When a monster is self-loving, and not self-loathing, he is inhabiting what Trocchi in his Paris days would have called a 'false consciousness'. He is certainly more of a danger to others than himself. Trocchi in fact had created two monsters: one of them he could control, and he exhibited it before the public on a leash; as for the other, as time went on it turned on its master, savaging him and all around him.

Rereading *Cain's Book* after many years, I am struck by a morbidity in the relationship between sex and drugs, and sometimes death. Whereas he never waxes lyrical over women, Trocchi forges a poetic mythology of junk, which fills the space marked 'Love' in the novel:

> I remember Jody saying: 'When we do make love, Joe, it'll be the
> end!' The end-love, she meant, the ultimate. – Like an overdose,
> Jody?

And again:

> I thought of Jody, and of how plump she is from eating too many
> cakes, of the soft wad of her belly, of our thighs without urgency
> interlaced, of her ugly bitten hands . . . into which she drives the
> needle each time she fixes. 'That's your cunt, Jody.'

At other times, Trocchi dwells on the separate parts of women's bodies
like a lecherous mortician: 'the flaccid buttocks like pale meat on the stone
stairs'; 'this first sex shadowy and hanging colourless like a clot of
spiderweb from the blunt butt of her mound'; 'her belly dangling like an
egg on poach'; 'the skin close, odorous, opaque, yellowish, and pitted
almost like Pumice-stone'; 'a French woman's vitals would be sweet to
the taste, while with those of an Englishwoman one risked being confronted with a holy sepulchre, a repository for relics'; and plenty more in
the same vein. In *Cain's Book*, from which all those quotations come, the
most affectionate liaison (apart from one with a man) is with Jake, a
woman with one leg cut off above the knee. Necchi desires her genuinely, but at the same time he cannot help whipping back the sheets and
saying to the reader, *Look what a monster I am.*

Trocchi's 'Divine Marquis' mode is even less gorgeous in his
pornographic *oeuvre*. It may be that artists reveal themselves more in their
moments of lowbrow frivolity than (as they like to think) at times of
highbrow seriousness; in any case, what is shown up by Trocchi's
obscene writing can be unappealing in the extreme.

The books were written mainly for money which helped keep the
magazine *Merlin* afloat, but Trocchi told me he considered them to be
'serious enough within their own limits'. Each book contains some good
passages, particularly the extraordinary *My Life and Loves: Fifth Volume*
by 'Frank Harris' (1954), which is about two parts Harris mixed with
three parts Trocchi, and is so stylistically convincing that it was later
published as part of a 'complete' edition of Harris's opus (much to others' mirth but Trocchi's annoyance, since he received no royalties). The

issue at stake is not sex, but the violence which sex in Trocchi's obscene books often conceals. In this passage from *Thongs* (1956), sex is hardly visible at all, appearing instead in the guise of power and pain:

> My father would mark her, a small cross cut with a razor on the soft inner surface of her left thigh; his cattle . . . Everyone knew about the mark. Fourteen women in the Gorbals had been cut already. Normally my father kept the woman for about two months afterwards. Then they were free to go. The men of the Gorbals fought each other to marry a marked woman.

The monstrosity was not confined to the printed page. Joe Necchi in *Cain's Book* does not actually say that he is responsible for turning Jody on to heroin, nor any other member of the novel's grotesquely fascinating cast of junkies, but it is a fact that in life Trocchi did just that, leading people to a 'far out' place, from which many could not return.

When he met his second wife, Lyn Hicks, she was a twenty-one-year-old from Hicksville, New York. Within months of meeting him, she was hooked, and six months after their marriage in Mexico in 1957, she was parading herself outside the casinos on Las Vegas Boulevard, 'The Strip' – Miss Hicks, the hooked hooker from Hicksville. It was just one more way to earn money for junk. In his biography of Trocchi, *The Making of the Monster*, Andrew Murray Scott tells us that at other times, 'she danced in a sleazy nightclub wearing silver spangles the size of half-dollar pieces gummed to her nipples and black satin stretched over a tiny piece of cardboard at her crotch . . .'

Trocchi told friends that on at least one occasion he had 'cooled out of a bust' by having Lyn offer herself to a policeman in the back of a police car. Whether this is genuine monstrousness, or mere bravado, it cannot be waved away by a gesture in the direction of the famous outrageousness and charm. Lyn died in London in her thirties, having tried unsuccessfully to kick the habit many times.

If Trocchi himself seems by now about ripe for dismemberment, not just by feminists but humanists of every sort, we might ask the question: What made the monster? What lay behind Trocchi's destructiveness? What is the key to his psychopathology? A clue can be found in an interesting diary jotting, uncovered by Andrew Scott and quoted in his biography, concerning the funeral of Trocchi's mother, who died when Alex was sixteen:

> the last vital link with existence [was] cut. Lowered into a grave that
> was my extinction. Men and women in black. Brothers. Aunts.
> Uncles. Lingered on the green slope like quavers on a musical score.
> Sixteen at the time. And my father said to me: 'You will never see
> your mother again,' like a drain running out. But she continued to
> exist. Her death was my direction.

The picture has the force of a dream, a vivid summary of the dreamer's
existence, which appears to him as his fate. The relatives motionless on
the grass, and the insensitive father, are less alive to the boy than the
corpse now underground.

This revelation about his mother connects in highly suggestive ways
with self-portraits in Trocchi's published writings. For example, in *Cain's
Book* there is an unexpectedly tender moment in which Joe tells how much
he enjoyed 'brushing my mother's hair to make it beautiful', when a child.
'I never knew my mother when she was young and, they said, beautiful
and sometimes when I passed my hand over her hair I was invaded by a
sense of outrage that she was not young and beautiful to have me.'

That 'have me' is awfully ambiguous, and it becomes even more trou-
bling once it is recalled that this passage follows hard on one in which the
narrator explicitly ties his liking for the red hair to subsequent revulsion
at the thought of her red pubic thatch. These associations are then made
concise, in a formula that links the 'red sex' to a fear – which duly became
a reality – of losing his mother's love: 'Only the mute knowledge of her
constant loving me was as vivid as the seditious thought of the red sex.'
This mother is both loved – for her unselfish loving – and loathed, for
her private sexuality.

At this point, we turn back to Trocchi's first novel, *Young Adam*, to
the part near the opening in which the narrator – also Joe, also living on
water, though on a barge and not a scow – discovers a female corpse
floating in the canal. As Joe describes what he has found, one detail in
particular stands out:

> As I leaned over the edge of the barge with a boathook I didn't
> think of her as a dead woman, not even when I looked at her face.
> She was like some beautiful white waterfungus, a strange shining

thing come up from the depths . . . But it was the hair more than anything; it stranded away from the head like long grasses. Only it was alive, and because the body was slow, heavy, torpid, it had become a forest of antennae, caressing, feeding on the water, intricately.

If this already gives off a whiff of necrophilia, the place is positively reeking once it emerges, in the second half of the book, that Joe himself is responsible for the woman's death. Wrap it all up together with further quotations offered by Andrew Scott, such as 'the conquest of a new female, especially a beautiful one, was closer to hate than to love' (from a letter to a woman Trocchi hoped to marry), and one would feel quite confident about quoting back to Trocchi his own judgement on his mother – 'Her death was my direction' – and concluding, 'Yes, you were right.'

Death was to be directed to Trocchi's house with an accuracy, and a swiftness, that he could not then have known about. But it appeared to some people, even in Paris days, that the celebrated charisma was a toxic cloud. Sometime around 1980, hoping to spark a few illuminating anecdotes about one old Left Bank trooper by another, I mentioned his name to James Baldwin. 'Trocchi?' Baldwin snapped, the nostrils flaring as the great eyes bulged. 'The junkie? I hate him. *I hate him*. Tell him that from me!'

If I never did, it was because I still felt that one great book, while it cannot excuse everything, gets you away with quite a lot. I kept in touch with Trocchi, off and on, over the years that followed our first encounter, more than once asking him to contribute to another magazine I was editing, the *New Edinburgh Review*. I had no success. The last time I saw him, in 1981, he again met me at the top of the stairs, sleeves rolled up. 'I'm just about to give myself a fix,' he said. 'Can you wait?'

This time I was alone, and although it would have enhanced my sense of the occasion to have glimpsed an evil aura about his still remarkably large and hardy frame, it simply wasn't there. 'My family's dying all around me,' he said, a vulnerable and most affecting grin pulling at his lips. Not long after Lyn's passing, their elder son Marcus had followed, losing a three-year struggle against cancer. He was eighteen. A woman friend from New Zealand had moved in, and he spoke fondly of her attempts to impose order on his flat, though to me the place looked a shambles. 'I must sort all this out,' Alex murmured, gazing with the visitor's eyes at the papers and envelopes, books and wooden sculptures, paint boxes and odd detritus that littered the floor. The way he said it told you he never would.

'I am a cosmonaut of inner space,' Trocchi had once proclaimed. Inner space was all that remained to him. He had few acquaintances left in the literary world. Between complaints about difficulties in getting his books relaunched in London, he spoke frustratedly, for once, of his addiction. Heroin, the young champion, had long since turned old tyrant. As much as anything, he missed the freedom to travel abroad. Alex was a francophile, but the channel was hard to cross. 'You have to make arrangements about drugs and all that. Ach, it's a drag.'

By this time, Alex was running a second-hand bookshop in Kensington High Street. We went there together, and I bought three modern American first editions (by Baldwin!), kindly sold to me for token prices. Then he took me to his afternoon drinking club, where he ordered us the Scotsman's favourite tipple, a glass of whisky with a beer chaser. 'A hauf-an-a-hauf, Jim-meh!' Alex said to the uncomprehending barman, and chuckled as if he and I were sharing a family joke.

Such moments, together with his knowledge of antiquarian books and stamps (in which he also traded), were to me curious and poignant little indicators of his 'insiderness', of the tameness of the monster. For years he was forgotten in Scotland, and *Cain's Book* has hardly ever been readily available in bookshops. It was while writing an article in 1984 in which I mentioned *Cain's Book* in passing as one of our country's three best post-war novels – the other two, Archie Hind's *Dear Green Place* and Alasdair Gray's *Lanark*, also feature artists who cannot finish their work – that I heard he was dead. Twenty months afterwards, his younger son Nicky climbed on to the roof of the empty Kensington flat and threw himself off. Like his late brother, he was eighteen.

I am horrified to discover – both because of the Trocchi tragedy and for my own failure to be 'perspicacious' – that my interview with the great man for the university magazine, twenty-five years ago, ended with the words: 'Trocchi's book is about living . . . Most of all, that is what *he* is about: life.' I know what made me put that down. Trocchi the cartographer, the flag-planter, opened frontiers for fellow travellers. He went far out, and then farther – he went so far that inner space swallowed him up.

ALEXANDER TROCCHI: A SURVEY

Edwin Morgan

Most of the critical writing on Alexander Trocchi – and it is not much in any case – has centred on his best-known work, *Cain's Book*. This is understandable, and no doubt that novel will remain his chief claim to fame, but it might be useful in the present essay to place it within a more ranging and comparative survey of his various writings, partly because there is not a greatly diffused sense or knowledge of these, even among the well read (a frequent fate of underground or semi-underground productions), and partly because he himself wanted all his writing to be seen as a continuum of communication, of self-definition, of modes of consciousness, rather than as a sculpture park of 'novels' or 'short stories' or 'poems' or 'essays'.

> It wasn't that writing shouldn't be written, but that a man should annihilate prescriptions of all past form in his own soul, refuse to consider what he wrote in terms of literature, judge it solely in terms of his living. (*Cain's Book*, p. 131)

Such existential beliefs help to account for the formidable amount of energy Trocchi put into editorial and publicistic writing. When he began editing *Merlin* in Paris in 1952, he not only created a magazine which would be a vehicle for talents he thought important – Christopher Logue, Henry Miller, Sartre, Genet, Beckett, Nazim Hikmet, Ionesco – but also through his own thoughtful, persistent, and unshrill editorials was able to map out a new direction for 'Europe's independent minds', or perhaps more strictly a new non-direction, since so much of his argument was directed against directionism, against absolutisms whether Russian or American, against the Cold War which had piled such a mountain of bitter fruit in the very marketplace of victory. Meanwhile the first Russian sputnik went up in 1957, and the exploration of space and the Russian–American space race began. Without ever being anti-science, Trocchi felt the writer's complementary task was to become a 'cosmonaut of inner space'; the independent minds might well be nonconformist, alienated, iconoclastic, but whatever effect they had or wanted to have on society should have a psychological rather than a political mainspring.

As coeditor (with Richard Seaver and Terry Southern) of the anthology *Writers in Revolt* (1963), Trocchi either wrote or underwrote the unsigned introduction, which asserted that both 'language and subject remain threatened by forces whose avowed purpose is to protect those unable to judge or think for themselves' and that what was needed was 'the deliberate avoidance of lip service to assumed values, and adherence instead to deeply personal impulse'. If this seems too inward-looking to justify the 'revolt' of the title, it should be pointed out that the anthology contained most of Allen Ginsberg's *Howl* and an extract from William Burroughs' *The Naked Lunch*, both works with strong contemporary sociopolitical implications, as well as Sade, Genet, Hesse, Baudelaire, Artaud, and the devious Malaparte. These and other names prefigured or were a part of Trocchi's 'invisible insurrection' as outlined in his article 'Invisible Insurrection of a Million Minds' (*New Saltire*, no. 8, June 1963) reprinted in America in *City Lights* Journal (no. 2, 1964); published as *sigma* portfolio (no. 2, London, 1964).

This is Trocchi's most important single essay, and although written with his characteristic clarity and precision it belongs so much to the widespread and endlessly ramifying alternative-society millenarianism of the 1960s that it is hard to clinch a descriptive account of it. Briefly, the aim was nothing if not ambitious: not a Leninist *coup d'état* but a *coup du monde* (his own phrase), a transformation of the mass of society, not from within the mass but through the influence of a 'nucleus of men', something like Plato's Guardians, who are 'capable of imposing a new and seminal idea' and who will work internationally and anti-nationally ('History will not overthrow national governments; it will outflank them'). Artists must have direct access to communities and 'eliminate the brokers', but thère is a mild sideswipe at Arnold Wesker's ill-fated Centre 42 and its 'church-bazaar philosophy'. He envisages everything starting with the taking over of a country house 'not too far from the City of London', and the creation within that environment of a spontaneous university', a combination of Black Mountain College, Newbattle Abbey, and an Israeli kibbutz; and this repeated from country to country, building up a worldwide network of cultural and educational rejuvenation. In the Sixties, these ideas did find some fertile ground, and the 1968 prospectus for the Antiuniversity of London, with its anticampus in Shoreditch, does indeed include among its antilecturers Alexander Trocchi, who will fortnightly 'describe in immaculate intellectual terms the spiritual attitudes and the new economic scaffolding which must be brought into play as the tactical bases of any possible evolution of man'. The severe deintoxication so many countries have had since these heady days gives such pronouncements the flavour of a document already historical. National governments, far from being overthrown or outflanked, have proliferated and will evidently continue to do so, and to gain or keep real power; psychology, inwardness, ideas of exile and expatriation now seem indulgent in a world which has so many immediate and basic problems and is again in the old Johnsonian phrase bursting with sin and misery; and who would not now be a shade suspicious of well-meaning phalansteries of potential commissars, even if all their cry was that they would leaven the lumpen millions into the light? Nevertheless, the whole antiuniversity movement, and Trocchi's thirty-odd sigma portfolios, attracted an impressive body of support, including Joan Littlewood, R. D. Laing, John Arden, Anthony Burgess, Robert Creeley, Kenneth White, Tom McGrath, Norman Mailer, Edward Dorn, Stuart Hall, Barry Flanagan, and Hans Magnus Enzensberger. Perhaps it is in the nature of things that such a dazzlingly loose congeries of idealisms must belong to a certain time and place and cannot be much extended or developed; which is not to say that an element of exemplum may not still linger, to tantalise later harder-faced decades.

These literary and paraliterary activities did not bring in much money, and it is usually thought that Trocchi's translations, and his pornographic novels, must have been potboilers. In a sense this is true, but by no means entirely so. The novels he chose to translate have themes that one can see must have appealed to him or offered him an attractive challenge, and they are well translated, in a manner that shows diligence and care. Jan Cremer's *I, Jan Cremer* (1965; translated from Dutch with the help of R. E. Wyngaard) is the picaresque portrait of an outsider, a young hipster out of reform school who fights and cons and whores his way across Europe and North Africa, smuggling, selling drugs, painting pictures, bullfighting, even working in a slaughterhouse (a passage uncannily reminiscent of Archie Hind's *The Dear Green Place*), and finally being interrogated by the police for a murder he has seen but did not commit, in a sort of mirror-image of the end of Trocchi's own novel *Young Adam*. One central, self-observing, self-defining character is found in all the novels he translated: in André Pieyre de Mandiargues's *The Girl on the Motorcycle* (1966) the entire book recounts the leather-suited girl's thoughts and memories as she rides out one morning from her husband to her lover (and her death); René de Obaldia's *The Centenarian* (1970) is the sprightly and inventive monologue of an engaging eighty-seven-year-old, recalling his past and looking forward to his century; Valentine Penrose's *The Bloody Countess* (1970) is a fictionalised biography of the terrible sixteenth-century Hungarian countess, Erzsébet Bathory, who bathed in the blood of over six hundred murdered young servant-girls before she was caught, totally unrepentant, and tried; and in Jean Douassot's *La Gana* (1974) we have a blowzy, bizarre, Henry Millerish Bildungsroman of an unhappy and outrageously treated boy growing up into some sort of damaged teenage semi-maturity, the maturity of a solitary, hiding at the end like an animal in his dead uncle's room.

Whether tragic or comic, these are all studies in isolation, as are Trocchi's own two novels, and there are many incidental similarities. The motorcycle in *The Girl on the Motorcycle* has a function similar to that of the barge in *Young Adam* and the scow in *Cain's Book*, where movement in space sets off a displaced movement in the character's perception of time, so that he/she shudders or rocks or drifts through memories, present impressions, and imagined futures in a disorienting way. Or again, the old man in *The Centenarian* is not merely monologising for our benefit, he is writing his story down on a series of jotters he buys at the beginning, just as Joe Necchi in *Cain's Book* is actually writing *Cain's Book*. Hangings occur or are about to occur at the end of *The Bloody Countess* and *Young Adam*, and in *Cain's Book* the hero mentions his obsession with the image of a hanged man and actually suspends a doll in a noose from the mast of his boat, fearing that he has been living or writing in such a way that 'it can lead me only to the hangman'; to which one should add that Trocchi closes an essay on Orwell in *Evergreen Review* (vol. 2, no. 6, Autumn 1958) by contrasting Orwell's 'vulgar democratic unreflectiveness' and passé concern for sociopolitical factors at the expense of all others with the occasional far deeper insight into the individual human soul he showed himself capable of in his 1931 essay 'A Hanging' – and Trocchi quotes the passage where the wretched Indian on his way to execution steps aside to avoid a puddle.

In some of these translated novels there is a marked erotic interest, as there is also in *Young Adam* and *Cain's Book*, in his poems, and in the flamboyant and bitty *The Fifth Volume of Frank Harris's 'My Life and Loves': An Irreverent Treatment* (1958) (which is about thirty-five per cent Harris and sixty-five per cent Trocchi). Explicitly erotic writers like Henry Miller, Jean Genet, Allen Ginsberg, and William Burroughs were among the heroes of the 'revolt' with which Trocchi was associated, and there would therefore be nothing very surprising if his potboilers turned out to be pornographic potboilers. Without trying to insert a 'so-called' before the 'pornographic', one can still see a great deal more in these books, in the whole context of Trocchi's work, than the panting punter might suspect. In the best of them, *Helen and Desire* (1954, under the pseudonym Frances Lengel), there is again the isolated single central character through whose present consciousness and relived memories an existentialist, libertarian, anti-work-ethic philosophy of life is clearly formulated; and again the teller of the tale (a woman from Australia, held captive for sexual purposes by Arabs in Algeria) is herself writing it down, as her own novelist. The book is fairly regularly punctuated by her sexual encounters, both straight and gay ('I moved in the hothouse world of scented boudoirs, and flirted with the husbands whom I cuckolded') so that there is something for everyone, and the erotic descriptions are lush with the sort of metaphors that would have appealed to the later Metaphysical poets ('writhed on soft gimbals', 'the amorphous sludge of my breasts', 'sliding on soft graphite'); but on the other hand the main conduct of the narrative is nicely matter-of-fact in a Moll Flanders mode. As the book's title suggests, she is desire incarnate. Her narrowly religious father (a Scottish immigrant, one suspects!) had precipitated her adolescent reaction of complete amoral promiscuity, and as she travels through Asia and the Middle East she comes to live for immediate, non-lasting encounters. 'What would I do with a man for twenty-four hours in a day?' 'All great lust is impersonal.' 'The Western God, the Jewish God, was invented to make the hatred of life logical.' 'I am anxious to record everything, to break through the shameful shell of civilised expression.' At the end, fed for aphrodisiac purposes on honey, almonds, and hashish, and eagerly awaiting the next unknown evening visitor, she feels she is beginning to disintegrate, like Joe at the end of *Young Adam*, and her story ends in mid-sentence. Despite the fact that it has to meet the demands of its underground genre, this is far from being a negligible novel.

Thongs (1969) (and the title says it all) is a more broken-backed and unsatisfactory book from any literary point of view, but it has features that deserve mention. Like *Young Adam* and *Cain's Book* it has a strong Scottish, and specifically Glasgow connection. Like *Helen and Desire*, it has an isolated female figure as its central character. And like *Helen and Desire* and *Cain's Book*, it uses the device of the central character writing the novel which (maybe) the reader is reading. As in *Helen and Desire*, or more to the point perhaps as in Hogg's *Confessions of a Justified Sinner*, an 'editor' is printing the woman's own story as written in her personal notebook. Gertrude Gault (the same surname as that of Ella and Leslie in *Young Adam*) grows up in the Gorbals district of Glasgow and is the daughter of the Razor King. A violent and vicious environment is described, in terms almost parodically reminiscent of McArthur and Long's *No Mean City* except for greater literacy in the style, and the heroine's predisposition to being a victim, a willing one as it turns out, is traced back to a brutal father and a brutish society. At the age of fourteen she watches her father in a squalid sexual assault on his mistress, Hazel; he then thrashes his daughter with his black leather belt, and she discovers her masochism. Hazel, it emerges, is also a masochist, and introduces her to the owners and clients of a West-End mansion devoted not only to sadomasochistic pursuits but to the furtherance of a secret order whose headquarters are in Madrid. There is a Holy Pain Father, there are twelve Pain Cardinals, and a whole descending hierarchy of whippers and whipped. Although more than half of the book is set in Glasgow, the action finally moves to Spain, where Gertrude becomes Carmencita de las Lunas, is advanced high in the order, and dies as a martyr, scourged and crucified, and eventually a cause of pilgrimage. The theme of 'hanging', it will be noted, is here too, as well as the familiar self-isolation from society's norms, so the book readily finds its place within Trocchi's *oeuvre*. But it is virtually two separate stories, neither of them very persuasive, and the melodramatic Glaswegian mythology he falls back on is very different from the moving and beautifully observed Glasgow scenes in *Cain's Book*.

Erotic, but rather more publicly printable, are many of Trocchi's poems, collected in *Man at Leisure* (1972). He is essentially a man of prose and not of verse, but the verse is in some danger of being forgotten altogether, so a brief comment, at least, is in order. These poems, reminding us sometimes of Christopher Logue, sometimes of Alan Jackson, sometimes of Tom Leonard, seem to bear out a statement Trocchi (or the narrator) made in *Cain's Book*:

> I find myself cultivating a certain crudity of expression, judging it to be essential to meaning, in a slick age vital to the efficacy of language. (p. 71)

Not all the poems have 'crudity of expression', but where it is used it is generally to underline sexual liberation or political satire. For the former:

> The stinking cauldron
> of inhibition soup
> had its lid lifted
> by Attacunt Peep
> the hairy mind-wrestler
> the child with which
> god blessed her
> womb, and the sweet lust
> by which it was irradiated.
> ('The Stinking Cauldron')

A characteristic political passage comes indelibly marked with the ampersands, contractions, and lowercase of the Beat era:

> Concerning white geese of dover
>
> now, the minister of aircraft production
> the hon. john dracula
> has just signed a contract fr a
> progressive manufacture 'f
> 1,000 dreadnaught mk fck
> tactical bombers
> their eventual delivery
>   'to procure
>   peace'
>   fr the geese
>   in 1980
>
>   &

in commending the governmental decision
brigadier general paralysis
    met with derision . . .
('Lessons for Boys and Girls II')

Probably the best poem is a long five-page piece, in a more straightforward style, called 'A Little Geography Lesson for my Sons and
Daughters'. It is about 'the East' and 'the West', and although it is not a
dialogue it is rather like a medieval 'dialogue of soul and body', where
strengths and shortcomings of two opposed subjects are set out. The wise
came from the East, but 'its wisdom is dried up'. The wisdom of the
West is a book of rules, 'not quite indispensable for those who travel by
Pullman'. The East is 'a dark uterus' waiting to be truly and fruitfully
impregnated by the West, but artificial barriers keep the two apart.

If there is anything that isn't clear
I refer you to the chronicles of Zarathustra
or to the Chieh-hein of the Llama Swingitup. [sic]
if you can't get hold of these,
see me, please.

Trocchi's short stories and novels are the literary centre of his work, and
bring together most of the ideas, attitudes, and themes already looked at.
The four stories in *New Writers III* (1965) emphasise human isolation. In
'A Being of Distances' a middle-aged son who has been to his uncle's
funeral returns by train to London and keeps thinking about his father, a
widower now and a lonely man like himself; meeting his father at the
funeral, talking to him, but not staying, has left him disturbed and empty,
'a being of distances'. 'The Holy Man' is a more grotesque,
Hoffmannesque story about a dilapidated French residential hotel inhabited by mostly ageing and variously handicapped persons – a hunchback,
two blind men, a dwarf, a dumb man, a one-legged woman, a one-eyed
man. Interest centres on the man in the attic who has boarded up his
window and never leaves his room; food is brought to him, excrement is
removed. No one knows anything about him, but he excites much speculation. Here, the isolated man does not present his own case but is seen
only through the eyes of others. In 'Peter Pierce', a man on the run from
the police takes refuge in a room below that of an eccentric ragman.

Before the narrator goes away at the end of the story, he has built up a tentative but never very illuminating relationship with the ragman who lives almost in a world of his own. The narrator feels he has been in touch with some mystery, 'face to face with the subhuman', and records the strangeness of the experience very much as Wordsworth relates his encounters with solitaries in *The Prelude*. 'A Meeting' is described elsewhere as being 'from a novel in preparation', and its characters appear also in the story 'The Rum and the Pelican' (*Merlin*, vol. 2, no. 3, 1954). It makes little impact, and hardly stands by itself, but its unprepossessing hero, a thin, round-shouldered bespectacled clerk making desultory conversation with a female colleague in a bar, shares the lost, dislocated, aimless quality of life we observe in the main characters of the stories. The *accidie* that seeps into these tales makes us think of *Dubliners*, and Trocchi's style, low-key but precise, is a cousin of Joyce's 'scrupulous meanness'. A certain obsession with naturalistic detail – making cocoa, looking at a greasy fork, comparing old pen nibs – is strongly reminiscent, in a Scottish context, of James Kelman; in both cases it probably comes from the *nouveau roman*. The short stories are a mixed bag as regards quality, though two of them, 'A Being of Distances' and 'Peter Pierce', are worth anthologising. But Trocchi seems to have sensed that he needed to propel his figure of the outsider into the more ample space of the novel, give him adventures, give him enough time to allow a fertile interchange between present and past, give him also enough interaction with other characters to define the exact nature of his detachment (the classic pattern: being alone and desperately wanting relationships, having relationships and wanting to be alone; not Sartre's *Huis Clos* but '*L'enfer, c'est les autres/moi-même/les autres/moi-même/les autres*, etc., etc.').

The fascination of all this for a Scottish author is not hard to see, and although Trocchi learned from Sartre and more obviously from Camus's *L'Etranger*, we also cannot help noticing links back to Hogg's *Justified Sinner* and forward to Alasdair Gray's *Lanark*: the dislocation of time, the problem of the hero's self-identification, the tension between natural guilt and its abnormal absence, the story within a story, the prominence of father-son relationships, the presence of serious crime, whether real, imagined, or uncertain – all these aspects would be picked up even if a Scottish background had not been given to his novels by Trocchi himself, the actual setting of the Forth and Clyde Canal in *Young Adam*, the poignant and humorous recollections of the hero's early family life in Glasgow in *Cain's Book*, the lurid Gorbals of *Thongs*. Whether Trocchi ever fully came to terms with his Scottish upbringing and early environment, in the sense in which Joyce and Beckett did in relation to Ireland, is arguable. Joyce managed it by compulsive memorialising and indeed re-mythologising of Dublin, Beckett by the occasional Irish setting, the flavour of Irish names and words, the marked un-Englishness of the tone of voice. But Trocchi, desperate to deparochialise, was swept into the new internationalism of the later 1950s and the 1960s, especially on its French–American axis, and it may be that decisions made too quickly at that time caused his difficulties in assimilating and using his own past. Nevertheless, it should be remembered that in his famous public clash with Hugh MacDiarmid during the Writers' Conference at the Edinburgh Festival of 1962 – an international event if ever there was one – Trocchi's claim was not a stateless or cosmopolitan claim: he was there on the panel of Scottish writers, and he claimed (if we strip off the colours of rhetoric) to have contributed more to Scottish literature during recent years than Hugh MacDiarmid had done. The argument was not so much a simple nationalism *v.* internationalism debate as it seemed at the time; it was rather an argument about how, in the early 1960s, a Scottish writer should go about his business, and whether a change of direction was due, whether it was time to take a closer look at what was happening elsewhere, whether openness of spirit rather than hugging of certainties would be good for Scotland. The significance of that moment in the McEwan Hall was that the evidence could not quite be brushed off by the largely Scottish audience, as it might have been if it had been given by one of the foreign speakers like Mailer or Burroughs; it was one of their own who was talking. With some, inevitably, he never passed the scandal barrier, the drugs-and-sex-rootless-drifter reaction and despite his obvious intelligence, and the controlled style of his prose, it seems likely that his unjust neglect as a writer was not unconnected with various sorts of moral disapproval. In actual fact, *Cain's Book* no more proselytises for heroin than *Young Adam* does for murder. It is true that Joe Necchi takes drugs, both by himself and in the company of friends whose wild lifestyle is rendered fairly mercilessly; but he is also a writer, who vividly recalls and evokes a past and a present unconnected with drugs.

When he was a boy in Glasgow his parents took in lodgers, at whose habits his father is always ready to explode:

> My father came in.
> 'I'm going out,' he said. It sounded like an ultimatum.
> 'You went out last night, Louis,' my mother said. 'I have nothing to give you.'
> 'I didn't *ask*, did I?'
> 'I gave you two shillings last night.'
> 'I didn't ask you for any bloody money!'
> 'Don't lose your temper, Louis.'
> 'I'm not losing my bloody temper. I didn't ask you for any bloody money! We've never got any bloody money because you're too bloody soft on them, the whole bloody lot of them! Pitchimuthu with his bloody fried sardines and that old bloody cripple in the blue room! Kept me out of the bathroom all bloody day with their bloody carry on!'
> 'Louis, you just stop this! Stop it at once! Go on out if you must, but don't begin that business all over again!' (*Cain's Book*, p. 251)

In his present, working on a scow off New York, he records immediate detail, fixing a flux as it passes:

> When I woke up this morning around eight I found I was the last scow in a tow of four moving like a ghost-ship in fog. I say 'a tow of four' because last night there were four of us. Actually I cannot even see the scow ahead of me. I know we are moving because the wrinkled brown water slides like a skin past my catwalk. I threw an empty can overboard. It bobbed in the wake of my stern for a few seconds and then, like something removed by a hand, it was out of sight. I suppose I can see in all directions for about fifteen feet. Beyond that, things become shadowy and at the same time portentous, like the long swift movement of the log which floated by a few minutes ago. (*Cain's Book*, p. 180)

In terms of plot and characters, neither *Cain's Book* nor *Young Adam* comes to an end. *Young Adam*, a thinner and less impressive book than *Cain's Book*, but in some ways a preparation for it and a story that does stick in the mind, leaves its hero, Joe 'Taylor' as he calls himself, listening to a judge condemning a man to death for a murder he did not commit but which Joe did commit (or it may have been an accident, though he accepts responsibility for it). It is as if he is frozen, paralysed, totally unable to save the innocent man. 'I cannot remember how the court broke up. All I know is that suddenly Mr Justice Parkington was gone and the disintegration was already taking place' (*Young Adam*, p. 162). The novel closes rather powerfully on that unspecified 'disintegration'; more like the end of a film than the end of a novel. *Cain's Book* likewise refuses to 'end', except that its last two paragraphs are almost lapidary in their attentiveness to the problem of making a non-ending satisfactorily close the book. 'This, then, is the beginning – a tentative organisation of a sea of ambiguous experience, a provisional dyke, an opening gambit' (*Cain's Book*, p. 251). We may be tempted to think that the man drifting and writing in his scow on the Hudson River is writing a drifting book about his scow on the Hudson River, but the 'organisation', the 'dyke', the 'gambit' all suggest control, forethought, shaping of material. At a second reading, the dramatic function of the 'embedded' scenes from his early life becomes clearer; there is a similar proceeding in Gray's *Lanark* and *1982, Janine*, and in some of the films of Tarkovsky. But was it written as novel or antinovel? Six years before he finished writing it, Trocchi wrote in one of his editorials in *Merlin* (vol. 2, no. 2, Autumn 1953):

> In a literary climate in which we are exhorted to remember that 'novelists ought to write novels' – where accent, that is, is laid upon plot – we might point out that the imperative is redundant, that novelists, we suppose, and by definition, do, although serious writers, we feel, may not.

Hm. Well. No more is said, but the gauntlet comes down with a distinctly glittery clatter. It is surely time now for critics, admitting the force and range and originality of Trocchi's work, to take it up.

THERE'S THIS FUCKIN' WRITER

Jeff Nuttall

Certain aspects of my relationship with Alex Trocchi make my skin crawl with embarrassment now as we survive as best we can in the wreckage of the revolution that had so few of its intended effects and so many unanticipated ones. At the time Bill Butler, the poet and bookseller who killed himself, perhaps wisely, before Thatcher was elected, said 'What Trocchi wants from you, Jeff, is half your salary. What you want from Trocchi is fame.' If there was a sour truth in his words why was I able to disregard it? What were the higher motives that served to sublimate such crass self-advancement?

Well there was always the terror, that daily expectation of the planet's immediate termination by nuclear holocaust which a few of us suffered consciously and which all of us suffered indirectly. Project sigma seemed at least something that could be attempted to obviate it. I had not yet encountered the difficulty and the sadness of living with and loving drug addicted people. In '65 I thought it merely hilarious when I raced up the stairs to the flat in Observatory Gardens one Saturday morning to find Dan Richter and his wife whirling their left arms round like yo-yos (windmills) trying to work up veins to get on with the heroin experience they had 'decided' (been persuaded) to 'go through' (sink into). Since then I, like many of us, have seen friends and relatives dwindle and die and it wasn't hilarious at all.

I was sufficiently sophisticated in my understanding of creativity to know that the transcendental vision is maybe the gross sexual abuse of somebody who doesn't see the face of infinity so clearly, that the majestic flight of genius may also be the trajectory of a psychopathic ego, that creative people, and particularly also the Beats, had long cheerfully claimed the right to theft. So I was able to rationalise the apparent corruption when quite large donations made towards project sigma, its publishing programme, its intended Arts Centre / Fun Palace, were frittered away on drugs, drugs and more drugs. Had not cultural revolution, far from merely tolerating drugs, become synonymous with drugs? After all, by this time we had contacted Tim Leary who preached acid as the millenial panacea.

When the Richter baby died as a consequence of its parents' addiction I thought Christopher Logue, who had known Trocchi longer than any of us, was really out-of-order acting up stroppy at the funeral.

The Trocchi family had, I believe, sustained one similar loss when I was called from Yorkshire, to which I'd escaped from psychedelic London, to act as character witness at a magistrate's court somewhere in Surrey I seem to remember, where Alex was monstrously accused of peddling smack to young people. Coasting on a (mountainous) wave of (mountainous) hypocrisy I presented my bourgeois credentials as a family man and polytechnic lecturer while Roland Penrose, in his fruity posh intonations, argued Alex's innocence – 'And perhaps I can help you to understand, Your Honour, how young and idealistic people gathered round a writer for whom they have profound respect, may imitate his debilities without his being in any way aware that this might be a consequence of their adulation.'

Or words to that effect, while I, just descended from the witness box, could imagine the street voices: 'There's this fuckin' writer. Pretend you've read his gear. I think we can score . . . '

Alex got off. He and I and his wife Lyn went to the pub and celebrated. It was good to see them, even if Lyn was using again and her looks were shockingly deteriorated. She died shortly afterwards and so did their lovely sleepy-eyed little boy. And so, of course, did Alex.

Yes, I feel creepy about that occasion. Not happy at all.

Jeff Nuttall, 1997

SALLY CHILD

How did Trocchi die?

Alex was diagnosed as having lung cancer about a year before he died, when he was operated on and part of his lungs removed and he was literally chucked out of hospital and just told to get on with things, which we did. He was much more fragile, obviously, after a major operation and then he got his strength back, was getting quite perky, and he'd stopped drinking and he'd stopped smoking while he was recovering from the operation but when he started feeling better he started feeling more sociable. So he was going back to the pub and drinking and he . . . he went to a sale, as far as I know, and caught a chill in a saleroom and we thought he had the flu and he didn't really want me to get a doctor because he thought he would be all right.

When the doctor came he ordered an ambulance . . . I – this isn't very pleasant, I don't know if you want to hear this because I get very angry about this bit – but the ambulance men were bastards, basically. They made him walk down the stairs, they didn't want to carry him. We got him to the hospital, they sort of threw him through the door and said that's where our responsibility ends, you know, get someone else to take him up in the lift. He was shunted into a ward with another person, by which stage he was hardly conscious. They threw me out and I remember, this doctor came out with a syringe and it had blue blood in it, and basically he was drowning, and then he died.[1]

What finally happened to Nicolas?

I think I probably feel a bit guilty because I think I probably came between Alex and Nick and I often wonder whether they'd be better off without me. I obviously took attention away from Nick. Alex loved Nick, there was no question about that. Nick loved Alex. In fact, Nick was very good with Alex, especially when he was younger, very caring. But I don't think anybody really realised how much the death of his mother affected him.[2] Alex used to say that it was like Nick had lost an ice cream cone. In other words, he didn't show anything at all which is, as everybody will tell you, a very bad sign. But nobody really picked up on it because at the time they were dealing with Mark and everything else. And then, of course, losing his father, his father dying so suddenly, was a horrible shock. But then my father died, so I wasn't in a very good state and then, of course, the flat burned down. Then in the meantime, Nick had gone to America to stay with his grandparents and had fallen in love . . . And I think all his emotions were just completely and utterly overwhelming. I just don't think . . . He just didn't know what had hit him. I bitterly regret not taking him back to New Zealand when I went back when my father died. I think that was a big mistake at the time, I had reasons to think that he'd be better off where he was. He was doing A-levels. I thought if he could get into university, he would find something that he would really enjoy and his life would take off from there. But by that stage, when I came back from New Zealand, he told me that he'd tried to commit suicide. I think the first time he took an overdose. That didn't work. Finally he jumped from the top of the building.[3]

CHRISTOPHER LOGUE

Oh god it was dismal. It was a cremation, and very few people came. It was in South London and I just remember it as being a very depressed occasion. There was no sense of power about it, there was no sense of loss even.

I was very depressed at the funeral. You're not supposed to be exactly gay at funerals, on the other hand they have a kind of strength and there is a formality in funerals and death is a serious business and not necessarily a very depressing business. It's something that's too serious for depression. But there was something sad about this. It was a funny way for the Alex I knew to end, with a very few people there. I didn't know many of them. It was in one of those ghastly crematorium chapels which don't seem to have any identity at all. I think I spoke and I didn't say anything very important or good. I think one or two other people spoke and then the coffin vanished through those doors into the furnace and some very slow sad jazz music, perhaps Charlie Parker, was played. It was just very . . . just too downbeat and nobody went anywhere afterwards. They all just dispersed and I gave a couple of people I didn't know a lift back into London, because it was down in Putney. And that was the end of it. Somehow I wanted something more . . . you know, but perhaps it just wasn't possible.

THE STREWN RAMPARTS OF JERICHO:

from *Cain's Book*

Alex Trocchi

— *What the hell am I doing here?*

At certain moments I find myself looking on my whole life as leading up to the present moment, the present being all I have to affirm. It's somehow undignified to speak of the past or to think about the future. I don't seriously occupy myself with the question in the 'here-and-now', lying on my bunk and, under the influence of heroin, inviolable. That is one of the virtues of the drug, that it empties such questions of all anguish, transports them to another region, a painless theoretical region, a play region, surprising, fertile, and unmoral. One is no longer grotesquely involved in the becoming. One simply is. I remember saying to Sebastian before he returned to Europe with his new wife that it was imperative to know what it was to be a vegetable, as well.

. . . The illusory sense of adequacy induced in a man by the drug. Illusory? Can a . . . 'datum' be false? Inadequate? In relation to what? The facts? What facts? Marxian facts? Freudian facts? Mendelian facts? More and more I found it necessary to suspend such facts, to exist simply in abeyance, to give up (if you will), and come naked to apprehension.

It's not possible to come quite naked to apprehension and for the past year I have found it difficult to sustain even an approximate attitude without shit, horse, heroin. Details, impressionistic, lyrical. I became fascinated by the minute to minute sensations and when I reflected I did so repetitively and exhaustingly (often under marijuana) on the meaningless texture of the present moment, the cries of gulls, a floating spar, a shaft of sunlight, and it wasn't long before the sense of being alone overtook me and drained me of all hope of ever entering the city with its complicated relations, its plexus of outrageous purpose.

– The facts. Stick to the facts. A fine empirical principle, but below the level of language the facts slide away like a lava. Neither was there ever a simple act; in retrospect I couldn't isolate such a thing. Even while I lived in my act, at each phase, after the decidings, it unfolded spontaneously, and frighteningly, and dangerously, at times like a disease run riot, at times like the growing morning sunlight, and if I find it difficult to remember and express, and difficult to express and remember, if sometimes words leap up, sudden, unnatural, squint and jingling skeletons from the page, accusing me and amusing me with their obscene shakes and making the world mad, I suppose it is because they take a kind of ancestral revenge upon me who at each moment is ready to marshal them again for death or resurrection. No doubt I shall go on writing, stumbling across tundras of unmeaning, planting words like bloody flags in my wake. Loose ends, things unrelated, shifts, nightmare journeys, cities arrived at and left, meetings, desertions, betrayals, all manner of unions, adulteries, triumphs, defeats . . . these are the facts. It's a fact that in America I found nothing was ever in abeyance. Things moved or they were subversive. I suppose it was to escape this without going away, to retreat into abeyance, that I soon came to be on a river scow. (Alternatives: prison, madhouse, morgue.)

I get up off the bunk and return to the table where I light an oil-lamp.

When I have adjusted the wick I find myself fumbling again amongst the pile of notes, extracting a certain page. I hold it close to the lamp and read:

— Time on the scows . . .

Day and night soon became for me merely light and dark, daylight or oil-lamp, and often the lamp became pale and transparent in the long dawns. It was the warmth of the sun that came on my cheek and on my hand through the window which made me get up and go outside and find the sun already far overhead and the skyscrapers of Manhattan suddenly and impressively and irrelevantly there in a haze of heat. And as for that irrelevance . . . I often wondered how far out a man could go without being obliterated. It's an oblique way to look at Manhattan, seeing it islanded there for days on end across the buffering water like a little mirage in which one isn't involved, for at times I knew it objectively and with anxiety as a nexus of hard fact, as my very condition. Sometimes it was like trumpets, that architecture.

I find myself squirting a thin stream of water from the eye-dropper through the number twenty-six needle into the air, cooking up another fix, prodding the hardened cotton in the bubbling spoon . . . just a small fix, I feel, would recreate the strewn ramparts of Jericho.

THE COMPANY YOU'VE KEPT

Brief Biographies

WILLIAM S. BURROUGHS is the influential novelist and former heroin addict responsible for *The Naked Lunch*, *Junkie* and *The Soft Machine*.

JOHN CALDER was a leading London-based avant-garde publisher in the Sixties, who brought the work of Samuel Beckett, William Burroughs and Marguerite Duras amongst others to British readers. He still runs Calder Publications.

JAMES CAMPBELL is a journalist, former editor of the *New Edinburgh Review*, and author of *Talking at the Gates: A Life of James Baldwin* and *Paris Interzone: Richard Wright, Lolita, Boris Vian and Others on the Left Bank*.

SALLY CHILD was Trocchi's last partner and now maintains the Trocchi Estate in London.

LEONARD COHEN is a Canadian musician, poet and writer. He now lives and works at a Zen retreat in California.

GUY DEBORD was the founding father of the Situationist International. He committed suicide in 1994.

ALLEN GINSBERG, poet and writer, came to public attention with *Howl*. Along with Burroughs and Jack Kerouac, he was a pre-eminent figure among the Beats. He died in 1997.

MAURICE GIRODIAS published both pornography and celebrated works such as *Lolita*, *The Ginger Man* and *The Naked Lunch* under his Paris-based imprint, the Olympia Press. He died in 1990.

KIT LAMBERT co-managed The Who with Chris Stamp during their peak between 1964 and 1974. He died in 1981.

CHRISTOPHER LOGUE is a poet, playwright, actor and journalist (he compiled the 'True Stories' column in *Private Eye* between 1961 and 1993).

JANE LOUGEE was the publisher of *Merlin* and a photographer. Now Jane Lougee Bryant, she is currently writing a history of her hometown, Limerick, Maine.

GREIL MARCUS, writer, founding Reviews Editor of *Rolling Stone* and cultural commentator, is the author of *Invisible Republic*, *Mystery Train*, *Dead Elvis* and *Lipstick Traces* – a history of, amongst other things, the Situationist movement.

EDWIN MORGAN is a leading poet and lecturer at Glasgow University.

JEFF NUTTALL is a poet, painter, theatrical producer and former writer/publisher of *My Own Mag*, a counter-culture magazine. His seminal survey of the Sixties underground, *Bomb Culture*, was published in 1968.

PETER ORLOVSKY, poet, was Allen Ginsberg's lover.

GEORGE PLIMPTON is an essayist, sports writer, novelist and founding editor of the *Paris Review*.

NED POLSKY is a writer and criminal psychologist. His works include *Hustlers, Beats and Others*.

GEORGE RODNEY – the Rt Honorable – was a friend of Trocchi's in the Seventies and Eighties.

RICHARD SEAVER was on the editorial board of *Merlin*, championed the work of Samuel Beckett and became a respected editor at Grove Press in New York. He currently runs his own imprint, Arcade Publishing.

HOWARD SLATER is a London-based journalist, with a long-standing interest in the Situationists, sigma and Trocchi.

PATTI SMITH, New York poet and rock singer, came to prominence in the late Seventies. She has recorded numerous albums, recently re-emerging after a period of retirement. A longtime fan of Trocchi's, she never got to meet him.

TERRY SOUTHERN was the acclaimed author of *Candy* (with Mason Hoffenberg) and *The Magic Christian*. His screenwriting credits include *Dr Strangelove*, *Easy Rider* and *Barbarella*. He died in 1995.

IRVINE WELSH documented Britain's chemical generation of the Nineties in the immensely successful *Trainspotting*. His other novels include *The Acid House* and *Marabou Stork Nightmares*. Although he never met Trocchi, his enthusiasm and that of the magazine to which he contributed, *Rebel Inc.*, helped bring about a revival of interest in the writer.

ACKNOWLEDGEMENTS

Special thanks to Sally Child for her generosity with often irreplaceable images and papers, and John Pringle for his help and patience. Thanks also to James Campbell and Edwin Morgan for general consultations and the loan of rare documents and books.

We would also like to note our appreciation for the work of Andrew Murray Scott. Both his biography of Trocchi and his Trocchi reader have been invaluable in the preparation of this volume. Thanks finally to May Miller and Mike Bolland of the BBC for indulging us.

All material copyright the editors, except the following:

Excerpts from *Cain's Book* copyright © John Calder Publications, 1992; excerpts from *Young Adam* copyright © Canongate Books, 1996. All other Trocchi material copyright © The Trocchi Estate, 1997 (with thanks to Sally Child); *Merlin* editorials by courtesy of Jane Lougee Bryant; *Censorship and Virtue*, *Letter to Maurice*, *Tapeworm* and Trocchi's Speech to the 1962 Edinburgh International Writers' Conference courtesy of Alexander Trocchi Papers, Special Collections, Washington University in St Louis Libraries.

Transcription of the Edinburgh Writers' Conference, 1962, courtesy of The Trustees of the National Library of Scotland.

Trocchi entry to the *Edinburgh Review Encyclopaedia* copyright © Howard Slater; *Alexander Trocchi: A Survey* copyright © Edwin Morgan, 1985; *Alexander Trocchi and the Beginning of Merlin* copyright © Christopher Logue, 1985, all courtesy of the Editors of the *Edinburgh Review*.

Excerpt from *Bomb Culture*, copyright © Jeff Nuttall, 1968; *There's This Fuckin Writer*, copyright © Jeff Nuttall, 1997.

Alexander Trocchi, Public Junkie, Prié Pour Nous, copyright © Leonard Cohen, 1961.

Transcription of *Scope* courtesy of The Trocchi Estate, Leonard Maguire and BBC Scotland.

William Burroughs interview, copyright © William Burroughs, 1995, reprinted by permission of The Wylie Agency, Inc.

Allen Ginsberg transcriptions copyright © Allen Ginsberg, 1979, reprinted by permission of The Wylie Agency (UK) Ltd.

Excerpt from *Lipstick Traces* copyright © Greil Marcus, 1989.

Sex and Drugs and Trocchi copyright © James Campbell, 1992, courtesy of the *London Magazine*.

NOTES AND SOURCES

INTRODUCTIONS

My Father had False Teeth: from *Cain's Book*

Extracted from *Cain's Book*, Calder Publications Ltd, London, 1992, 21–3. This passage is a part of a short story, entitled 'The Citadel', originally published in the *Paris Review*, 1958.

Sort of a Blessed Curse: Patti Smith

Interview by the editors, Glasgow, August 1996.

1. *Poems of a Millionaire*. This is a mistaken reference to *Man at Leisure*, Calder & Boyars, London, 1972, Trocchi's collected poems.

A Scottish George Best of Literature: Irvine Welsh

Interview by the editors, Glasgow, July 1995.

1. Matthew Collin is a former editor of *ID* magazine.

2. Kevin Williamson is editor of *Rebel Inc.* magazine. Barry Graham's *Book of Man* (Serpent's Tail, 1995) owes an obvious debt to Trocchi.

3. *Dream State: an Anthology of New Scots Poetry*, edited by Donny O'Rourke, was published by Polygon in 1994.

An Encyclopaedia Entry: Howard Slater

Originally published as part of the *Encyclopaedia Supplement* in *Edinburgh Review*, 83, 1990, 132–4.

1. This is incorrect. Logue was closely involved with *Merlin* but not officially its coeditor.

2. Trocchi didn't meet Burroughs until 1962 when he had returned to Britain.

3. *Sappho of Lesbos* was first published by Castle Books of New York, not by Girodias' Olympia Press.

4. 'Potlatch' is the more usual spelling.

GLASGOW

Free to Choose from the Beginning: from *Cain's Book*

Extracted from *Cain's Book*, Calder Publications Ltd, London, 1992, 85–7.

Edwin Morgan

Interview by the editors, Glasgow, June 1995.

Tapeworm

From *Invisible Insurrection of a Million Minds: A Trocchi Reader*, edited by

Andrew Murray Scott, Polygon, Edinburgh, 1991, 46–54. This is one of a number of fragments found by Andrew Murray Scott in the Alexander Trocchi Papers, Special Collections, Washington University in St Louis Libraries, Missouri.

This piece is of uncertain date, but its references to Trocchi's first wife, Betty Whyte, whom he married in 1949 whilst still a student at Glasgow University, as well as other internal evidence, suggest that it was written in the early 1950s while Trocchi still resided in Glasgow.

PARIS

Dear Jack and Marjorie

From *The Invisible Insurrection of a Million Minds: A Trocchi Reader*, edited by Andrew Murray Scott, Polygon, Edinburgh, 1991, 71–3. Written in October 1950 for the *Scots Review*, Edinburgh.

Jane Lougee

Interview by the editors, New York, September 1995.

1. The magazine was originally to have been entitled *Mss.* The Scots poet Alan Riddell was to have been its co-editor, but Trocchi sacked Riddell from the magazine before its first appearance as *Merlin.* See James Campbell, *Paris Interzone*, Martin Secker and Warburg, London, 1994, 55–6, for an account of Riddell's ejection.

Merlin, *Autumn 1952: volume 1, number 2*

The first edition of *Merlin* was published on 15th May 1952. *Merlin* editorials were always credited to 'the editors', but in practice were almost always clearly Trocchi's work – *Words and War* (*Merlin*, Summer/Autumn 1954, vols 2 and 3, 67–70 in this volume) was an exception.

Alexander Trocchi and the Beginning of Merlin: *Christopher Logue*

Reprinted from *Edinburgh Review*, no. 70, August 1985, 59–65. The editor of the *Edinburgh Review*, Peter Kravitz, produced an edition largely devoted to Trocchi and his work. In addition to Logue's, the edition contained essays by Edwin Morgan, Tom McGrath, and John Calder.

Letter from Paris

Trocchi also published some poems in *Nimbus* in 1952.

Richard Seaver

Interview by the editors, New York, September 1995.

1. *Points,* a Paris-based bilingual review, was edited by Peggy Guggenheim's son Sinbad Vail. It was launched in 1949 and ceased publication in 1955.
2. *Collection Merlin* was an imprint of the Olympia Press, editorially controlled by Seaver and Trocchi.
3. Alex Trocchi and Betty Whyte had two daughters – Jacqueline Ann and Margot Françoise. Betty and the girls were eventually to emigrate to New Zealand.
4. Maurice Girodias (1919–90) was the publisher behind the notorious Olympia Press, renowned not only for its pornographic output but also for its publication of such texts as *The Story of O, The Ginger Man, Lolita* and *The Naked Lunch.* The Olympia Press was launched in the spring of 1953 with Henry Miller's *Plexus* and De Sade's *Bedroom Philosophers* (a translation of *La Philosophie Dans Le Boudoir*). See *The Good Ship Venus* by John de St Jorre and *Une Journeé sur La Terre,* Editions de la Différence, Paris, 1990, Girodias's autobiography, for more detail on his life.

Young Adam *Before*

Extracted from *Young Adam,* Canongate Books, 1996, 8–12. This edition is based on a text published in 1966 by New English Library and described by Trocchi in a manuscript note as 'definitive'.

Merlin, *Summer/Autumn 1954: volume 2, number 3*

This editorial continues for another fifteen pages in the original and moves on to American politics, an area in which Trocchi was no expert. John Pringle suspects that these latter passages were not written by Trocchi himself.

George Plimpton

Interview by the editors, New York, September 1995.

Merlin, *Spring/Summer 1955: volume 2, number 4*

This was the final edition of *Merlin.* In *Paris Interzone,* James Campbell notes that this last issue was in fact assembled by Austryn Wainhouse. So the authorship of this editorial is questionable, but it deals with Trocchi's usual concerns.

Terry Southern

Interview by the editors, New York, September 1995.

The Dirty Young Adam*: An Afterword*

Reprinted from *The Olympia Reader,* edited by Maurice Girodias, Grove Press, New York, 1965, 457–8. In *The Olympia Reader,* Girodias retained Trocchi's pseudonym, Frances Lengel, although the afterword blows the gaff.

Censorship and Virtue

From the Alexander Trocchi Papers, Special Collections, Washington University in St Louis Libraries, Missouri. This was originally written for inclusion in the Olympia Press catalogue.

1. Here the manuscript suggests that 'quotes if possible from *The Times*' might be appropriate. None were inserted.

Young Adam *After*

Young Adam was published in dirty book form by the Olympia Press in 1954, under the pseudonym Frances Lengel. The publishing history of this much-pirated text is tortuous in the extreme, and some editions of the pornographic version have been further rewritten and amended by authors other than Trocchi.

Jane Lougee

Interview by the editors, New York, September 1995.

1. Midhou was an Algerian drug-dealer friend of Trocchi's from Paris.

What the Hell am I Doing Here: from *Cain's Book*

Extracted from *Cain's Book*, Calder Publications Ltd, London, 1992, 185–9, 194–7.

NEW YORK

Jane Lougee

Interview by the editors, New York, September 1995.

1. In fact, Trocchi's mother died on 4 January 1942, poisoned by an infected tin of pilchards. Trocchi was aged sixteen.

Half an Hour Ago I Gave Myself a Fix: from *Cain's Book*

Extracted from *Cain's Book*, Calder Publications Ltd, London, 1992, 9–11.

Ned Polsky

Interview by the editors, New York, September 1995.

Richard Seaver

1. 'It is different from other books, it is true, it has art, it is brave,' commented Mailer on *Cain's Book*, whilst the *New York Herald Tribune* noted, '*Cain's Book* is the genuine article on a dope-addict's life . . . Trocchi's heritage goes back to the Marquis de Sade, the Romantics, and Beckett and Ionesco. In fact, Joe Necchi [the Trocchi-like central figure] might be called the

modern, male counterpart of Sade's 'Justine' . . . This is honest writing –
truth, but not fiction.'

George Plimpton

Plimpton had returned to New York in 1956. In effect, the *Paris Review* moved
with him and became a Manhattan-based magazine, although a managing editor
was appointed in Paris.

From Cain's Book, *volume 2*

Reprinted from *Evergreen Review*, volume 5, number 19, July/August 1961.

A Fifteen-year-old Chick and a Double Bass

Recorded by Allen Ginsberg at Trocchi's flat in London, 8th November 1979.
Transcribed and edited by Simon Pettet. Previously unpublished.

1. One of the most significant charges made against Trocchi, threatening the
   most stringent punishment, was that he had supplied drugs to a minor.
   This would appear to be his side of the story.

Hands Off Alexander Trocchi

1. Trocchi spent brief periods in prison in New York, but no other source
   refers to a stay as extended as this.

Alexander Trocchi, Public Junkie, Prié Pour Nous

Reprinted from *Flowers for Hitler*, Leonard Cohen, McClelland and Stuart,
Toronto, 1964, 45–7.

LONDON

Respectable Yet Sinister: Interview for Scope, *BBC Radio Scotland*

Trocchi interviewed by Leonard Maguire, recorded in Glasgow for the BBC,
1962. Transcribed by the editors.

John Calder

Interview by the editors, London, July 1995.

1. One such notable occasion was when Trocchi and Burroughs were interviewed by Dan Farson on *Something To Say* (Rediffusion Television, 1963).
   A transcript of the conversation exists.

The Edinburgh International Writers' Conference, 1962: Tuesday, 21st August;
the Scottish Writers' Day

Transcribed by the conference organisers. From the collection of the

National Library of Scotland.

This transcript is riddled with errors and misprints. Suggestions for correct, or at least better, readings are included in square brackets. In some places, of course, and presumably by accident, the transcriber has captured the normal incompleteness and grammatical errors of speech.

1. Henry Miller, who was one of the reasons Trocchi went to Paris in the first place.

2. It seems more likely that this and the following remark, both of which the transcript tentatively assigns to MacDiarmid, were made by Trocchi. Equally, though, for that reading to work, it seems likely that a further remark has been left out.

Trocchi's Speech to the 1962 International Writers' Conference: Edinburgh Festival, August 1962

From the Alexander Trocchi Papers, Special Collections, Washington University in St Louis Libraries, Missouri.

1. These were Trocchi's manuscript notes for his speech at the conference. A comically inaccurate transcript of his speech as it was actually delivered is held in the National Libraries of Scotland, Edinburgh. It refers, for instance, to 'Kim's Book'. At the end of his speech, Trocchi read only from *Cain's Book*, a single passage: pp. 12–13 in the Calder edition.

William Burroughs

Interview by the editors, Lawrence, Kansas, September 1995.

1. *Faithfull*, Marianne Faithfull's autobiography, with David Dalton, Michael Joseph, 1994.

2. Burroughs is referring to Austryn Wainhouse.

3. A psychoanalyst, R. D. Laing was the founder of the Philadelphia Foundation and author of *The Divided Self*.

4. Michael X was a British-based race rights activist. He was incarcerated and eventually executed for murder in Trinidad.

5. Felix Topolski was an illustrator.

6. *Towers Open Fire*, Dir. Anthony Balch, Supreme Films, 1963.

7. Phun City, held on Ecclesdon Common near Worthing in 1972, was a three-day rock festival and science fiction convention.

The Invisible Insurrection of a Million Minds

First published in the *New Saltire Review*, Edinburgh, 1962. Reprinted from

Invisible Insurrection of a Million Minds: A Trocchi Reader, edited by Andrew Murray Scott, Polygon Books, Edinburgh, 1991. This essay achieved something of Trocchi's aims as far as its dissemination was concerned; it was reprinted in *Anarchy* (London), *The International Situationist Review* (Paris) in 1962, the *Evergreen Review* (New York) and the *Los Angeles Free Press* in 1963, as well as being circulated as a sigma pamphlet. It was also reprinted along with *Sigma: A Tactical Blueprint* in *City Lights Journal*, number 2, 1964, edited by Lawrence Ferlinghetti.

Trocchi circulated a sheet inviting subscriptions to the sigma portfolio, which described the sigma project in the following terms:

> The *sigma portfolio* is an entirely new dimension in publishing, through which the writer reaches his public immediately, outflanking the traditional trap of publishing-house policy, and by means of which the reader gets it, so to speak, 'hot' from the writer's pen, from the photographer's lens, etc. In a sense you might be said to be subscribing to an encyclopaedia in the making; in another sense you will be participating in a tactical historigem, to coin a word. In subscribing to the *sigma portfolio*, you are stimulating the growth of an interpersonal log constructing itself to alert, sustain, inform, inspire, and make vividly conscious of itself all intelligence from now on. You will receive various future informations and tactical objects and can judge for yourself at what points you can participate. Again, the portfolio is what we call a 'futique' (what will be prized as an antique tomorrow); you will possess a first edition in this new dimension of publishing, the expanding file of our activities.

The footnotes reproduced below are Trocchi's own, unless otherwise stated.

1. *The Theatre and its Double*, Grove Press, New York, 1958.
2. The *prise de pouvoir* by an avant-garde is obviously only an early stage in a larger, more universal movement, and it must not be forgotten that our group of originators *'ne pourra réaliser son projet qu'en se supprimant . . . ne peut effectivement exister qu'en tant que parti se dépasse lui-meme'*. (Added to French version – A. Murray Scott)
3. *Notes éditoriales d'Internationale Situationiste, 3 décembre, 1959*. Freely adapted from the original.
4. *The Secret Reins*, (Centre 42) *Encounter* no. 102, March 1962. All quotations from Mr Wesker and Lloyd George are from the same source.
5. I believe international policies have been attempted since this article was written. However, my criticism is still relevant.
6. *Documents Situationistes*, Guy Ernest Debord. At present, town-planning

is determined by and tends to reinforce conventional functions, conventional attitudes. You sleep here, eat there, work there, die there. A revolutionary architecture will take no account of functions to be transcended (cf. Essay no. 2). [It is likely that the second essay here referred to is *Sigma: A Tactical Blueprint*, in which Trocchi argued for the development of an architecture designed 'for and around the participants' in the sigma project. A full version of this essay can be found in *The Invisible Insurrection of a Million Minds: A Trocchi Reader* [Editors' note]

Bomb Culture

Reprinted from *Bomb Culture*, Paladin Books, London, 1968, 156, 159, 181, 182–216, 221–3, 228–230. The notes below are Nuttall's own – at this point in the text he is intercutting two poems:

1. Allen Ginsberg, 'The Change', *Writers Forum Poets No. 5*, also in *The New Writing in the U.S.A.*, Penguin.
2. Harry Fainlight, 'The Spider'. *Fuck You* magazine ed. Ed Sanders, and *Wholly Communion*, Lorrimer Films.
3. Allen Ginsberg, op. cit.
4. Harry Fainlight, op. cit.

project sigma: Cultural Engineering: Manifesto Situationiste, *1960, sigma edition*

Reprinted from the original sigma pamphlet, 1964. The copy is poorly reproduced and missing some lines at the bottom of some pages. Typically it is the footnotes which have suffered; such as they are, they are reproduced below.

1. Whole footnote missing.
2. We have retained the French here, because 'in plain English' it might provoke a more stock response.
3. To regard life as finally a superior game is a metaphysical attitude [line missing].

The Long Book

From *The Hashish Club: An Anthology of Drug Literature*, volume 2, ed. Peter Haining, Peter Owen, 1975. This text, with its obvious similarities to *Cain's Book, volume 2* was presumably supplied by Trocchi directly to the editor of *The Hashish Club*. The similarities between the two are so striking (whole pages are reproduced with only the slightest changes) that it is difficult to see *The Long Book* as much more than a bit of literary goldbricking. Trocchi had promised

The Long Book to so many publishers by 1975 that a little 'work in progress' must have seemed a necessity. At the same time, both *Cain's Book, volume 2* and *The Long Book*, whilst on the one hand owing very obvious debts to Burroughs and Joyce, also contain passages of appallingly lacerating, and compelling, self-description.

The text of *The Long Book* as printed in *The Hashish Club* contains a number of obvious inaccuracies and dubious coinages. The notes below indicate either better possible readings, or that no obvious alternatives exist for particularly Joycean inventions.

1. Probably 'Turn on cooler!'
2. 'Oh God'.
3. Probably 'pseudo-entity'.
4. Probably 'pairoknees'.
5. Probably 'Romans'.
6. 'dicte of koanst' – *sic*.
7. 'telescope'.
8. Probably 'gleaming'.
9. Probably 'metacategorical'.
10. In *Cain's Book, volume 2*: 'Llareggub', the town of *Under Milk Wood*.
11. Probably 'Horst Wesel', as in *Cain's Book, volume 2*.

John Calder

Interview by the editors, London, July 1995.

1. A film version of *Young Adam* is under development by Lomond Television, Glasgow. At the time of publication shooting had still not commenced.
2. Although some accounts suggest that copies of *Cain's Book* were burnt by Sheffield City Council in 1964, it appears that several boxes of them still lie in the basement of Sheffield City Library, never to be released to the public.
3. It seems much more likely that the earlier passages of *Thongs* are actually a parody of *No Mean City*, MacArthur and Long's classic novel of Glasgow's gang culture.

£ S D (love, sex, death / pounds, shillings, pence / lysergic acid)

Reprinted from *Children of Albion, Poetry of the 'Underground' in Britain*, ed. Michael Horovitz, Penguin, 1969, 294–6. The volume's commentary provides a fascinating survey of the Underground, written in April 1968.

Letter to Maurice

From the Alexander Trocchi Papers, Special Collections, Washington University in St Louis Libraries, Missouri.

John Pringle, who found the letter, dates it to between 1965 and 1970, and suspects that it was a draft, never sent.

1. 'As a elusive pimpernel Girodias' – *sic*. But the sense is clear.

Michael X

Recorded by Allen Ginsberg at Trocchi's flat in London, 8th November 1979. Transcribed and edited by Simon Pettet. Previously unpublished.

Sally Child

Interview by the editors, London, July 1995.

1. Trocchi's eldest son, Mark, died in May, 1977.
2. In the late Seventies, Trocchi had book stalls on Kensington High Street and King's Road.

I Could Have Told It Much Better I'm Sure

Recorded by Allen Ginsberg at Trocchi's flat in London, 8th November 1979. Transcribed and edited by Simon Pettet. Previously unpublished.

We Drive Each Other Up the Wall

Recorded by Alexander Trocchi at his flat in London. Transcribed and edited by the editors. Previously unpublished.

1. In 1964, *Cain's Book* was seized by the authorities in Sheffield. Trocchi had to appear in court there to answer charges of obscenity – he lost. This was a few months after the more celebrated court case regarding *The Memoirs of Fanny Hill*.
2. Peggy Guggenheim, the noted art collector and patron, was then living in Venice.
3. Sinbad Vail was Guggenheim's son.
4. The late Hans Hartung was a painter of the School of Paris.
5. Songwriter Lionel Bart was composer of the musical, *Oliver!*
6. Here, Trocchi is probably referring to a visit to London by Californian publisher Milton Luros and his wife in 1967. Luros ran Brandon House and republished five of Trocchi's Olympia Press titles, reportedly enjoying healthy sales. Trocchi was hoping for a sizeable royalty cheque from him, but only received a thousand dollars.

Do You Know De Quincey?

Reprinted from *Lipstick Traces*, Martin Secker and Warburg, London, 1989,

385–8.

1. Apparently, Trocchi had shared a flat with Wilson, author of *The Outsider*, in London, probably in the mid-Fifties. [Editors' note]

AFTERWORDS

Sex and Drugs and Trocchi

A version of this piece first appeared in the *London Magazine*, April–May 1992, 45–59, under the title, 'Alexander Trocchi'. It is reprinted here with the author's amendments.

Alexander Trocchi: A Survey

Edwin Morgan's 'A Survey' is from *Edinburgh Review*, number 70, August 1985, 48–58. It is reprinted here with the author's amendments. The notes below are the author's own.

Quotations in the text are from the following editions:

Cain's Book (Calder, 1963) (first published 1960); *Young Adam* (Heinemann, 1961) (first published 1954, under pseudonym Frances Lengel); *Man at Leisure* (Calder & Boyars, 1972); *Helen and Desire* (Olympia Press, London, 1971) (first published 1954, under pseudonym Frances Lengel); *Writers in Revolt*, ed. R. Seaver, T. Southern and A. Trocchi (Fell, New York, 1963); *New Writers III* (Calder, 1965).

There's This Fuckin' Writer

Written for this volume, 1997.

Sally Child

Interview by the editors, London, July 1995.

1. Trocchi died on 15th April 1984. He was cremated at Mortlake Crematorium, South London on 25th April. His ashes, which were kept on the mantelpiece of his and Sally Child's flat, subsequently went missing.

2. Lyn Trocchi died of hepatitis with complications in November 1972, aged thirty-five.

3. Nicolas jumped from the roof of Trocchi's and Sally Child's burnt-out flat at Observatory Gardens in 1984. He was eighteen.

Christopher Logue

Interview by the editors, London, July 1995.

The Strewn Ramparts of Jericho: from Cain's Book

Extracted from *Cain's Book*, Calder Publications Ltd, London, 1992, 11–14.

BIBLIOGRAPHY AND FURTHER READING

ALEXANDER TROCCHI

NOVELS

Helen and Desire, Olympia Press: Paris (1954).

The Carnal Days of Helen Seferis, Olympia Press: Paris (1954).

Young Adam, Olympia Press: Paris (1954).

School for Sin, Olympia Press: Paris (1955).

White Thighs, Olympia Press: Paris (1955).

All of the above first published under the pseudonym 'Frances Lengel'.

Thongs, Olympia Press: Paris (1956) published under the pseudonym 'Carmencita de las Lunas'.

Frank Harris: My Life and Loves, vol. 5, Olympia Press: Paris (1954). Largely written by Trocchi, using only a nucleus of Harris's papers.

Sappho of Lesbos, Castle Books: New York (1960).

Cain's Book, Grove Press: New York (1961) and John Calder: London (1963).

Young Adam, Canongate Books: Edinburgh (1996).

TRANSLATIONS

Apollinaire, Guillaume, *The Debauched Hospodar*, Olympia Press: Paris (1953). Published under the pseudonym 'Oscar Mole'.

Cremer, Jan, *I, Jan Cremer*, Calder & Boyars: London (1965). With R. E. Wyngaard.

Pieyre de Mandiargues, André, *The Girl on the Motorcycle*, John Calder: London (1966).

Penrose, Valentine, *The Bloody Countess*, Calder & Boyars: London (1970).

de Obaldia, René, *The Centenarian*, Calder & Boyars: London (1974).

Douassot, Jean, *La Gana*, Calder & Boyars: London (1974).

POETRY

Man at Leisure, Calder & Boyars: London (1972).

SHORT STORIES

New Writers 3, John Calder: London (1965). With David Mercer, Sinclair
   Beiles and Nick Rawson.

AS EDITOR
Writers' Revolt, Fell: New York (1960). With Terry Southern and
   Richard Seaver.

ANTHOLOGY
Andrew Murray Scott (ed.), *The Invisible Insurrection of a Million Minds*.
   Polygon: Edinburgh (1991).

FURTHER READING

Campbell, James, *Paris Interzone*, Martin Secker & Warburg: London
   (1994).
Horovitz, Michael (ed.), *Children of Albion: Poetry of the 'Underground'
   in Britain*, Penguin Books: London (1968).
de St Jorre, John, *The Good Ship Venus – The Erotic Voyage of the
   Olympia Press*, Hutchinson: London (1994).
Marcus, Greil, *Lipstick Traces*, Martin Secker & Warburg: London (1989).
Nuttall, Jeff, *Bomb Culture*, MacGibbon and Kee: London (1968).
Rosenthal, Irving, *Sheeper*, Grove Press: New York (1967).
Scott, Andrew Murray, *The Making of the Monster*, Polygon: Edinburgh
   (1991).
White, Kenneth, *Travels in the Drifting Dawn*, Mainstream: Edinburgh
   (1989).

INDEX

Started in 1992 by Kevin Williamson, with help from established young authors Duncan McLean and Gordon Legge, Rebel Inc. magazine set out with the intention of promoting and publishing what was seen then as a new wave of young urban Scottish writers who were kicking back against the literary mainstream.

The Rebel Inc book imprint intends to develop the magazine ethos through publishing accessible as well as challenging texts aimed at extending the domain of counter-culture literature.

The first four titles point towards the future direction of Rebel Inc

Children of Albion Rovers
Irvine Welsh, Alan Warner, Gordon Legge,
James Meek, Laura J. Hird, Paul Reekie
A collection of novellas from six of the best young writers to emerge from Scotland in the 90s - £8.99

Hunger
Knut Hamsun
A new translation by Sverre Lyngstad
with an introduction by Duncan Mclean
Classic first novel by the Nobel prize-winning Norwegian - £6.99

Young Adam
Alexander Trocchi
Introduced by John Pringle
Seminal first work from the Scottish Beat writer - £6.99

Drugs and the Party Line
Kevin Williamson
Introduction by Irvine Welsh
A polemic on the politics of recreational drug use - £4.99

The above are available from all good book shops
or can be ordered directly from:

Canongate Books, 14 High St, Edinburgh EH1 1TE
Tel 0131 557 5111 Fax 0131 557 5211
email canongate@post.almac.co.uk

All forms of payment are accepted and p&p is free to any address in the U.K. Please specify if you want to join the Rebel Inc. mailing list.

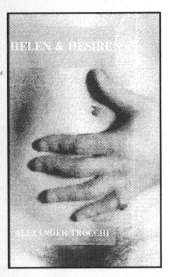